DESERT AND DELTA

By the same Author

YESTERDAY AND TO-DAY IN SINAI (Blackwoods)

THREE DESERTS (John Murray)

ORIENTAL SPOTLIGHT *Published anonymously under pseudonym RAMESES* (John Murray)

THE BACK GARDEN OF ALLAH (John Murray)

DESERT AND DELTA

MAJOR C. S. JARVIS
C.M.G., O.B.E.

LONDON
JOHN MURRAY, ALBEMARLE STREET, W.

First Edition . . . October 1938
Reprinted . . . . January 1942
Reprinted . . . September 1944
Reprinted . . . February 1947

PRINTED IN GREAT BRITAIN BY
LOWE AND BRYDONE PRINTERS LIMITED, LONDON, N.W.10

CONTENTS

LIST OF ILLUSTRATIONS

LIST OF ILLUSTRATIONS

SKETCH MAP *for* DESERT & DELTA

OUR POSITION IN EGYPT

Good, which they dared not hope for, we have seen ;
A State whose generous will through earth is dealt.

WORDSWORTH.

IN writing a book on Egypt, even one so light-hearted as this, it is impossible to avoid politics entirely and to dissociate oneself from the various situations that have arisen from time to time owing to the British occupation of the country. There are no politics in Egypt that are entirely divorced from this question, and as politics are the salt of life to the educated Egyptian and, moreover, persist in butting into the affairs of the British official, one cannot ignore the rather involved and difficult question altogether. The history of the occupation and the subsequent nego-tiations that have taken place during the last fifty years, however, has been so fully dealt with by abler and better-informed pens than mine that I do not propose to go deeper into the matter than is absolutely necessary.

In the year 1882, owing to a mutiny in the Egyptian Army, a state of complete anarchy ensued in the Nile Valley involving among other things the murder of Europeans and looting of their houses and shops. The rising was organized primarily to call attention to the inequitable treatment of Egyptian officers in the Army and the preference shown to Turks ; but in a few days the object of the rebellion was lost sight of completely and degenerated into a massacre of Christians and the extermina-tion of all foreigners.

The three Powers then interested in Egypt—France,

I

B

Russia, and Turkey—were invited by Great Britain to take joint action but refused, with the result that England acted alone and in a few months occupied the country and restored order. Having once taken over the responsibility, Great Britain has never been able or willing to shift the burden to other shoulders, but it is useless to maintain that our attitude is dictated solely by altruistic motives or that it would be the same if Egypt's geographical situation were other than it is. There is no denying the fact that the Suez Canal is vital to the existence of Great Britain and her Dominions and if present-day proof is necessary one need only call attention to the German coercion of Turkey into the Great War in 1914 with the object of denying this important water-way to the Allies.

To ensure that the Suez Canal is not closed to our country during a war we must of necessity keep a controlling interest in Egypt, whose history during the last two thousand years proves convincingly that she has never in this period succeeded in governing herself with her own nationals. Whenever, since 332 B.C., there has been a strong and efficient government in the country—and these periods have been extremely rare—it has been a government of foreigners; and Mohammed Ali, whom the Egyptians point to as their greatest and most successful ruler, was as much an alien as was Lord Cromer. He went to the country in the early part of the nineteenth century as an Albanian subaltern in a Turkish regiment and the regiment in question had been sent to assist in the drastic quelling of an insurrection by the Egyptians against Turkish rule. From this humble beginning Mohammed Ali became the greatest and most far-seeing of all Egyptian rulers, but the fact that he established a dynasty in the country after ruthless extermination of the Egyptian Mamelukes and Beys does not make him an Egyptian.

From 1922 until 1936 Egypt had a measure of independence, electing her Parliament by what amounted to manhood suffrage and appointing her own ministers who were free to govern the country subject to the " Four Reserved Points " which, however distasteful they may have been to Egyptians with a marked sense of nationalism, did not interfere in the slightest degree with the internal government of the country, provided the country was properly governed. During the fourteen years between 1922 and 1936 Egypt had sixteen governments—one of which resigned after the murder of the Sirdar, one was dismissed by H.M. King Fuad at a period when its futility had made it the laughing-stock of Europe, whilst a third resigned in 1930 in a fit of childish pique. Despite the fact that in 1922 the whole country combined together with the aim and object of obtaining its independence and the freeing of the land from British occupation, the main idea was almost immediately lost sight of in unseemly political squabbles, the mazes and ramifications of which were so confusing and savour so much of comic opera that it is impossible to follow exactly what happened ; and what was the reason of it all beyond the fact that certain individuals were seeking office and meant to have it at all costs.

During this period there were dangerous risings and demonstrations, aimed not at Great Britain but at the purely Egyptian Government then in power ; and when the mob gets the upper hand in Egypt history proves there is only one result—looting and attacks on Christians and foreigners. Great Britain's argument in favour of her continued occupation of the country, to put it into very simple and plain words, is as follows : if we evacuated Egypt entirely and left to the Egyptian Government the protection of the large number of foreigners of all nationalities who live and have businesses in the bigger towns and there happened, as most assuredly there would happen sooner or later, to be a revolution against the government of the day and some foreigners were murdered, what would be the result? It is idle to ignore the fact that there are at least two European Powers at the present time, and there may be more in the future, who would sacrifice anything to get a footing in Egypt; and it is safe to assume that battleships would arrive at Alexandria and Port Said with the greatest promptitude and that Egypt would be occupied by a landing force to protect the nationals of the particular country that happened to get there first. This might be England, and if so all would be well; if, on the other hand, it were another country it would mean that we should be either involved in a great war or would have to accept the foreign occupation of Egypt and, what matters so vitally, the loss of control of the Suez Canal.

As a proof that this is not an exaggerated or fanciful view one need only remember Alexandria and the many demonstrations that took place in this excitable city between 1919 and 1923. On one occasion a mob, which with the best possible intentions had started out to show their disapproval of the British occupation in an orderly manner, for some unaccountable reason became imbued with anti-Hellenic views and three Greeks were killed and innumerable Greek shops looted. Another mob at a later date with the same laudable intentions in their minds seized an unfortunate Italian, poured petrol over him and burned him to death.

If further proof of the unreasonableness of Egyptian mobs is required, one might recall also the episode which happened in Assiut in 1919 when the whole of Egypt blazed up into open revolt against the British. Assiut is a large town on the Nile, half-way between Cairo and Luxor, and is the dwelling-place of most of the rich Copts in Egypt. Here they have wonderful palaces on the banks

4

of the Nile and live in the lap of luxury. The Copt, the Egyptian Christian, had for generations experienced a not particularly happy time in Moslem Egypt, but with the strong British control during Cromer's days he came into his own. He has, as a rule, more brain and business acumen than his Mohammedan brother, and with the bar of religion removed the Copt rose to eminence officially and vast wealth commercially. When all Egypt rose against the British, the Copt, who is essentially an opportunist for his hard life since the Arab invasion has taught him the necessity of always backing the winning horse, considered that he also must strike a blow for freedom if only for the sake of effect, so certain of the young Copts stirred up the Moslem *fellaheen* of Assiut against the British.

The resulting mob, some thousands strong, advanced upon the town and found a company of British infantry behind hastily erected sandbags; this looked decidedly unhealthy and most unprofitable, and the mob scratched its head for a moment. The British were Christians and unbelievers and it was primarily against the unbelievers that they had assembled together; if certain of these unbelievers were unsporting enough to arm themselves with machine guns and rifles and get behind sandbags there were other unbelievers who had not taken these precautions and who were far better endowed with this world's goods. And so as one man the mob moved on to attack the palaces of the rich Copts and the long-suffering British infantry had to go forth and protect the lives and property of the people who had actually instigated the revolt. These incidents happened only nineteen years ago and there is not the slightest reason why they should not happen again.

Who could blame Great Britain, therefore, if she adopted the very reasonable attitude of refusing to believe that there were any immediate signs of Egypt being able to govern herself successfully or, what is more important, of being able to protect the very large number of foreigners who own businesses in the Nile Valley. The much-discussed Four Reserved Points really hinged on this and nothing else. Everybody has read about these Four Reserved Points at least a hundred times, and as I have never yet met a British or Egyptian official in Egypt who could think of more than two, it would perhaps be wise to enumerate them as the possibility of the ordinary individual remembering more than one is remote. They were:

1. The security of communications of the British Empire in Egypt.
2. Defence of Egypt against foreign aggression direct or indirect.
3. Protection of foreign interests in Egypt and of minorities.
4. The Sudan.

The first three meant the Suez Canal and side issues that might compromise it. The Sudan reservation was dictated partly from sentimental and partly from national reasons. Gross maladministration of the country by the Egyptian Government prior to 1886 led to a fanatical rebellion that swept northwards as far as Wadi Halfa and might have meant the conquest of a great part of the Nile Valley by the Mahdi's troops. A recurrence of trouble in the Sudan would affect all the trade routes in Northern Africa and have repercussions in Uganda and possibly Kenya; in other words, the necessity of a strong and equitable government in the Sudan is an absolute essential.

Also a certain amount of British blood was spilt in its reconquest and some British money expended, and we are loath to see our efforts wasted. The Sudan is a model of the perfect government of a very savage country peopled by mixed races, and it has all happened in thirty-nine years, so why spoil it ? If it were handed back to the Egyptians it is more than probable that they would be thrown out again in the first year of their occupation, and after all what is sauce for the goose is sauce for the gander. If the Egyptians demand self-determination for themselves and all other nations, does not this apply to the Sudanese also ? One of the many Egyptian premiers realized this and pressed for a speedy solution of the Sudan difficulty for, as he remarked very ingenuously, the settlement of this question would become increasingly difficult with the growth of education and national feeling in the Sudan— in other words, what would be the reply if the Sudanese should raise a cry of " The Sudan for the Sudanese " ?

The arguments raised in favour of Great Britain maintaining a control in Egypt are somewhat one-sided and one answer is, *Necessitas est lex temporis et loci,* " Necessity is the law of time and place "; and secondly, that British guidance has in fifty years resulted in a completely bankrupt State becoming, if not one of the wealthiest nations in the world, the country that balances its budget and pays its way with far greater ease and less taxation than any other. It must be borne in mind that Great Britain, by virtue of her position in the country, obtains no financial benefit whatsoever; we have no special trade treaties with Egypt and no preferential tariffs, and all other countries compete, and compete most successfully—far too successfully—with our business men. There have been times when Great Britain could have obtained without the slightest difficulty a preferential tariff for British products, but we have never done so, and as a contrast one may point to a mandated country not a thousand miles away where the mandatory Power sees to it that her goods and manufactures predominate to the almost total exclusion of those of any other country.

7

There has, however, been a complete change in public opinion during the last twenty-five years with regard to the occupation of foreign and backward countries. Previously we saw only our own side of the question and, whilst congratulating ourselves on the inestimable benefits we had conferred upon the countries and people we controlled, quite overlooked the other side of the argument, flatly refusing to believe it possible that the nation in question might prefer to rule itself in its own way. Our attitude was that they should be everlastingly grateful for having such a capable and honest race to look after their affairs, and that they should ask us to remove ourselves was not only incredible but ranked as the grossest ingratitude.

Nowadays, however, we are not quite so certain of ourselves nor so intolerant and irreconcilable, and we are beginning to realize and understand the point of view of a people who are ready to suffer some inconvenience and a trifle of inefficiency if they can be free from foreign domination and control. We Britons are fully alive to, and exasperated by, the fact that in some respects the government of our own country is out of date and not in keeping with modern opinion, and we know that so far as internal legislation is concerned Mrs. Grundy, wearing an outsize in red flannel drawers—that symbol of mid-Victorianism—has the last word to say in many things. In proof of this is the fact that our governments flatly refuse to recognize that ninety per cent. of the population are going to have a mild gamble occasionally and that nothing will stop them. As our legislators will not see this the exchequer of the Irish Free State has had the handling of millions of pounds of British money, and the greater part of the population are now filling up football coupons and adopting the hole-and-corner method of sending their money a week later to evade our futile anti-

8

gambling laws. There is no doubt whatsoever that if either Hitler or Mussolini were directing our legislation they would accept the inevitable and devise some scheme by which this *penchant* for a mild gamble benefited the State financially. Nevertheless, I think we would all prefer to continue under Mrs. Grundy's rule than have either German or Italian domination.

In 1936 a treaty between Great Britain and Egypt was signed which has settled for the time being all the points at issue. The Treaty provides for the removal of the British forces from Cairo and Alexandria to the Canal zone; Egypt accepts responsibility for minorities and foreigners; and the Sudan has become a condominium by which Egypt is allowed to maintain a force in that country. The Egyptian Army is to be trained under the direction of a British Military Mission, which acts in an advisory but not executive capacity, and the internal government of the country is entirely in the hands of the Egyptians.

Although this Treaty has solved the British-Egyptian *impasse* it does not appear to have had quite the beneficial and peaceful effect in the country that the Egyptians anticipated, for there has been a further series of political squabbles leading to changes of government and divisions of existing parties. At the time of writing these differences of opinion seem to have been settled temporarily and all appears to be well, but as Egypt is a country in which the most unsuspected developments occur with startling rapidity, it is never safe to attempt a prophecy.

Shortly before the Treaty was signed King Fuad, who had ruled for nineteen years during a particularly difficult period in his country's history, died and his young son, Farouk, ascended the throne. Personally, I consider that in King Fuad Great Britain has lost a good friend and Egypt a very sound and astute monarch. His motives in

Signing the Treaty between Great Britain and Egypt

The shades of Lord Cromer and Zaghoul Pasha, and seated at the table Mr. Anthony Eden, Sir Miles Lampson, Nahas Pasha, Hafez Afifi Pasha, Makram Pasha and others

certain of his actions may not have been dictated always by actual friendship for our country but rather by the trend of circumstances; the fact remains that he had a wiser grasp of the situation and understanding of his people at all times than his own ministers and in many cases than our own Foreign Office. He was always in a difficult situation, for not only did the policy of his own government change from time to time but also that of Great Britain; in other words, having grasped what Sir Austen Chamberlain required in 1928, he had to reconcile himself to the views of Mr. Arthur Henderson and Mr. Ramsay Mac-Donald with Dr. Dalton intervening; and that which these politicians said out of office hardly coincided with their actions when in office. However, as an Oriental this probably did not surprise him to any great extent.

I do not think that our policy in the country during those troublous times made King Fuad's difficult position any easier. We rapped him over the knuckles for being undemocratic and autocratic whenever he threw out a violently anti-British and anti-Monarchy Egyptian Ministry; we found fault with his advisers and demanded their removal from time to time; and all the while we expected him to maintain in the country a government that was not openly antagonistic to our ideals and aims.

King Fuad was certainly not appreciated for his many good qualities while he was alive, neither by his own people nor by our own government; but I think that when the time comes to write the history of his reign and weigh up his actions and aims in a calmer atmosphere, and in the light of the happenings of some five years hence, scant justice will be done to this Monarch if he is not credited with being possibly the wisest and most far-seeing of the many rulers who followed Mohammed Ali.

CHAPTER I

HIGH COMMISSIONERS AND NOTABLES

The tumult and the shouting dies,
The captains and the kings depart.
RUDYARD KIPLING.

THE question that one is asked always by publishers and editors when it is a matter of writing reminiscences is: "And what notables or great men did you meet during your career?" The truth is, of course, that though one comes in contact with a very large number of prominent men if one is an administrator on the confines of Egypt one cannot pretend that one gets to know them very well; nor that one has discovered any particularly intriguing or private sides to their character of which the world in general is ignorant.

High Commissioners and men of that ilk, though they are quite prepared to explore the brains, if any, of governors and officials and obtain their views of local affairs, are not in the habit of giving much of the same coin in return. British residents and officials in Egypt one might almost say are notoriously indiscreet, and if any man that matters discloses to some minor light details of the policy he proposes to carry through the disclosures are usually common property at the various clubs after the lapse of twenty-four hours. For this reason there is greater need for discretion in the East than there is at home, where the horizon is so much wider and there are so many affairs and so many policies to discuss.

During my service in Egypt I came in contact with

five High Commissioners : Sir Reginald Wingate, Viscount Allenby, Lord Lloyd, Sir Percy Loraine and Sir Miles Lampson. Of the five, I imagine all but Sir Miles Lampson were suffering from the disability of having to run a most difficult job with no definite policy to follow and no clear instructions as to the line they should take. Our position in Egypt was so unusual and so ill-defined that the Foreign Office never had any very fixed ideas on the subject, and possibly never understood the different mentalities of the people of the Nile Valley. Governments in England also changed with frequency during the period 1919 and 1936, and the various Secretaries of State for Foreign Affairs naturally differed in their views as to the policy to be adopted, so that the High Commissioners were very much in the position of navigators trying to steer an ill-found ship through seas beset with shoals and reefs with no course set nor charts available. Sir Miles Lampson, I imagine, was better off, as he, apparently, was sent to Egypt with definite instructions to arrive at a treaty at all costs. The others, one concludes, were told to do the best they could in the circumstances, to take no drastic action but to maintain prestige, and to keep Egypt quiet whatever happened ; and this was not easy.

Sir Reginald Wingate was the only one of the five with any real inside knowledge of the country prior to his appointment. Lord Lloyd from his youth had travelled frequently in Egypt, and during the War had served on the Palestine and Trans-Jordan fronts ; whilst, as everyone knows, Lord Allenby had been in command of the Expeditionary Force in Egypt, but neither had experienced the same close contact with the country as had Sir Reginald, who joined the Egyptian Army in 1883, and had served in either the Sudan or Egypt until he accepted the High Commissionership in 1916.

There was, therefore, very little about Egypt and her people that Sir Reginald did not know, and he had one very great asset in being able to speak Arabic both fluently and grammatically. Arabic is a most difficult language, and so hard to master that during the whole of my service in the East I never met an Englishman who spoke it well enough to pass as a native. I should say Sir Reginald was easily the best Arabic scholar serving in the country, and this ability to have real heart-to-heart talks with all and sundry, and last but not least use the correct titles and designations for all classes and walks of life in that country of studious politeness and attention to petty details, was one of the very greatest assistance to him.

I served only a matter of eight months under Sir Reginald's régime, for he was replaced by Lord Allenby in the High Commissionership in 1919 after the rising in Egypt in the spring of that year, the British Cabinet apparently holding him responsible for the outbreak, despite the fact that he had clearly foreseen what would happen and had frequently warned the government at home of the state of affairs. I was then too new to the service in Egypt to have any personal views on the very complex question, and my knowledge of the situation is based entirely on the various books I have read.

I, however, met Sir Reginald in the Western Desert on two or three occasions, and one could not help being struck by the extraordinary effect he had on the Libyan Arabs. So far as I knew, he had never previously been in contact with these particular tribesmen, for the whole of his long service had been in the Sudan or Egypt proper, but there was not an Arab in the West who had not heard of him and his fame as a soldier and administrator and who longed to meet him personally. The Arab, of course, is a natural tuft-hunter, and there is no difficulty in obtaining a crowd and good *claque* for any notable who comes into the Province: but in Sir Reginald's case there was genuine enthusiasm, and every Sheikh was longing to have private speech with him and touch his hand. His ability to talk fluently with them on all subjects made a most lasting impression, and when one takes into account that this popularity of his extended all over the country and in all walks of life, particularly in the Army where he was almost worshipped, it seems a pity that better use was not made of his undoubted ability and wide influence in the country.

During the War Sir Reginald adopted the custom set by the late King George V that no alcohol was allowed in his house until peace was proclaimed; I happen to know, however, that—far from this abstention being utilized to augment the totally inadequate financial resources of the High Commissioner, in those strenuous War days, as the Club gossip was inclined to hint—it enabled Sir Reginald and Lady Wingate frequently to entertain at tea large numbers of soldier convalescents and nurses, a thousand at a time, in the beautiful Residency gardens, a form of rest and relaxation they thoroughly enjoyed. It was, of course, a wonderful example, and would have been still more wonderful if it had been more generally followed. The lamentable fact remains that with one or two exceptions very few people denied themselves alcohol during the war. Dinner at the Residency in those days was, therefore, rather a gloomy business, and the butler who came round with the drinks did nothing to enliven matters, for the tone of his voice, when asking the question "Lemon-ade or barley water, sir?" suggested the death sentence at the Old Bailey. Whatever the High Commissioner's views on temporary teetotalism may have been, one was not left in doubt as to his butler's attitude.

The British Army officer and British official in Egypt are, however, a resourceful and far-seeing class, and forewarned is forearmed, therefore people were in the habit of priming themselves up for these state dinner parties and imbibing sufficient before arrival to carry them through six courses. The result, however, was not entirely happy, for until one has tried one does not realize how difficult it is to get sufficient alcohol on board to make one a cheery dinner companion when one is diluting the stock the whole time with barley water or lemonade. It takes a considerable amount of practice to discover the exact quantity one must consume at 7.50 p.m. to carry one through till 10 p.m. without becoming too cheery and forthcoming with the soup. The marked feature at the Residency dinners in 1918 was the extraordinary cheerfulness that started with the *hors d'œuvre* and lasted to the entrée, and the rather funereal gloom that fell on the party when they reached the dessert stage. I hope I am not giving the impression that we are a race of heavy drinkers in Egypt, because, compared with other countries East of Suez, we are actually most moderate. We are, however, nearly all of us men who are accustomed to drink a whisky and soda or half a pint of wine at dinner with probably a sherry to see the soup course through, and if deprived of these we are not at our best and *bon mots* are conspicuous by their absence.

The first time I dined at the Residency they were in their summer quarters at Alexandria, and I received warning of the lack of alcohol too late to take action. I had driven in from Amria in the Western Desert in a very thirsty and frail condition, and as I imagined dinner was at 8 p.m., I had no time to deal with the situation.

I arrived at the Residency door at 7.55 p.m., and the butler of " barley water and lemonade " fame met me.

" What time is dinner ? " I asked excitedly.

" Eight-thirty p.m., sir."

I looked at my watch hurriedly.

" Good," I said, " I've just time to run round to the Summer Palace Hotel and get some kit I have left there."

" It will be *quite all right*, sir," said the butler distinctly. " Let me send someone to fetch it."

" No, no," I exclaimed, " I must go myself." As there was no kit in existence, this was absolutely essential.

" I tell you, sir, it will be *quite all right*."

By this time, however, I was down the steps into my car and bearing north-east for the Summer Palace, where a strong whisky and soda put me on my legs again and in a fit frame of mind to face a state dinner. At 10 p.m., as the guests were filing away downstairs to the doorway, I saw several of the old habitués of the country heading for a small room on the ground floor. I followed them and found a small but select party quietly but very thoroughly putting away long whiskies and sodas that the butler was serving out in his pantry. He put a brimming glass of a strong mixture in my hand.

" As I told you before, sir, you would have been quite all right," he said solemnly.

Lord Allenby took over the High Commissionership of Egypt with all the prestige of the most successful Palestine campaign behind him. He was the General who had inflicted one of the greatest defeats in the world's history on the most powerful nation in the mid-East, and this counted for much, as the Egyptian dearly loves a conqueror. Perhaps " dearly loves " is hardly the expression to use, but their attitude towards a strong and relentless soldier is something more than fear and reverence and savours almost of devotion. One imagines with his reputation and the renown connected with his name

18

that Allenby could have accomplished anything he wished, and the Egyptians would have accepted the situation without a murmur.

Presumably, however, he had had instructions to go gently and to use diplomacy, and this was not his natural line. All his great qualities as a fighting soldier and an indomitable driving force were stultified by this new and unusual rôle. If a diplomat changes front, shows indecision, and evolves a weak policy, it is more or less what is expected of him and in keeping with his calling. Moreover, one has always the hope that his vacillation is a pose to cover some masterly stroke of diplomacy; this hope is usually a vain one, but one buoys oneself up with it, or, alternatively, if one belongs to the opposite camp, dreads the hidden strength. When a great soldier, however, adopts this policy, the result, to say the least, is apt to be misunderstood by both sides, and the fact remains that the Egyptians, when they had recovered from their surprise, mistook the benignancy of Allenby's régime for weakness.

To understand the need for diplomacy and a strong policy in Egypt at this particular period it is necessary to have some idea of the situation. Although the Nationalist or Wafd party, who were demanding complete independence, apparently represented some ninety per cent. of the population of Egypt, there were other and powerful factors to be considered. First and foremost there was King Fuad, who, whatever his official attitude may have been, was definitely against national freedom and removal of British rule. There were also the Pashas and big landowning classes, who saw and dreaded the thin edge of communism in the Wafd party, and last but not least, many influential and brilliant Egyptians, who disliked the Wafd largely for personal reasons and who, given encouragement, would have been willing to take office and carry on with a policy that more or less reconciled itself to British ideals. When one realizes that in 1930, during that period when the country was solid for the Wafd party, Sidky, backed by King Fuad, took over the reins of government and maintained his rule for five years against, apparently, the wishes of the whole nation, one obtains some idea of how one strong man can control the destiny of his country in face of all opposition. Allenby with his great reputation for strength, not to say ruthlessness, and his nickname of " The Bull," had the ball at his feet, but instead of shooting a goal he kicked it into touch—and there the ball has remained with some vicissitudes ever since.

During Lord Allenby's High Commissionership I cannot say that any of us—the British officials of the country —came in very close contact with him. He was a very great soldier and a great personality, but one never obtained the impression that he concerned himself to any extent with the views and affairs of the small fry. This may be a purely personal impression, but neither during the War nor later, when at the Residency, did he appear to take much interest in the rank and file of his army, nor the British officials of the country. During the War he inspired the troops with the greatest confidence, which was badly needed when he took command in 1917. He saw to it that their rationing was perfect and their well-being all that it should be ; but he never strove to obtain personal contact with the men, and he never, at any time, achieved that adoration that Plumer, Birdwood, Shea and others obtained. He was at all times Olympian and, despite his small clipped moustache, Jove-like and just as unapproachable.

When Stack Pasha was murdered by Nationalist assassins in the streets of Cairo in 1924 a wave of horror and consternation went through the country. The Egyptians, terrified at the reprisals that might be inflicted on the inhabitants, remained shut up in their houses and for two nights the cafés—those gathering places of the educated classes—were deserted, for no man knew how the blow would fall or when. When Allenby delivered the British ultimatum to the Houses of Parliament, with the regiment of the 9th Lancers clattering beside his carriage, the streets of Cairo were deserted, and Parliament itself with visions of members strung up to lamp-posts had scuttled for safety. The ultimatum, when it was read, was strong, but not strong enough, and unfortunately there was included in it a diplomatic blunder of the first water—a purely commercial clause concerning water supplies from the Nile to the Sudan that obviously favoured the Sudan Plantations Syndicate and nothing else had been inserted amongst the other terms of a more punitive nature fitting to the situation. The foreign Press, never very amicable towards the British position in Egypt—a relic of the eighteen-eighties—were not slow to comment on the weak spot, and the Egyptian newspapers, who invariably receive their inspiration from outside, then followed suit. There ensued what one might call one of our sloppy periods during which we allowed the Egyptian Government to argue; the Egyptians themselves crept out of doors again in the streets and cafés, and everyone breathed a sigh of relief. The lion's roar had died away to a feeble whimper and whining complaint. The natural reaction to intense fear, the moment the danger is passed, is annoyance and aggravation with the cause, and from that day British prestige in the Nile Valley was on the wane.

The only times I came in personal contact with Lord Allenby, except as a very junior official at big luncheon parties at the Residency, was when I dined at G.H.Q. mess at Kelab in Palestine just before the third battle of

Gaza. The army had been encamped for five months in this uninteresting stretch of sand country, and it was exceedingly difficult to find any form of recreation beyond riding about in very featureless scenery.

The only people who were really happy were a small group of skilled ornithologists who occupied their spare time by increasing considerably the world's knowledge of migratory birds. The leaders of this community, Colonel Meinertzhagen, Lord William Percy and Major Portal, were more or less in their element, for fate had dumped them down in the very best spot for studying the big annual migration at the right time, and they made the most excellent use of this exceptional opportunity. I doubt if these three lucky individuals, unlike the majority of the Expeditionary Force, experienced a moment's boredom, but the remainder of us found time very heavy on our hands.

One of our childish amusements was to keep tarantulas and scorpions in cigarette-tins and after dinner to match them against each other in fights to the death. These unpleasant insects—sometimes two scorpions, sometimes a pair of tarantulas at catch weight, but more often a scorpion and a tarantula—were placed in a tin washing bowl to fight it out, and there was heavy betting on the results. Usually the tarantula would win as he sailed in to close quarters, snipping off the legs of the scorpion with his mandibles until only the trunk was left. He would then methodically eat the scorpion's head away, apparently oblivious of the fact that his opponent was busily digging in his envenomed sting the whole time. Actually the stings did him no good at all, as he almost invariably died as the result soon after the bets on the result had been settled.

At the dinner I attended at G.H.Q. some tarantula

versus scorpion fighting took place and Lord Allenby's entry, a magnificent heavy-weight tarantula, presented by one of the divisions in the command, was put in the ring. As luck would have it, he met my scorpion, who was only a middle-weight and had no reputation whatsoever. Whether the representative of the Commander-in-Chief took matters too easily, despising his opponent, or whether he was off colour that night, the fact remains that my scorpion dashed in in the first round, planted his sting in some vital spot and Palestine's champion at catch weights rolled over dead. It was all very lamentable— there was no question of foul play, of course, and the fight was a perfectly fair one, but it was definitely regrettable that a scorpion owned by a junior major should publicly defeat the tarantula of the Commander-in-Chief.

When Lord Lloyd arrived in the country in 1925 the first task he had to undertake was the restoration of the respect and deference due to the dignity and position of Great Britain's High Commissioner. It has always been the desire of Egyptian Nationalists to relegate our High Commissioner to the limbo of being merely one of the various foreign ministers that serve in the country, and purposely to ignore and disregard the fact that the post was something far more important. At an official opening of Parliament a short time before the appointment of Lord Lloyd no special arrangements had been made for the arrival, seating or departure of Lord Allenby from the ceremony, and he was seen by all and sundry in the midst of a surging crowd of diplomats, officials and press correspondents almost fighting his way to his seat.

The average Englishman with his democratic ideas rather enjoys this sort of thing, and the " man in the street " appreciates it highly. Nothing commands the respect and admiration of the people for members of our Royal Family more than some occasion when they mix in a crowd and shed all pomp and dignity for the time being. "There's a Prince for you," you'll hear them say, "come right among us just as if he were one of the mob and drinks his glass of bitter with the best. Gawd, I'd do anything for a chap like that."

The East, however, most definitely does not understand this democratic descent from dignity. In its eyes a big man must be big all the time, and, if he does not insist on the utmost respect being paid to him and his position on every occasion, it thinks there must be something wrong with him and his breeding—or that the country that appointed him has a poor opinion of him.

You will see this all day and every day in Egypt. The *fellah* who has made a success of his little plot of land immediately advertises his newly acquired position by buying a first-class trotting donkey, and, here's the important part, hire's a man to run behind it. This type of donkey is the most willing and energetic beast in the world and definitely does not require a whipping-boy behind; but since the days of the Pharaohs the great have ridden with slaves running with them and customs die hard in the East.

A fourth-class clerk drawing £9 a month comes to your house after office hours with a correspondence file weighing about eight ounces. It is quite impossible for him, an *Effendi* and a Government official, to degrade himself by walking through the streets with a file in his hand, so, pacing behind him at a respectful distance, is a uniformed orderly carrying the small packet of correspondence.

At some unguarded moment I have occasionally picked

up a trowel in my garden with the idea of putting in
bedding-out plants, and immediately there has been a
blind rush in my direction, the trowel has been snatched
from my hands and I have been sat firmly into a chair
on the lawn, whilst a group of men under the eyes of
the gardener put in the plants in the wrong position.
Innumerable British officials with the normal British scorn
for these silly ideas of dignity have endeavoured to step
down from the eminent position in which they find themselves ; but their subordinates, wearing the expression of
shame and confusion one sees on the face of British police
when they are dealing with a drunk who insists on taking
off his trousers in the street, immediately rush up and
replace him on his throne.   The Egyptian is most obliging
and polite and he is willing to try to understand and put
up with many British idiosyncrasies, but over questions
of the dignity of power and office he is adamant and
admits no backsliding.

Lord Lloyd with his knowledge of the Orient understood this and was horrified on arrival in Egypt to
find how the post of High Commissioner had fallen from
its high estate.   He at once insisted on the reintroduction
of all the special rights and privileges that had been accorded
to High Commissioners in the past.   Whenever he travelled
he demanded a special train ; he arrived at, and departed
from, Cairo Station by the royal gates ; and at all functions and ceremonies special arrangements had to be made
to ensure his arrival just before the King and his departure
immediately afterwards.   People who did not understand
the situation or the country imagined that Lord Lloyd
was unnecessarily concerned about his personal dignity,
but there was no question of this at all.   Lord Lloyd
clearly realized that for Great Britain's representative to
be herded among the ministers of minor powers at state

Lord Lloyd: "*I hear a lot about your movements and your sayings. What's your little game?*"

Mahommed Mahmoud Pasha: "*I hear a lot about your movements and sayings. What's your little game?*"

functions was to advertise to all and sundry that England no longer insisted on a special position in the country. Egypt is the land where the expression " the thin end of the wedge " originated, and at the first signs of the insertion of this tool one must take adequate steps. In a country where dignity is such an esteemed and fragile flower any apparent discourtesy of this description is not a matter of forgetfulness or oversight—it is done deliberately and with an object in view.

Another point in which Lord Lloyd's policy differed from that of his predecessor was over the question of the British officials in the country. Under a clause in the agreement of 1922 all the British officials were to leave the country by 1927. The first batch—an enormous number—had been relieved in 1924, a second consignment left in 1925, and when Lord Lloyd took over in the autumn of that year only a skeleton force then remained in the country. The result of this sudden removal of almost every head of department in the country was confusion, dissatisfaction and, last but not least, peculation. Lord Lloyd decided to do all that was possible to save something from the wreck, and it was due to his firmness and tact that control of the more essential and important posts remained in British hands until 1936.

To enable him to judge what posts to save, and to discriminate between those that were essential and others that were not so vital, he made it his business to get into personal contact with almost every official in the country. From the British constables serving in the streets of Cairo and Port Said to senior officials of the Army, Lord Lloyd knew not only almost every man personally, but also the details of his special post and the difficulties he had to contend with. Lord Lloyd took over the High Commissionership of the country at one of the most difficult periods of its history, and only those who worked with him realized the devotion and untiring energy with which he undertook his task. In the midst of the most delicate and worrying situation he could always find time for a short and encouraging interview with some ill-used British official in some minor post, and his sympathetic grasp of the matter in hand and his friendly helpful attitude made him a host of friends who will always look back on Lord Lloyd as the best High Commissioner Egypt has ever seen.

The officials in the country obtained the impression that Lord Lloyd was not only mindful of their welfare, but regarded them as very necessary and vital cogs in the machinery of Anglo-Egyptian affairs—men who were performing a difficult and essential job—and it is always satisfactory to feel that one's work is appreciated. With some of his predecessors and successors they at times felt as if they were not only troublesome and redundant, but that their presence constituted a definite embarrassment and obligation.

On the other hand, Lord Lloyd with his very quick and virile brain and his desire to get to the point at once, had very little time for a few officials in the country who, from long residence in the East, had become more Oriental than the Egyptians themselves. If he asked a question he expected a direct answer, and any attempt to haver or shelve the issue brought forth a reprimand in a rasping cutting voice which accounted for a certain amount of unpopularity among the class known in Egypt as the " goldfinches," those who wear a touch of scarlet on their heads—a tarbush—and line their own nests with consummate skill. There were, during Lord Lloyd's régime, a few British officials of long standing who desired only to hold down their own particular jobs to the bitter end, and were unmindful of the fate of more junior officials under them and the well-being of their departments. Lord Lloyd detected them at once, and his enemies may be numbered among those whose dilatory and self-satisfied methods met with his disapproval—and Lord Lloyd's disapproval is very shattering to one's *amour propre*. One is left in no doubt as to one's failings and shortcomings.

In Sir Ronald Storrs' vastly entertaining and clever book, *Orientations*, he mentions how Lord Kitchener carried on in the country, "in face of that detraction which, in the East, is the natural pastime of undirected leisure." There is so much in this little sentence that might convey nothing to the man who does not understand the mentality of the British official in the Orient, for it is his habit—a bad one—to crab the High Commissioner or Governor-General, or whoever is in charge of affairs, with a constant chatter of derogatory remarks both as regards his personality and his policy. Probably Sir Eldon Gorst suffered from this little failing more than anyone, but every High Commissioner in Egypt had his share. When a new High Commissioner arrived one would hear on all sides nothing but praise for him, his manner and his methods, and then, after a few short months, the undercurrent of gossip would start and permeate the clubs and houses of those who entertain. It was all very cheap and despicable and suggests that there must be many in Egypt who have insufficient work to do.

Another community in Egypt who owed much to Lord Lloyd's High Commissionership were the members of the British business firms, for, in his eyes, being Great Britain's representative in the country did not mean that he was to concern himself solely with diplomacy, but also with more mundane matters such as trade. With his very wide vision and his devotion to the British Empire he realized the importance of furthering and encouraging business with the Nile Valley. This side of the British régime had been sorely neglected in the past, and with the general feeling in Egypt against our occupation of the country our trade was not in a very flourishing condition and badly needed assistance when Lord Lloyd was first appointed.

For the personal help and encouragement that he gave British officials he expected in return that if there should be a question of the purchase of goods, cars or other commodities in their special department, they should see to it that British contractors and firms secured the order. This was not always easy, for the Ministry of Finance at that time was showing definite bias in favour of German or Italian contractors; but if a big contract went the wrong way despite one's efforts, one realized that one was in for a difficult interview with this very much alive and dynamic High Commissioner.

Compared with other nations Great Britain is very badly represented in Egypt as regards schools and hospitals, and in this respect it was very evident as far back as 1925 the steps that Italy was taking to impress the Egyptians and the mid-East generally with the importance of her position in the Eastern Mediterranean. In every town of any size in Egypt there is a vast and imposing Italian Consulate, a school for Italian boys and any Egyptians who might wish to attend, and an up-to-date hospital. France, too, has not been backward in this respect, and many of the leading Egyptian politicians and their wives owe their education to French schools. England alone was backward, and here again Lord Lloyd stepped into the long vacant breach and strove to awake British nationals to their shortcomings, with the result that the success of the British schools in Egypt to-day owe much to his encouragement and initiative.

Unfortunately Lord Lloyd's term of office was a short one, as he resigned the High Commissionership on the accession to office of the Labour Government in 1929. His galvanic activities and very strong Imperial views had proved too drastic altogether for the weak Conservative party in power prior to Mr. MacDonald's Government; and Mr. Henderson on taking over the Foreign Office decided from the start that he and Lord Lloyd would never see eye to eye. It was, however, both foolish and hasty to force a resignation of this description within the first few weeks of taking office, as it meant, not only a repudiation of Lord Lloyd but everything for which he stood. The Egyptians were not slow to grasp this point, and they have never forgotten it. The difficulties with which his successors have had to deal during the years between 1929 and 1936 are almost entirely due to Mr. Henderson's hasty and misguided action in 1929.

In the history of the British Empire there have been many Proconsuls whose views and activities have not met with the approval of the existing Government at home. Sometimes they have won through despite opposition, and posterity has reason for gratitude to them and their imperial attitude, and sometimes they have failed; but always, for the sake of the country, there has been some attempt to " save face "—not so much for the sake of the official in question as for his position, his policy and his successor. I imagine that Lord Lloyd cared not one jot whether his face was saved or not by the Labour Government that compelled his resignation, but by so doing Mr. Henderson made it extremely difficult for every High Commissioner that has followed; for the Egyptian Nationalists, rather naturally, construed the action as indicating the complete reversal of British policy in every detail. The seed that was sown in 1929 germinated very rapidly, but we have not reaped all the harvest yet.

I imagine that possibly Lord Lloyd hardly fits in with the scheme of things to-day. When I looked at the photograph of the Conservative Conference at Scarborough in 1937 I realized the reason, for the hall was packed with old ladies. I am sure they were one and all most kindly and benevolent old ladies; but I wonder if they really grasp the mentalities of Egyptians, Hindus, Palestine Arabs, Sudanese and Abyssinians. I served with Lord Lloyd in the War, and again with him for four years in Egypt during his High Commissionership, and the feeling that I have is that I would like to set the calendar back to 1894 and go out with him as one of his lieutenants to South Africa, the Sudan or even Egypt, and to have taken an active part with him in the administration and general advancement he would have accomplished in those countries.

Lord Lloyd visited Sinai several times during his term of office as High Commissioner, and those who imagine that he was unpopular with the Egyptians owing to his very strong policy should have seen the welcome he obtained from the local people. His Arabic was not in the same class as Sir Reginald Wingate's, but it was quite good enough, and the inhabitants of Kantara and vicinity who, on his first visit turned up in hundreds to meet his train, though rather sullen to start with by reason of the activities of politicians, were at once won over by his disarming and friendly manner, so that he received a most enthusiastic welcome on his return a few days later.

At El Arish waiting on the platform to greet us were all the Egyptian Army officers of the station. Among them was one who had been with Lord Lloyd during the Hedjaz campaign with Lawrence. He was a very good fellow, but of recent years had rather lost his enthusiasm for the British and was definitely turning Nationalist and hostile. He had said to his brother officers, as I knew, for one hears most things in the desert : " He will have forgotten me. He is a great man now and will not want to know a small one like me."

When Lord Lloyd stepped out of his coach and I started to introduce the officers in order of their rank, he suddenly exclaimed :

" Oh, you need not introduce me to my old friend— *Mahommed Effendi*. We served together in the Hedjaz. Do you remember that camel ride we made from Akaba when my saddle-bags were burnt ? "

A few days later I heard this officer holding forth in the local club.

" You all saw it—every one of you. He, the High Commissioner of England, with all the worries of Egypt on his back, remembered me after thirteen years, who was but a *mulazim* (lieutenant) at the time. I ask you, would any of our great ones have done the same ? Give me the English officer—he does not forget his old friends." And after this Lord Lloyd's war-time comrade persisted in driving about the country with a Union Jack on his car. This is an honour reserved for the High Commissioner only, but in the circumstances we said nothing about it.

Later on in the day when we were some fifty miles south in the desert a big gathering of Beduin were at the roadside and some of whom had seen Lord Lloyd with Lawrence during the War. These he recognized instantly, to their great joy ; and then, to while away the time, he had a happy inspiration. He said he would offer a prize of £2 for the best camel amongst them, and this recognition of the importance of the camel is always a happy thought with Beduin.

Lord Lloyd asked me if I were good enough judge to pick out the best of the two hundred odd animals that were being trotted past us, but I shrank from the ordeal.

"I expect your *shawish* (sergeant) knows—he's an Arab," said Lord Lloyd.

The *shawish* when appealed to was quite sound. There was no argument about it—the camel of Sheikh Salem was easily the best—and so, amid loud clapping, the award, which gave complete satisfaction, was made.

"*Wallahi*," said one old Sheikh afterwards, "I have heard much of this *Mandoob el Sami* (High Commissioner), but no one ever told me that he was the best judge of a camel in the country. A man who knows a good camel at sight knows all things."

This was typical of Lord Lloyd, for wherever he went his attractive and dynamic personality had the same effect on the mass of the people who turned up in the first place rather sulkily but went away to enthuse. Unfortunately pressure of work in Cairo made his visits to the country few and far between; but some indication of the effect his presence had may be gained from a furious press attack in the local papers who protested against the High Commissioner's visits to country towns. This, they stated, was no part of a British High Commissioner's duties, and an abuse of his prerogatives. Lord Lloyd's instant popularity whenever he came in contact with a crowd was such that the Nationalist or Wafd party feared for the future of their cause which relied on keeping the feeling against Great Britain at boiling-point.

Sir Percy Loraine, who followed Lord Lloyd, had a very much more peaceful and less eventful time in Egypt than either of his predecessors; but this was due entirely to the fact that the Egyptians were far too busy fighting amongst themselves to find time to annoy and attack Great Britain. It was shortly after he took office that the Wafd were returned to power for the second time, and after an abortive attempt at signing a treaty with Great Britain, proceeded to pick a quarrel with King Fuad which led them into the wilderness for five years. All Sir Percy Loraine had to do after this was to keep the ring for the combatants and occasionally warn them; and he did this from outside the ropes and at no time scrambled inside to break clinches.

Both Lord Allenby and Lord Lloyd had had to deal with a series of the most difficult situations when the Egyptian Government took action that was definitely aimed at weakening our position in the country, and they were forced constantly to deliver strong notes and ultimatums to counter these machinations. Sir Percy had nothing of this description to deal with, for Sidky's Government was definitely pro-British, and desired above all things the continuance of the occupation for the time being. I imagine Sir Percy was asked occasionally as to the possibility of bringing off a treaty, but with a virtual dictatorship in the country that represented at the best not more than ten per cent. of the electorate it was obviously a waste of time. If Sidky had obtained the most favourable terms imaginable for his country, the Wafd on their return to office would have repudiated his treaty, lock, stock and barrel, at the first opportunity as a gesture of personal spite.

Sir Percy merely had to sit tight and watch events, and during his years of office he showed no desire to travel about the country and get in contact with the people. I personally never saw him except at the Residency, and as I was the *vade mecum*, as it were, of one of the most interesting and inaccessible antiquities in Egypt—the Monastery

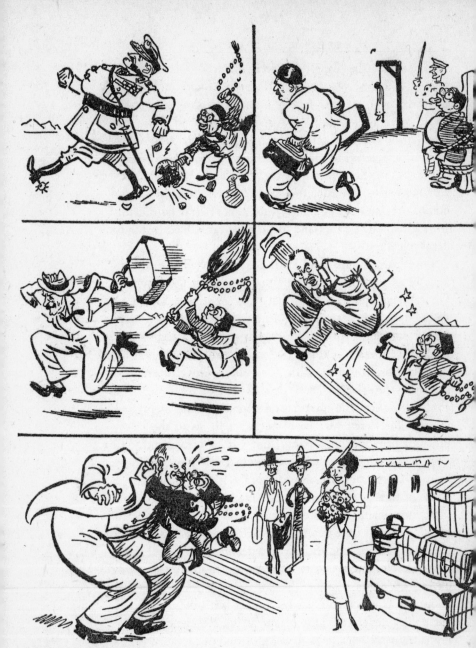

Five High Commissioners of Great Britain and Masri Effendi, the John Citizen of Egypt

From right to left: Sir Reginald E. Wingate, Viscount Allenby, Lord Lloyd, Sir Percy Loraine and Sir Miles and Lady Lampson

of Mt. Sinai—this was remarkable. He was the direct antithesis of Lord Lloyd in every way; where one was all galvanic energy and enthusiasm with a " for God's sake get on with the job " attitude, the other was suave and rather languid, with " Foreign Office " at its best stamped all over him.

Sir Miles Lampson arrived in the spring of 1934 with a record for smoothing out difficulties and achieving treaties in China. He is very large and very imposing with a markedly genial manner. He was known among the Egyptians as S'Miles, which was a very suitable pseudonym. English names usually present considerable difficulties when used by those who speak Arabic, as the Arabic tongue resents two consonants adjoining without a vowel between, and such letters as " P " or " V " do not exist. Maxwell was therefore christened as Makaswilly, and Sir Percy Loraine as S'Bercy. Lord Lloyd constituted a difficulty as he arrived in the country as Sir George Lloyd, and the ordinary people very naturally thought he must be the Lloyd George who had negotiated the Peace Treaty, and he was known at first as *S'Joge Loid Joge* and later as *Lode Loid*.

Sir Miles held the view, and a very sound one, that it was impossible for a High Commissioner to deal with Egyptian affairs and negotiate a treaty unless he knew the country thoroughly. He spent the first year of his term of office seeing everything, from the whole of the Sinai Province to the Western limits of the Libyan Desert, together with the four big oases, and then did an exhaustive tour of the Sudan. He was definitely air-minded and travelled as far as possible by aeroplane—a proceeding that was not at all popular with his then private secretary, who loathed the air and always suffered from sickness.

Sir Miles' activities were not understood by the Egyptians, who saw in his peregrinations an unhealthy interest in their country that boded ill for the future. The local Press was greatly concerned over his visit to Sinai, which they construed as an intrigue with me to annex the peninsula to the British Empire. One paper giving a circumstantial account by an "eye-witness" of how I had smuggled that other arch-conspirator, Sir Arthur Wauchope, from Jerusalem so that the two High Commissioners could meet secretly on some mountain in Southern Sinai—a Moses and Aaron conception—to discuss their fell designs on the integrity of Egypt's territory.

The effusions of the Arabic Press are so delightfully humorous and naïve and so very ignorant. If these two High Commissioners had had anything secret to talk over they had innumerable opportunities when they stayed with each other in Cairo and Jerusalem respectively, or when they played golf together. They would hardly arrange such a conspicuous and unwieldy thing as a meeting in the desert where everything attracts notice and everything is known; I have frequently discovered one has only to drop a pin in the heart of Sinai for the reverberations of its fall to resound in the clubs of Gezira within twelve hours.

The Egyptians as a race, however, are such natural intriguers that they see something suspicious in every movement that is made by a man in the position of High Commissioner. There is, or was, at the Residency some member of the native staff who was in the pay and secret service of the *Nationalist* party in the country. This is proved by the reports of all happenings and movements of guests that appeared in the local Press, and when the scare of the annexation of Sinai was in the news I happened to be staying at the Residency, with the result that my peregrinations were fully reported. It said amongst other things that one night I was closeted with Sir Miles in

"*The man who knows everything—the Kavasse at
the Residency*"

his office till past midnight examining maps and documents. Actually we were discussing duck-shooting and fishing and looking at a selection of photographs of bag and baskets.

The Egyptians, realizing that we regard the Peninsula as being of some importance, are quite unable to grasp the fact that we are interested in it from the point of view of the Suez Canal and nothing else. It is only a desert at the best and little can be made of it. Its mineral wealth is in the same category as its cultivation, namely, hardly worth while; and though it was once regarded as having possibilities as an oil-field the various attempts at boring that have been made in different parts of the Peninsula were one and all failures. All this is common knowledge, but the interest which we take in the country compels the Egyptians to believe that it must hold some hidden wealth that will be exploited to the full immediately Great Britain gets her hand on this triangle of desert. One erudite correspondent in an Arabic paper wrote a long article describing the wealth of Sinai, and said that it was "rich in valuable minerals such as lime." This is quite true, as I imagine about two-thirds of Sinai is solid lime-stone—unfortunately the same description applies to almost every country in the world.

Sir Miles Lampson will go down to posterity as the High Commissioner who brought off the long-delayed Treaty, and on paper I imagine it is as good a treaty as we could expect in the circumstances. I say "in the circumstances" advisedly because actually the negotiations took place after, and seemingly as the result of, a particularly unhappy state of affairs in the country. In other words, the agreement reached appeared to be a concession to force.

In October, 1935, the invasion of Abyssinia was beginning; the futile and irritating policy of sanctions was being applied; Italy was most aggressive and unyielding, and war looked a possibility. For the time all Egypt was terrified, and with very good reason, for if hostilities had occurred she would have been in the hub of things. There was never at any period a happier moment for bringing off a treaty of friendship with Egypt than the autumn of 1935, when she realized that the only thing that stood between her and invasion by Italy was the occupation of the country by Great Britain.

Unfortunately the opportunity was missed. One imagines the Foreign Office were engaged too busily with the Abyssinian affair to worry about Egypt unduly. The Treaty had been in the air for thirteen years without taking any tangible form, and a few months more would not make much difference. The trouble is that in Egypt situations occur very quickly and in a most unaccountable and unexpected fashion—the horizon that is clear without a cloud in sight at daybreak is often overcast and most threatening by nightfall.

There was a sudden wave of anti-British feeling inspired and fanned by the Wafd party as a purely political move to discredit the existing ministry. There was reason to suspect also foreign propaganda and foreign financial assistance. Great Britain was accused, among other things, of treating Egypt with contempt in that she had taken active steps for the defence of the country without consulting or informing the Egyptian Government of her intentions. Heavy reinforcements of British troops had landed at Port Said, and Alexandria had been turned into a British Naval base without the permission of the Egyptians. It was the most excellent propaganda, and was most skilfully applied, for in a week the whole of Egypt blazed up into anti-British rioting, and every school and university in the country went on strike.

It was in this atmosphere some six months later that the

" *The Removal of Abrashi Pasha from the Palace.*"

Ziwar Pasha : "Have you seen anything of Abrashi Pasha lately?"
Sir Miles Lampson : " I have searched for him everywhere but cannot see him."

Treaty was signed—and it was unfortunate for both Great Britain and Egypt. Unfortunate for us because the Egyptians entertain the feeling that the generous concessions it contained were wrung from us by active demonstrations and as a concession to disorder; and unfortunate for Egypt because the schoolboys and students of the country are firmly of the opinion that they succeeded where a legion of cabinet ministers failed and that they won Egypt's freedom by striking and rioting. The result is that never a day passes without some school or other in the country going on strike for a variety of childish reasons, and it is very difficult for a Government that owes its position to rioting schoolboys to take the necessary steps to reinstil the discipline they destroyed deliberately for their own purposes.

To sum up the situation, one can only say with regard to this Treaty that if we had been prepared to make all the concessions we have we might have obtained an agreement with the country on these lines at almost any time during the unhappy period between 1919 and 1936. The fact that we gave way on almost every point after seventeen years of unrest and disturbance provides another object lesson to the world that Great Britain—or the post-War Great Britain—will always surrender to the forces of disorder.

As Sinai lies on the road to Palestine, I came in contact from time to time with distinguished sight-seers, from Royalty, both serving and ex, to well-known writers, Parliamentarians and straying journalists. On one occasion I had the supreme honour of sitting at table with four kings—the poker-player's dream—but it is only fair to state that two of them were definitely ex, one of them had been deposed and reinstated, and the fourth was a ruling Prince. They were the ex-kings Hussein and Ali of the Hedjaz, King Feisal of Iraq and the Emir Abdulla of

43

Trans-Jordan, and they had gathered together at Port Said on the occasion of King Hussein's retirement to Cyprus after Ibn Saud's successful invasion of his country.

The Emir Abdulla I knew well, as I frequently went to Trans-Jordan to see Peake Pasha, the commander of his Arab Legion, and when in Amman I never failed to pay my respects to this very charming and urbane Prince. Of the Emir, Lawrence in his *Seven Pillars of Wisdom* says in connection with his search for an Arab leader in the revolt: " As our conversation continued I became more and more sure that Abdulla was too balanced, too cool, too humorous to be a prophet: especially the armed prophet who, if history be true, succeeded in revolutions. His value would come perhaps in the peace after success." This prophecy has come true, for Abdulla as Emir of Trans-Jordan has been an unqualified success as a ruler of a large Arab state populated almost entirely by nomads.

Trans-Jordan might so easily have had a stormy unrestful post-War period such as Iraq has suffered, and that it has experienced some twenty years of peace and harmony is almost entirely due to the wisdom and well-balanced mind of this very charming Arab Prince working in complete harmony and friendship with his chief-of-staff, Peake.

As Lord Lloyd said in a speech at a dinner given in his honour during the Coronation festivities: " Ismuhu [1] Sherif, Shakhsuhu Sherif, Nafsuhu Sherif." (" His name is noble; his character is noble; and he himself is noble.") A more apt and true description of the Emir could not be devised, and one can only congratulate Lord Lloyd on being able to put into classical Arabic such a happy description of this delightful and charming ruler.

After the Egyptian notables with whom I was accus-

[1] The family name of the Emir Abdulla is Sherif, which means: noble.

44

tomed to work in Egypt I found Abdulla such a pleasing
antidote, for here was a man who was an aristocrat in the
best sense of the word; a man born to rule, very sure of
himself, and one who blended dignity and a strong personality with a most delightful sense of humour. He was
greatly interested in natural history, and our discussions
on liaison matters concerning our frontiers sooner or later
turned to hunting, shooting and hawking. Among other
things, he wanted a pet leopard, and asked me if I could
obtain one for him from Sinai. I said I would do my best
to obtain one if he would get me a pair of oryx from
Trans-Jordan, as I wished to re-establish this antelope in
the Peninsula. Unfortunately both these animals are very
rare, and by no means easy to catch, so that nothing materialized. The Emir used to ask me if I had got him his
leopard, and I would retaliate by inquiring after my oryx.

The last time we met was after my retirement at a big
reception in London in connection with the Coronation.
I was wearing a deaf aid to counteract my disability, and
as he had not seen it on me before, he asked what it was
and how it worked.

" And is it working now? " he said, picking up the
reception box.

" Yes," I replied.

He then lifted the box to his mouth and shouted:
" Feyn fahadi? " (" Where is my leopard? ")

Kipling came through Sinai during an inspection of
the War graves in the mid-East, and the idea of this big
peninsula with its Arab population being run by one
solitary Briton was the sort of thing that intrigued his very
busy and inquiring mind—it was so entirely Kiplingesque.
He got out at El Arish Station and had a look at the barren
sand country, peering at it from under his jutting eyebrows.

" Yes," he said in his brisk manner, " and I suppose most of your troubles here are in connection with land ownership—that and smuggling."

This, to my mind, was a fairly good testimonial and proof, if it were needed, that Kipling was not only a great writer, but also a man of more than ordinary insight and intelligence. In one minute he had grasped the innermost details of my job. Most men, on seeing Sinai and its picturesque nomads with their big, curved swords and fast-trotting camels, might have thought my time was occupied with fighting recalcitrant tribesmen or preventing raids and pillage; but Kipling in his wisdom and wide knowledge saw that it was land and " my neighbour's land mark " that proved the bone of contention. And though the land is nearly worthless he was right.

He was a great student of the Old Testament, and on the principle that there was nothing new under the sun held the view that most of the world situations of to-day were merely wider repetitions of those recorded in one or other of the books of the Bible, and that our various leaders and soldiers had their counterparts in the kings and patriarchs mentioned in Joshua, Judges and Samuel. Once when I was puzzling over the title of a book he said, picking up the Bible, " This is the best place to look for one," and promptly read out half a dozen in as many minutes.

My friendship with Kipling lasted till his death. Every summer during my leave I used to motor 130 miles to lunch with him at Batemans, and I cannot think of anyone else for whom I would drive through two counties for a single meal. One of my most pleasant recollections is walking with him beside the little brook at Batemans and having the various fields and fords pointed out to me by the author of those two wonderful books, *Puck of Pook's*

Hill and *Rewards and Fairies*. I saw where the Centurion met the children, where the Norman knight spurred his horse across the ford, and the house without iron.

I remember commenting on the life-like picture he had drawn of the two Roman Centurions on the Great Wall, and he said, " Oh, that was quite easy. I merely took the subalterns who serve on the North-West Frontier of India as my characters. The type has not changed in any detail."

It is the fashion to-day to decry Kipling and his works, the reason being, apparently, that it is now considered bad form to mention the Empire which the past generation won for us so hardly, so naturally a poet and writer who sang and wrote of the Empire before all things must bear the blame for the change of thought. It riles me, how-ever, to hear the younger generation, who do not under-stand the outlook of the late eighties and the nineties, scoff at him as a jingoist, a war-monger and worst of all an Imperialist. Kipling at least dealt with, and wrote of, men, and his works will live and be remembered. This, one hopes fervently, will not be the case with at least one product of the younger generation—the songs that crooners sing. One hears on the wireless to-day plaintive and discordant noises that suggest more prisoners must have been taken by the Abyssinians than the Italians admitted, and that the unfortunate creatures earn their living by wailing for their lost manhood. The pseudo-male crea-tures who howl so mournfully are, however, preferable to the female of the species, for the noises they give vent to bring back memories of rough channel crossings and bad attacks of laryngitis. In an age when the B.B.C. have to provide an hour of this sort of entertainment every evening or offend their listeners, it is small wonder that Kipling, his writings and his ideals of Empire find little favour—but this phase will pass.

CHAPTER II

THE WAFD—THE PLAYBOYS OF THE EASTERN WORLD

Patriots are grown too shrewd to be sincere,
And we too wise to trust them.

COWPER.

THERE is an old and very true saying that countries get the governments they deserve, but there are exceptions to every rule and one can safely say that Egypt certainly has done nothing whatsoever to deserve the Wafd; no country in existence has merited such an infliction. In course of time the Egyptians will look back upon the years between 1919 and 1938 and realize this for themselves, for never in the history of this world has there been a popular party that has so shamefully misused its power and thrown away wilfully so many golden opportunities of achieving the objects for the furtherance of which it was created.

The whole history of Egypt's efforts to obtain her independence between the years 1919 and 1936, when the Treaty with Great Britain was finally signed, is a record of the Wafd's extraordinary methods of government when in power and their still more extraordinary and short-sighted policy when out of office. During this stormy period there were several extremely sound and far-seeing Ministries not of the Wafd persuasion who took office, one might say unconstitutionally, either at the instigation of King Fuad, who was no believer in the voice of the people as interpreted by the Wafd, or by one of the

British High Commissioners holding office during these periods.

It was the desire of these governments to prove to Great Britain and the Capitulatory Powers that Egypt was capable of ruling herself and that the country was fit for complete independence in every way. It was necessary to give proof of this to the other Great Powers as well as Great Britain, as they were more vitally concerned with the Capitulations than we were.

Egypt possesses some first-class, intelligent and far-seeing politicians, qualified in every way to direct the affairs of the State, but they one and all belong to other parties and not to the Wafd. Invariably, when there has been a period of complete peace and sound government with these politicians in office, and Great Britain and the Powers concerned were beginning to think that a treaty was possible, the Wafd, jealous that any other party should speak for the nation, has stirred up the schoolboys and riff-raff of the towns to open riot in an effort to unseat the government in power. The result was that all thought of a treaty was put on one side until Egypt could give better proof that she was competent to produce a government able to restrain the dangerous and fanatical elements in the country; and this was one result only, the other being that as these disturbances almost invariably started at the beginning of the winter and were duly reported, not to say exaggerated, in the British, American and Continental press, Egypt lost again and again practically all the tourist traffic which would normally arrive in the country in December bringing considerable sums of money into the country.

During the seventeen years between 1919 and 1936 there were only five winters when conditions were peaceful enough in the Nile Valley to tempt tourists to come to

Cairo in any numbers, and this constant state of unrest in the country has given Egypt a bad name, so that the winter visitors who were wont to flock there in thousands now give it a wide berth. There are at the present time fewer hotels in the country than there were in 1914, and many of the larger ones in Cairo and Luxor now open up one wing only during the short " rush " season.

As a proof of the lengths to which a Wafd-incited mob will go one might quote the lamentable occurrence in the early months of 1936 when the delegates to a World Surgical Conference were surrounded by a crowd of howling rioters, who tried to upset the cars of the various foreign representatives as they arrived with their wives for the inauguration ceremony. The Conference broke up before its task was completed in consequence and many of the delegates left the country in disgust. Egypt is now spending thousands every year on advertisements and propaganda striving to win back to her shores the tourists that the Wafd party's minions insulted and turned away.

The Wafd owed its inception in 1919 to the popular cry for complete independence and self-determination, the general demand for which made the post-war settlement of Europe and the Near East such a difficult and unsatisfactory problem. The head of the party—in fact, its creator—was Saad Pasha Zaghloul, an Egyptian of *fellah* stock who had served as an official in the Egyptian Government. There was nothing very remarkable about Zaghloul beyond the fact that he had a considerable amount of confidence in himself, a certain strength of purpose and was a good orator. His brain was in no way outstanding and there were far cleverer men in the party, but he caught the popular fancy and in the eyes of the Egyptians ranked with Washington, Garibaldi, and other great leaders in the struggle for freedom. This popularity went to his head and towards the end of his career he suffered from megalomania, so that in one of his interviews with a senior British official of the Residency he referred to himself not as " I " or even the regal "We," but as "Saad," and spoke in the third person.   He believed implicitly that he was the saviour of his country and had been appointed by God to carry out His will, for there was something of the fanatic about Zaghloul ; but the trouble was that the party became too strong for him and during the latter part of his life he was more or less in the position of a piece of flotsam being swept away on the bosom of a flood—the fact that he was floating at the head of the waters gave the false impression that he was leading it, whereas in fact if he had tried to check his headlong flight the flood would have swept over him and swirled him into a side eddy.

The Wafd came into power in the election of 1923 and practically carried the country for the simple reason that it was very dangerous for an elector to vote for anyone but a member of the popular party.   The Parliament that sat after the election was the most deliciously funny institution that has ever happened in Egypt or anywhere else. Its keynote was lack of discipline and at every debate half the House were on their feet at the same time shouting their views whilst the other half yelled to them to sit down.   The President at the opening of Parliament was provided with one of those small bells that one strikes with one's forefinger ; this he broke at the first sitting by hitting it with his fist, and small blame to him.   At the next sitting he was presented with a more efficient Mark 1 bell that also proved useless, and, having tried a railway station-master's variety, he was finally equipped with an electric fire-alarm buzzer, the noise of which was so terrific that the whole House including the President had to rush into the lobbies to save their ear-drums.

This government fell in 1924 owing to the murder of the Sirdar, Sir Lee Stack, for which they were held responsible, and a moderate party was formed which carried on with various changes until the autumn of 1929, when, after a general election, Egypt once more saddled itself with a Wafd Parliament.

The Ministries that took office during the years between 1924 and 1929 had not a majority in the House, and how they managed to survive so long is one of those mysteries of the East that cannot be explained. Parliament was still overwhelmingly Wafd, but a slight change of feeling was apparent in the country generally and it was evident that the popular party was no longer quite as popular as it had been. Exactly how far this change of feeling went it is difficult to say, as, if a voter wished to dissociate himself from the people's party, he had to be either a very influential man or a very brave one.

The Wafd, swollen with power and extremely jealous of any dissension, had changed from a people's party fighting for its country's freedom to a dictatorship desirous of office, and backed by a form of Mafia or Secret Society. It adopted methods of terrorism and it was unsafe, not to say disastrous, for any man to hold or express anti-Wafd views. The average *fellah* (cultivator) has no particular political ideas, as he is not a very intelligent man and listens readily to any nonsense talked by the wearer of a tarbush and European clothes. Every village in Egypt contains a large number of half-educated so-called *Effendis*, who are the sons of the *fellaheen* and who have been sufficiently educated to despise manual labour, but who do not come up to the standard required by the government offices even if the government could find room for them all. These products of this craze for indiscriminate education on unsound lines are all ardent Wafdists, as the party when in power endeavour to find employment for them. The *fellah* is a Wafdist partly because he has never heard the other side of the question and partly because he might get a bang over the head with a *nabbut* if he dared to think or speak otherwise.

The junior clerks, tax collectors, etc., and other minor employees in the smaller towns were almost solidly Wafd, as they had an idea that they would have better prospects of promotion and increased pay with that party in power, though as a matter of fact, during its various terms of office, the Wafd, except for some very flagrant cases of favouritism, did nothing whatsoever to improve the conditions of service for the junior ranks, and usually passed an order postponing promotion and increases of pay.

Among the senior and executive staff of the government there was a large number of men who did not see eye to eye with the popular party, but they were always inarticulate for the very simple reason that it was unsafe to express any other political views. On the three occasions when a Wafd Government took office it was plainly evident that they had a black list of all officials in the government service who were antagonistic to their party, and a clean sweep was made of them. The Wafd had secret agents in every office in the country and a very close watch and records were kept on the movements and remarks of every official, particularly those who were in actual touch with British chiefs.

The Egyptian Government normally is not remarkable for the expedition with which it manages its affairs, but the celerity displayed by the Wafd party on taking office in ridding themselves of all officials of the wrong political views would have been an object lesson in promptitude to the rest of the world if only it had been shown in a better cause. In 1930, for instance, after the fall of Mohammed Mahmoud's Cabinet, every *Mudir* (Governor), sub-*Mudir*, and most of the Under-Secretaries were placed on pension during their first twenty-four hours of office, and before a fortnight had elapsed over two hundred officials had been either retired or transferred from their positions to others less attractive and less remunerative.

The chaos and inefficiency that this caused in the administration of the country was beyond belief, for not only were executive officials penalized and transferred, but also those holding necessary and purely technical posts in such departments as Agriculture, Customs and Railways. The Ministry of Agriculture is not only the most important but probably the most efficient department in the country, and owing to the nature of its work should certainly be outside politics in every way, but in the clean sweep of 1929 highly technical officials engaged in some special research were ruthlessly rooted out on account of their supposed political views and sent to some other department in the provinces where their special knowledge could not be employed to any advantage. That is to say, citrus fruit experts during some important experiment were sent to do ordinary clerking in a minor office, cotton-worm entomologists were despatched to outlying poultry-farms, and horticulturists were turned on to survey work. This was done with two objects in view: firstly, to show the officials in the country that adherence to any other party than the Wafd would be regarded as a crime to be punished at the earliest opportunity, and secondly, to reward those ardent Wafdists in minor positions who had been acting as secret agents during the party's absence from office.

When another party came to power after the inevitable fall of the Wafd, namely in 1924, 1928, and 1930, their successors in common justice had to see that wrongs were righted and another complete change of senior government officials took place. This "Box and Cox" system persisted for the thirteen years between 1924 and 1937, necessitating a double staff of senior officials, one on pension and one serving, and it still remains to be seen if the leopard can change its spots, or if this very vindictive party, if it returns to power again, can resist the temptation to penalize all those who are not in complete accord with its views.

One rather amusing episode during this "quick-change" period concerned a police officer in Cairo, whose unpleasant task it had been to remove a prominent and very vociferous member of the Wafd party from an assembly during a period when the all-powerful faction were not in power. There is no saying what were the original political views of this particular officer; for all one knows he might have been a keen Wafdist himself, but he was called upon to use force in the execution of his office and he did his duty. When the Wafd came into power at 10 a.m. on March 18th, 1928, the officer was placed on pension at 10.5 a.m. precisely! About fifteen months later when the National party fell, this unfortunate policeman was immediately reinstated, promoted, and given his back pay, to fall with another and more resounding crash on the 1st January, 1930, when the Wafd once again returned to office. In less than six months' time like a phœnix he rose again from the ashes of half-pay and sprang to still greater eminence on Sidky Pasha taking over the reins of government. Exactly what his fate is at the present time I cannot say, as I have lost touch with the situation, but it must have been extremely awkward for his subordinates during those years, as his upward and downward movements were so rapid and entirely ephemeral that they were probably at a loss to know whether to greet him with a low obeisance of deep respect and humility, or to tip him ten piastres to tide him over a bad period.

The greatest mistake made by the Wafd party, however, was in allowing unbridled licence to their Parliamentary deputies. These gentlemen, who had been elected solely for their enthusiasm for the national cause and not on account of any special ability or knowledge of the country and its affairs, were under the impression that they had been selected to function in an active administrative capacity. They invaded the offices in Cairo, demanded to peruse secret files, gave direct orders for certain actions to be taken and for certain transfers to be made, and generally terrorized the senior staff and clerks. In the provinces in some cases the situation was even worse, for here the local deputy—often a low-class *effendi* of consummate ignorance—usurped the position of the local Mudir or Governor and, calling for a table and a chair in the office, proceeded to administer justice, or that particular form of bias and fanaticism that passes for justice in Wafdist eyes. My local deputy in El Arish imagined that he was going to carry on on these lines, but on his first appearance at the office two enormous Sudanese policemen took him firmly by the arms and literally " saw him off " before I was called upon to deal with the situation myself. When the storm they had aroused had blown over they were both promoted to Corporal's rank, but though an English Governor might dare to offend an all-powerful Wafdist delegate such action would have brought speedy retribution on the head of an Egyptian Mudir and the greater part of his staff would have fallen with him.

As a contrast to the extraordinary methods adopted by the Wafd when in power, one must admit the general administrative ability and excellence of the governments that intervened, notably those of Mohammed Mahmoud and Sidky Pasha. In the case of Sidky Pasha it is a fact that during the latter part of his term of office, after his breakdown in health, affairs went somewhat awry and the charges of corruption made against his government by the Opposition went far to discredit it; but one must give Sidky Pasha the fullest credit for having steered Egypt through the world economic crisis of 1931 and for first-class statesmanship and strength of purpose during the troublous times from 1930 to 1933. It may be said that Sidky Pasha and his very able Finance Minister, the late Ahmed Abdel Wahab Pasha, foresaw the coming economic crisis and took steps to deal with the situation long before any of the great European Powers and America had realized that the general slump was anything more than a temporary trade depression, and for this reason the people of Egypt suffered less than the population of any other country. For this, however, they received no credit whatsoever from their own people, who could see them only as Dictators who had taken office unconstitutionally.

The extraordinary part about the whole situation was the British Government's attitude towards the Wafd. This party appealed apparently to their sense of constitutional government because it represented what they fondly imagined to be the people's representatives elected by the free vote of an intelligent democracy. They had no conception of what " the free vote of an intelligent democracy " means in the Nile Valley or how big a part the local *Omdeh* (Mayor) with his *nabbut*-(staff)-armed henchmen plays, or how a police commandant of the correct political views can sway an election. If the Wafd was elected by the demo-cracy, the government must as a matter of course be good in every way, and so the Foreign Office and British Parlia-ment with the democratic " bug on the brain," or what one might call its " wet " policy, backed the party and its various governments, and frowned upon King Fuad and the excellent Ministers appointed by him whenever the popular party became too impossible. The amusing and satisfactory part about the whole business being the fact that King Fuad on his own responsibility and without prompting did the " dirty work " of our Foreign Office from time to time and sent the Wafd Governments packing whenever their actions became so palpably anti-British that a definite crisis was in sight. It is admitted that his policy was dictated by a desire to preserve the prerogative of the Throne rather than to assist British aims, but at the same time there is every reason to believe that King Fuad had no very marked objection to the British occupation of his country.

The situation rather resembled a long and somewhat ineffectual game of chess between the Wafd party and the Foreign Office, and whenever the Wafd made a definite and menacing onslaught with a knight, King Fuad would take a hand in the game and upset all the pieces on the board.

A marked feature of all the Wafdist Governments was their dislike of King Fuad and their antagonism to the Monarchy. Their desire to curtail his powers caused them frequently to lose sight of the fact that the real *raison d'être* of their existence was the removal of the British occupation of the country. This feeling of dislike was reciprocated and King Fuad showed no hesitation whatsoever in picking up the gauntlet when a Wafdist premier cast it down. In this he showed both political and personal courage, for in 1928 he dismissed the Nahas Ministry out of hand and appointed Mohammed Mahmoud as virtual dictator when at least eighty per cent. of the population were ardent Wafdists. Whilst in 1930, when the whole country, lock, stock and barrel, were behind Nahas Pasha, he refused to sign a Bill that had been passed by Parliament and the Senate unanimously, and cheerfully and most willingly, accepted the resignation of the Cabinet when this action was threatened.

On this occasion Nahas Pasha with the whole country solidly behind him felt convinced that no man in the country would dare to take office if he resigned, and it was a definite shock to him and to his party when Sidky Pasha formed a government and proceeded to rule the country with an exceedingly firm hand, which he managed to do successfully owing to the marked Egyptian characteristic of invariably rushing to the assistance of the strong.

The Wafd at once preached revolt, and to open the ball Nahas went to the small town of Zagazig to hold a political meeting at which it was hoped that he would succeed in stirring up the mob sufficiently to overwhelm the police and the small detachment of the Egyptian Army who were sent to maintain order. It was touch and go, for in all probability the majority of the police and army were Wafdist at heart, and it was a doubtful question whether their loyalty would stand the strain. Luckily they stood fast and in some scrambled fighting a few men were killed before the mob was dispersed, but it was on the whole an inconclusive battle. A few days later Nahas went to the town of Mansourah, where a huge and unruly gathering can always be counted upon, and it was confidently expected that here the Wafd would win the day. The slightest wavering of the police and army on this occasion would probably have meant the fraternization of the forces with the mob, and the whole of Egypt would have blazed into revolution.

The soldiers were drawn up outside the house at which Nahas Pasha was to deliver his address and orders were given that he was to be refused admittance. The troops fixed bayonets and the car containing Nahas Pasha charged the line endeavouring to break through. Apparently this annoyed the normally rather lethargic Egyptian soldiery, for they swarmed over the car, stabbing the tyres, and one private aimed a blow at Nahas Pasha with the butt of his rifle, which broke the arm of Sinnot Hanna Bey, who was sitting beside him. This blow settled the fate of Egypt for the next six years, as it completely pricked the bladder of Nahas Pasha's courage and, realizing his narrow escape and believing implicitly also that men had been told off to kill him, he never again attempted during Sidky's term of office to lead the people against the forces of the Government, and this made all the difference to the zeal of the mobs.

The officer in charge of the Army detachment at Mansourah was very possibly a man with no very marked political views. Like the policeman who incurred the ire of the vindictive party and became a " quick-change artist " in consequence, it is quite possible that he was himself a Wafdist; but after the affray at Mansourah he realized very clearly that his career was finished most definitely if ever Nahas and his party returned to power and that his only hope of salvation was to maintain the Sidky Government in office. Sidky Pasha, who is a good judge of character, realized this also, and therefore in all the subsequent riots this officer was shifted from pillar to post to take command of troops, and there was never any question of wavering or hesitation after this. " With his back to the wall," to quote Lord Haig, he was here, there, and everywhere—a striking example of devotion to duty and martial zeal—and it is no exaggeration to say that the crushing of the Wafdist revolt against the Government was due very largely to the energy and example displayed by this officer who was faced with disgrace and extinction if Sidky fell.

There were serious riots after this in Alexandria, where a looting mob of many thousands can be enlisted at a moment's notice on any excuse, and Wafd supporters were busy bribing the worst elements to attack the police and organizing lorry-loads of stones for window-breaking, but the police and army maintained the upper hand. The rioting at Alexandria was followed by a much-advertised attempt on the part of the dismissed delegates with Nahas at their head to break into the closed House of Parliament in Cairo. The mob, bribed by the Wafd party—the payment was two shillings for the day—turned up dutifully and in their political zeal smashed practically every street lamp in Cairo, but as neither the " Dignified Chief " nor any of the prominent Wafdists could screw up their courage to sally forth and lead their battalions, the rioting fizzled out rather tamely by midday.

After this Nahas and his adherents figured in some comic-opera events, the most amusing of which was when, on a previously proclaimed visit to Alexandria which Sidky had forbidden, they forced their way on to the Cairo platform and boarded the express which was due to start. They were so busy jeering at the police officials whom they had outwitted that they did not notice when their carriage began to move that they had been detached from the Alexandrian express and that they were outward bound on a non-stop circular desert tour. The engine with its carriage full of infuriated politicians was then run all round Cairo, and finally fetched up at Helouan, some twenty miles away in the desert, where it was turned round and run back again. It stopped in the evening after an interminable and exhausting day at a deserted level-crossing some five miles outside Cairo, where a police officer awaited the party with cars. He politely informed them that they could return to their homes if they wished by car—if not the train was at their disposal, and they could continue to make the journey to Helouan and back for as long as they pleased. As Nahas and party had boarded their carriage at 10 a.m., and it was then 5 p.m.—and as the dining-car had been detached with the remainder of the train—hunger proved to be stronger than their political zeal, and with diminished heads they went quietly home.

It was believed that the original and distinctly humorous idea of sending Nahas on a desert trip had been ordered by Sidky himself; in any case he got full credit for it and full marks not only for outwitting the Wafd but for heaping ridicule on their heads. Even the most ardent Wafdists could not help laughing at the thought of the infuriated " Dignified Chief " and his satellites, crawling about the desert railway in a solitary coach, and ridicule is the most deadly weapon, especially in a country that puts dignity as the all-important attribute of a man.

Nahas figured in another farcical performance when he attempted to visit Sohag in Upper Egypt, where he and his party were shut up on a wayside station for two days and a night. On this occasion there was a station buffet, but it was a lamentably inefficient one, and when its meagre supply of food was exhausted the party were willing to board a special train and return to Cairo bereft of all dignity but equipped with the most excellent appetites.

Both these episodes made Cairo rock with laughter and there is very little doubt that they were mainly responsible for firmly consolidating Sidky's position and weakening the enormously strong hold that the Wafd had on the country.

Sidky's most difficult task, however, was the disciplining of the schoolboys and University students who had received every encouragement, and in fact had been definitely incited by the Wafd to go on strike and organize demonstrations at different periods during the time they were out of office. This is a most short-sighted and foolish policy, as there is nothing quite so impossible and swollen-headed as a youth of sixteen or seventeen who considers he is his country's chosen representative. The harm done to the youth of the country while Nahas and his party were indulging in unseemly struggles for office will bear fruit for many years to come in the form of a brood of undisciplined and conceited young men who have so many rough corners on them that they will not fit into any walk of life.

Having demonstrated in the streets of Cairo and other cities for the benefit of the party that sponsored them, they were very loath to return to work when they had achieved the object for which they had gone on strike. They therefore proceeded to down books and rush into the streets whenever they found an examination paper too difficult or disliked the expression on a master's face. In a yelling mob they would invade the offices of Nahas Pasha and his Ministers demanding instant redress, and these officials were in the invidious and uncomfortable position of having to surrender to the absurd and childish demands of their youthful adherents.

Sidky took this deplorable situation firmly in hand by issuing an order that any youth who went on strike would be at once dismissed from his school or University. The students were well used to orders of this description, and imagined that Sidky would tamely surrender in the same fashion as his predecessors, with the result that some hundreds of boys were rusticated, and he flatly refused to budge from his decision when frantic parents besought him to relent. This had the required effect and for five years the students of Egypt went diligently to school and took no further part in the affairs of the country.

In 1935, when the Wafd after five years in the wilderness once more fought their way back to power, the schoolboys and students were again called upon to play their part. The Ministry, that of Tewfik Nessim Pasha, was a weak one, for King Fuad, owing to failing health, had ceased to play a prominent part and provide a staunch backing to the government, and therefore the Cabinet foreseeing their downfall and a return of the Wafd were afraid to take active steps against the rioting students. The police received instructions not to interfere and for six months Cairo and the other towns in Egypt were literally controlled by schoolboys. On several occasions, having chased the police off the scene, they took over the management of traffic and from dawn to sunrise swollen-headed little boys and silly little girls were allowed to parade the streets and constitute themselves a public nuisance.

The schools and Universities were practically closed for the whole of the winter months, as, even after the return to power of the Wafd, the boys struck and continued to strike on every possible pretext, varying from the trivial to the purely fantastic. When the examinations were held in the early summer of 1936 for all the schools there were as the natural result an unprecedented and startling number of failures. A demonstration to call attention to this state of affairs paraded before Nahas Pasha, whereupon he lowered the pass standard from sixty per cent. to forty per cent. ! Therefore not only is the batch of students of the 1936 class twenty per cent. more ignorant than their predecessors, but the Wafd can congratulate themselves on having lowered the general standard of education and efficiency of the nation in the same ratio.

And this is by no means the end of the story, for one cannot tamper with the youth of a country with impunity, and this particular batch of Wafdist chickens will most certainly come home to roost.

* * * * *

The foregoing pages were written in the late winter of 1937, and I had hoped there would be no great change in the political situation to warrant further work on this chapter before the book went to the printers. This proved to be a vain hope, however, because on the 30th December, 1937, the young King Farouk dismissed Nahas Pasha and his Cabinet and invited Mohammed Mahmoud Pasha to form a Ministry. After only eighteen months of office, during which the Anglo-Egyptian Treaty was negotiated, the tactics of the Wafd had been sufficiently true to type to warrant the King taking the drastic step of dismissing them.

The actual points at issue were the appointment by the Cabinet to senior and key positions in the government, certain members of their party whose sole qualification for the post was their adherence to the Wafd cause; an attempt to pass a Bill making it treason for any Minister to take office unconstitutionally; a change in the oath of loyalty taken by the officers of the Army by which they swore allegiance to the King and Constitution and not the King only; and the question of the Blueshirts. The first three points concerned the abrogation of the power of the King, and were deliberate attempts to deprive the Throne of its right to control the government of the country in any way. This had proved the bone of contention between the late King Fuad and Nahas Pasha, and King Fuad was always prepared to face a revolution rather than lose any portion of his powers.

The Blueshirts were, like most of the " Shirt " fraternity that function in other countries, a consummate nuisance. During the latter part of the 1935 student troubles signs were not wanting that the youth of the country were not so whole-heartedly Wafd as they had been previously, and when the young King began to take

65

an active part in affairs it was at once apparent that he had caught the popular fancy, for wildly cheering and enthusiastic crowds greeted him on every occasion. King Fuad's best friends cannot pretend that at any time he aroused the spontaneous affection of his people, and, though they clapped and cheered him when he passed through the streets, one had the feeling always that it was a very lukewarm and forced welcome for a volatile and easily moved nation like the Egyptians. The wonderful reception accorded to King Farouk on his return from his visit to England during the Coronation of King George VI was something quite different and gave definite proof that he had, as actors put it, " got across the footlights." From that day his appearance in the streets was always a signal for the students to turn up in large numbers and cheer their King as fervently as they had cheered Nahas Pasha in the past.

The Wafd, realizing that the students were transferring their affections, then formed the gang of roughs and toughs who were called the " Blueshirts " and the opposition leaders retaliated by creating another organization called the " Greenshirts." There was not much to pick between these organizations, for there was little of a voluntary nature about their enlistment and they undoubtedly received pay for their doubtful services. These gangs of roughs fought openly in the streets on any pretext, and the students joined in impartially until the Wafd Government disbanded the Greenshirts as being an illegal body but ingenuously allowed their own organization, the Blueshirts, to remain, and in fact added to their numbers and efficiency. King Farouk, who had as his adviser the ablest man in Egypt, Ali Maher Pasha, insisted upon the disbandment of the Blueshirts also, for he foresaw that there never could be peace in Egypt when one political party would be in a position to control the country by the employment of a disciplined and armed gang.

During the controversy between the Throne and the Cabinet there were the usual wild demonstrations, and in one which took place in front of Abdin Palace, Makram Ebeid Pasha, the lieutenant of Nahas and an ex-idol of the students, was man-handled by a gang of Azharites and his car overturned. It was a most regrettable business that the Minister of Finance should be assaulted in this fashion, but there was a certain hint of poetic justice in the occurrence, for the disorderly behaviour of the students and their interference in the government of the country was very largely due to the machinations of the party of which Makram was one of the leaders, and no one minds very much if a man is hoist by his own petard.

King Farouk in dismissing the Wafd from office called attention in no uncertain terms to their maladministration and their inability to accomplish anything. Their programme of work when they took office in 1935 had been a most inspiring and laudable one, but in actual fact they had accomplished nothing in their eighteen months of government beyond committing projects to writing and giving official tea-parties and talking. With the Treaty of Alliance with Great Britain and the appointment of a British Mission to advise on military matters, the first thing they should have undertaken was the increase and modernization of the Egyptian Army, but after eighteen months' office and the most wonderful intentions nothing whatsoever had been accomplished beyond putting schemes on paper and filling posts with Wafdist adherents.

The new Prime Minister, Mohammed Mahmoud Pasha, is a most talented and capable statesman and he has in his Cabinet all the ablest men in Egypt. King Farouk is still in his teens, but he has given early signs of possess-

ing all the qualities of his distinguished family—a brilliant
intelligence, breadth of vision and genuine love of his
country. With the added advantage of great personal
charm and a most attractive appearance—and one must
not overlook the advantage of a well-decorated shop
window even with Monarchs—the barometer for the
moment appears to be " Set Fair " in Egypt, and after
nineteen years of political strife and disaffection it is to
be hoped that nothing will occur to retard or destroy the
progress that should follow this combination of a clever
and popular Sovereign backed by a most capable and
efficient Ministry.

The political history of Egypt during the last nineteen
years has been very regrettable, for there is a great deal
of natural charm and ability in the Egyptian character ;
one feels that under a settled government something of
the old Egyptian magnificence, which once dominated
the known world, might be brought to life again. As for
the *fellaheen,* or cultivators, they are naturally the most
delightful and charming people with whom one can come
in contact, and as a hard-working and decent-living peas-
antry they have no equal in the world. The official and
educated classes are well above the standard of those that
hold office in Eastern Europe and there is no lack of brilli-
ance and devotion to duty, but the general advance of the
country has been held up again and again by the malign
influence of the erstwhile popular political party, the Wafd.

The Stock Exchanges in Cairo and Alexandria provide
a useful illustration of the business man's opinion of this
national party and its governments, and the considered
judgment of the speculator and investor is free from bias
of all kinds and is not dictated in any way by political
feelings. Whenever there has been a prospect of the
Wafd party returning to power there has been a marked

slump in all shares on the markets and the depression has remained so long as they held office. Immediately, however, there were signs that the Wafd were likely to be expelled a general hardening of prices was evident, and on the day they were cast out into the wilderness, despite the risk of internal trouble and possible revolution, there has always been a veritable boom on the Exchange with a general upward tendency.

This picture of the machinations of the Wafd tends to show the Egyptian in a bad light, and it is unfortunately true because Wafdism during the years between 1919 and 1936 was a form of evil blight, a disease that produced a warping effect on the character of its adherents. There is some excuse for this in the fact that in some ways it was a secret society inaugurated to free Egypt from foreign occupation, and secret societies tend to produce underhand and ruthless methods. On the other side of the picture, however, was the wonderful loyalty and affection British chiefs obtained from their immediate staff during these troublous years, and this loyalty was all the more remarkable and appreciated because one's subordinates fully realized the risk they were running from the vengeance of the Wafd.

During my eighteen years' service in Egypt I came into close contact with a hundred or more Egyptians—officers, clerks, soldiers and police—and with one or two rare exceptions they were all delightful to work with, loyal and polite to a degree, and above all most hospitable and sympathetic. They were of all classes and creeds, with Copts predominating in the clerical staff and Mahommedans filling the executive posts and the ranks of the police and mechanics. In our solitary desert station they were cut off from those breeding grounds of dissatisfaction and disaffection—the coffee shops—and one saw them therefore as they are naturally a simple-minded, hard-working people and interested only in their work, their family life and their gardens. From the Sub-Governor down to the lowest-paid mechanic they showed the most enthusiastic oneness of purpose, a desire to prove that Sinai was entirely independent of outside help and to make our little town of El Arish as up-to-date and civilized as possible. If any new departure on these lines was mooted the complete staff pulled together in the most amazing manner and everyone was willing and eager to work overtime to achieve the object in view. Among other things the Sub-Governor built a social club complete with tennis courts; the chief clerk devised a new method of filing; the mechanics did not rest until they had achieved a modern workshop with lathe, foundry and paint-spraying machine; whilst the blacksmiths invented a new model wind-mill pump, which was an unqualified success and which was installed all over the Peninsula.

The *Akhwan*, or brotherhood as we called ourselves, was a happy community, and when I left Sinai I left behind also many faithful friends. I shall never forget the wonderful and genuine sympathy they extended to me on the occasion of a bereavement in my family, and it was always somewhat of an enigma how a race individually so charming could be so hostile and ruthless in the mass. If I have shown spleen against the Wafd political party and its adherents it is not due to any direct personal matter, but because of the treatment they extended to certain members of my loyal staff when they came into power. Their actions on those occasions were dictated by their policy of forcing every Government employee in the country into the Wafd fold and hampering the work of the few British officials remaining in the service. Probably their attitude was that it was necessary that a few should suffer for the general good of the cause, and it was a very salutary lesson to others when the right-hand man of the Governor of a Province was refused his promotion and increase of pay when he was legally entitled to it for no other reason beyond the fact that he had served his chief faithfully and well.

One very excellent officer of mine was given a direct order by the Ministry, without reference in any way to my Administration, to get out of the Province within twenty-four hours and proceed at once to a most insalubrious post on the Red Sea. Openly to disgrace a man in this fashion is a far more drastic action in Egypt than it would be in England, for the dignity of the official is his most cherished possession. It was also a very shrewd blow at myself, for the average Englishman reciprocates loyalty, and inability to protect one's faithful staff from wanton attacks of this description is most galling. The only satisfaction I enjoyed from this particular episode was that it figured in the High Commissioner's Note of 1928 as a case of direct Ministerial interference with the inner administration of the country, and after a time this unfortunate scapegoat of Wafdist spleen was reinstated.

CHAPTER III

OFFICIALS HIGH AND LOW

I have done the state some service, and they know't.
SHAKESPEARE.

EGYPT has on the whole been lucky in the men that Great Britain has sent to serve in her Civil Service and Army during the last fifty years, and the most rabid Nationalist will admit, grudgingly perhaps, that for some unexplained reason the British official has taken a personal interest in his work for the work's sake and, stranger still, has sometimes shown a tendency to be actively pro-Egyptian and even willing to take a stand against his own Government's demands if he considers them unfair. This puzzles the Egyptians, who find it very difficult to believe that the British official can sink his nationality over minor matters and see things from a purely Egyptian standpoint.

The wonderful work performed by Lord Cromer, Lord Kitchener and other well-known administrators who did so much for Egypt has been fully described in various books on the subject, so that it is unnecessary to mention them here except to say that they gave of their best to the country they served. There were others holding comparatively minor posts who did almost as much for Egypt, men who spent the best years of their lives in a trying climate and who at the end of their career retired one and all poor men with small pensions of some £700 as a reward for their services. They went to the country poor, they worked for thirty years on a sufficient but none too generous salary, and they retired at the age of fifty-five or sixty with the pension to which they were entitled—and nothing else. In our eyes there is nothing very remarkable in this, but to the Egyptians it is inexplicable, puzzling and upsetting, for, as Egyptians have pointed out to me many times, no one of their own countrymen, after holding such a position for thirty years, would retire on his pension only.

The feeling against Great Britain generally and the British officials in particular, which became apparent in the years just prior to the war and afterwards, was caused by the fact that all the important positions in the country and practically all the executive posts were in the hands of the British to the total exclusion of Egyptians. There were very solid reasons for this complaint and the state of affairs that caused the irritation had been arrived at gradually and as a natural sequence of our national characteristic of striving always for perfection.

In the very early days of the British occupation of Egypt it was the intention to administer the country as a temporary measure only with the minimum of British advisers in the various Ministries, leaving the executive control of government work to the existing Egyptian officials. This was a most excellent idea in theory, but in practice did not work because the normal Briton with his very rigid standards of efficiency and moral integrity is very rarely sufficiently plastic to reconcile himself to the laxer methods of the East, and is quite unable to carry on in his department when he knows that it is permeated by peculation, nepotism, and all the other adjuncts of Oriental officialdom which have existed since the days of the Byzantine Empire. The position was a very difficult one, for as a race we do not recognize anything but the highest standard of official honesty, and it is against all the traditions of British administration to put a man in charge of a department and say to him: "There is a vast amount of bribery and corruption in your department, but Rome was not built in a day and you cannot make a silk purse out of a sow's ear. So go easy and do your best without causing an upheaval." This possibly would have been the best line to adopt in the circumstances, but, owing to British rigidity, the chief who will give these orders does not exist and neither does the subordinate who could act upon such instructions.

The secret of success in administering an Oriental people is the ability to discriminate between the essential and the non-essential and not to strive for the full hundred per cent. of efficiency and morality in some particular branch of official curriculum to the neglect of general control. The very able men who assisted Lord Cromer in his work of reconstruction in the country were too thorough and too enthusiastic and, desiring to clean out immediately the Augean stable of Ismail Pasha's administration, demanded more and more British officials in executive positions to assist them in the task. These in their turn, suffering from the same laudable desire to achieve perfection, insisted upon British subordinates till finally in 1922 there were over a thousand English officials in the country, many of them serving in quite minor and entirely subordinate posts.

As a case in point one might quote the case of British confidential clerks ; it was proved and proved again that as a confidential clerk the Egyptian is a definite failure, for in the first place he is a confirmed chatterbox and his national conceit causes him to desire to appear as a man of considerable importance in his little circle at the café of his choice. The direct result of this is that there is nothing private or secret in Egypt and in my own Administration the confidential decisions as to promotions and transfers made by the senior officials' committee, which was held twice a year in Cairo, were known as a matter of course to all the Provinces the same evening, despite the fact that at every meeting the delegates were pledged to secrecy. Owing to this consistent leakage there were a considerable number of British confidential clerks and typists employed in every Ministry, and this filling of minor positions in a country where the aim and ambition of every young man is to hold a Government clerkship or post was one of the chief causes of complaint against the British.

The Egyptian looks at matters always from an entirely personal point of view; the question of sovereign rights, hostility to the Capitulations, and the occupation by British troops did not affect him very vitally and compelled merely his lukewarm adherence, but the fact that he could never rise higher than a second-class clerk in his department because the senior posts were reserved for the British was a matter that he took very much to heart. One might say, therefore, that to a very large extent the universal clamour for independence owed its origin to the unnecessary number of English officials in the country, for the Government employé is a very powerful and numerous class in the Nile Valley.

During the years between 1927 and 1936 it was discovered that the country could be run with only a sprinkling of British officials in place of the thousand odd who had previously managed the affairs of the country. There was, of course, a very definite falling off from the old standards set during Cromer's days and various scandals came to light, such as the pension commutation ramp when, immediately after British control had ceased in a certain department, a large number of the leading officials in the country commuted portions of their pensions for Government land, which land they sold the following day to contractors at its real market value, i.e. treble the amount they had paid. Then there was the finger-print scandal when minor officials, inspired by the example of their seniors, sold at a reasonable price the finger-prints and police records of the leading drug-smugglers of the country to the people most interested in their disappearance, for in the drug trade it is a very definite advantage to appear as a first offender and not a hardened criminal. The business, one must admit, was carried out with scrupulous fairness and no ex-criminal was asked to pay more than the actual value to him of his finger-prints and police record.

There was also the memorable occasion when at the annual school examinations in the early summer there was a most satisfactory and quite phenomenal return of successful candidates at which some of the dullest students obtained the full hundred per cent. of marks. All might have been well, and the year 1934 would have gone down to posterity as a vintage year for youthful Egyptian brains, but unfortunately a small minority of students, who had been unable to obtain or had been unwilling to pay the market price for an advance copy of the examination papers, began to complain and the whole scandal came to light. The only people who suffered on this occasion were the unfortunate British school-masters who had their leave curtailed by one month to enable them to preside at a second series of examinations at which the number of successful students was if anything below normal.

It is, however, impossible to achieve in the short period of fifty years a perfect state of official integrity in a country which for four centuries has experienced all the evils and open corruption of Turkish administration, in which the taking of bribes and exploitation of a Government post is a recognized and entirely legal form of emolument. One cannot effect a complete change in the outlook of a nation in five decades, and perhaps the mistake that we made in Egypt was this constant striving after perfection from the start, or in other words trying to run before we could walk.

At the conclusion of hostilities in 1918 Egypt, in common with many other countries, found it incumbent upon herself to recruit a large number of new officials to bring her Civil Service up to strength. This was necessary to replace not only those who had volunteered for active service and had lost their lives, but also others who had retired on reaching the age limit. The greater part of the officials required to bring staffs up to strength were obtained from the nearest and most suitable source—in this case the British Army serving in the country—and it is a common thing nowadays to hear the old pre-war officials of the country, if you care to listen to them, voice the opinion that most of our unpopularity in the country between 1919 and 1936 was due to the employment of the wrong type of official. It all sounds very convincing, but the fact remains that the most serious rising in Egypt occurred in the spring of 1919 before the majority of the war-time officials had been taken into the service.

One of the peculiarities of Great Britain is the fact that if one has served one's country in the Army during a war it is the greatest bar to civil employment one can have. It is not merely a question of this black mark in the past against one at the time when one applies for a post but, like a sentence of penal servitude, it counts against one for the rest of one's life. It is a definite bar sinister and away back in the seventeenth century Francis Quarles commented upon this peculiar attitude of ours in his lines :

> Our God and soldier we alike adore
> When at the brink of ruin, not before ;
> After deliverance both alike requited,
> Our God forgotten, and our soldiers slighted.

77

During the war one was called a hero and other noble things, and elderly gentlemen came down to Victoria to see one off to Flanders, saying, "If I were a younger man I'd be coming with you, my boy." When one returned on leave or wounded one was petted and fussed over by well-meaning women, but immediately after the last shot was fired on the 11th November one became a troublesome drug in the labour market, suffering from that disability which effectually prevented one from being of any real use—one had been a soldier and served one's country.

One of the reasons for this, I think, is that some of the most gallant and dashing of the officers who led their men into action in the latter stages of the war were singularly hard to place in civil life. They belonged to the type of buccaneering " hard case " that laid the first foundations of Empire in Elizabeth's days, and such men do not fit in in days of peace. In war they were invaluable and equal to two ordinary men, and on account of their wonderful records of gallantry and endurance they were the first people to be found responsible civil posts in 1918, but temperamentally they were absolutely unsuited to take up a humdrum office or routine life, and as civilians their failure to " make good " was just as marked as their success had been as leaders of men when courage and endurance were the two essentials that counted. Such men, however, were rare, and as the great mass of temporary and auxiliary officers were quite normal individuals, lacking possibly the spirit of the Elizabethan corsair but with all the intelligence and application of ordinary civilians, it was unfair that this spirit of depreciation should have persisted because, through no fault of their own, four years of their early lives had been wasted at war.

It is exceedingly difficult to find a man to-day who

suffered from avoiding service during 1914–18; all of those who managed to hang on to their civil jobs prospered exceedingly with accelerated promotion, whilst on the other hand we all know of hundreds of cases of men who, owing to a variety of causes, were ruined by their war service.

As a nation we have very short memories, and we have not only forgotten entirely the sacrifices that some men made but we have also lost all recollection of how others failed to do anything at all. I know of two cases where men, who had been leading lights in their counties, prominent in the hunting-field and all other activities, failed most dismally to come up to scratch during the war and who, despite the fact that everyone expected them, on the strength of the part they had played in the past, to be the first to spring to arms, nevertheless managed by various devices to escape active service altogether. Feeling was so strong against them at the time that they removed to some other part of the kingdom to hide their diminished heads, but somewhere about 1920 they both crept back to their old haunts, playing a subdued note at first, but by 1923 all had been forgotten and they were once again, " Good old ——" without whose assistance and approval it was impossible for anything to happen in the county.

There were among the pre-war officials who remained in the Egyptian service after the war a few, a very small minority, who had never pulled their weight in the country and who from their earliest days had been regarded as slackers. This state of affairs is inevitable where there are upwards of a thousand men in a service and it would be a most remarkable phenomenon if everyone was of the same standard of excellence. The fact remains, however, that these quite useless but very charming individuals

79

had been allowed to remain in the service and receive their promotion to senior posts to the detriment of most capable Egyptians below them. Any dissatisfaction that the Egyptians may have felt about British officials in the country was caused by these rather useless and limpet-like drones and not by the hard-working ex-Army officers, who were brought into the service in 1919 and 1920 and who were mostly on contracts that could be terminated by three months' notice. A contract term of service may be unfair to the official, but on the other hand it does eliminate the risk of a man filling a post and regarding it as a sinecure for the rest of his life.

There is no desire on my part to crab the pre-war British official, for as services go they were definitely above the average, being most carefully selected in the first place. As Sir Ronald Storrs tells us in *Orientations*, after all but the "Firsts" and "Blues" had been eliminated, the final choice was made by discovering if the would-be official smoked Turkish in preference to Virginian cigarettes, but despite the acid test—this "Gasper" bar—an idler occasionally slipped through the meshes. As our failure in the country is so constantly attributed to the misdeeds of the category to which I belong, the war product, I think it is only reasonable that I should endeavour to shift the responsibility.

On the whole the British officials in the service were most popular with their Egyptian subordinates and when the outcry for their removal went up in 1922 the usual attitude was, "Sack every British official in the country except my own chief." The reason for this was that the Englishman invariably treated his Egyptian juniors with respect and consideration, whereas in the East it is considered a sign of weakness and detrimental to dignity to be polite or kind to a junior. I have heard Egyptian Heads of Departments speaking to their subordinates as if they were members of a labour gang, and I have very seldom seen a senior official ask a junior to take a seat during an interview; he is expected to stand in a respectful attitude the whole time.

Another reason why the British element in an office was popular lay in the fact that it definitely prevented favour-itism and nepotism with their concomitant evil, unfair promotion. During the last ten years, when the British officials remaining in the country were shorn of much of their executive powers, it has been one constant struggle on their part to prevent their loyal and hard-working subordinates from being passed over and even demoted to make way for some Ministerial pet or political pawn for whom a place had to be found. On these occasions the wiles and unflagging persistence of the Egyptians in power found its Waterloo in the endurance and watchful-ness of the Briton in the case, and I have known struggles, particularly in the Army and in my own department, that have lasted for years with moves and counter-moves to save from Oriental spleen some unfortunate subordinate whose place was desired for a nominee of " one who must be obeyed." Invariably I think the British element won in the end and every phase of the prolonged war was watched assiduously by all the Egyptians in the depart-ment. I was never quite certain, however, what the general reaction was; I think there was grudging admiration for the dogged endurance of the Briton, but it was mingled with amazement that any senior should allow himself to be worried almost into the grave over the welfare of some quite insignificant officer.

The general attitude in Egypt towards the official under-dog whose luck is out reminds one very much of the average poultry-run; in the chicken world, if a bird

is sick or wounded in any way there is no sympathy wasted
—he has got himself into this condition by some means or
other, and the sooner he is put out of his misery the sooner
will one be able to forget his miserable state, so every
member of the run gives him a savage peck and hack with
the spur to hurry him on to oblivion.   This is rather
remarkable, for as races go the Egyptian is usually most
sympathetic to anybody who has suffered a bereavement
or financial loss.   There is no such thing, of course, as
organized charity and no attempt is made to better the lot
of the submerged tenth, but a beggar will never die of
starvation in Egypt.   I can only conclude that this heart-
less attitude over the down-and-out official is due to the
atmosphere of injustice which has persisted in the country
from the days of the Hegira onwards, which creates a feeling
of " it cannot be helped so why worry ? "

Most of the old British officials of the Egyptian Government left the country during the early days of my service
owing to the generous retirement scheme initiated with
the Declaration of Independence.   Therefore with the
exception of those who served in my own Administration
I did not get to know them very intimately before their
departure on pension.   Some, however, remained in the
service and have even outstayed me, and among them
may be mentioned Sir Thomas Russell, the popular
Commandant of the Cairo City Police.

Russell Pasha is one of the very few men in the country
who really served his apprenticeship and learned his trade
as an Egyptian official and a policeman.   His early days as
a junior officer were all of them in the Provinces, and for
a long time he was in command of that excellent force,
now fallen somewhat from its high estate, the Police Camel
Corps.   The result of this is that Russell knows intimately
a very large number of the *Omdehs* (local Mayors) and

" *Lewa Thomas Wentworth Russell Pasha, Commandant of Police in the capital, guardian of law and order in the country—and then some !* " *Akher Saa.*

notables of the country together with hundreds of the villagers and has, moreover, a wide selection of old cronies of all types from big-game *shikaris* to duckboys and high-waymen to smugglers. I imagine that every inhabitant in Cairo knows him at least by sight and has something more than a healthy respect for him. They must entertain for him a feeling approaching affection, for during the all-too-frequent rioting in the capital the commonest sight one sees is Russell riding on a conspicuous white horse with a totally inadequate escort, or driving about the town in an open car. He has undoubtedly given the rioters and malcontents of Cairo every conceivable oppor-tunity to assassinate him, and his action has not been dic-tated by bravado ; the point is that if a dangerous Oriental mob allows a most conspicuous six-foot police officer to ride or walk through them unharmed they have un-consciously let the wind out of their sails for the time being, and it is very difficult to work up again that state of blind fury that was driving them to stone and assault the police. Russell's sudden appearance during a riot has usually caused a complete reversal of feeling for the moment and the disgruntled mob has moved off with a feeling of frustration to look for some part of the city where they can demonstrate without interference of this annoying description.

Personally I think Russell's strong card has been his ability to serve without friction and without appeal to the Residency under a variety of Ministries, from the violently anti-British to the pathetically Anglophile. His position has been extremely delicate and uncertain for many years, as the disgruntled politician his police hustled out of Cairo station in a dishevelled condition on the Monday night has sometimes been the Minister of the Interior on the following Tuesday with the whole force in the hollow of his hand. It is to Russell's credit that, despite the fact his police had to obey orders and "move on" the leading men of the opposition on frequent occasions, he himself invariably behaved with such supreme tact that there was no personal feeling—and this was remarkable, for it is naturally difficult for the Egyptian to see matters on broad lines and not to harbour resentment.

The most difficult situation that Russell was called upon to handle was an episode described in another chapter when Nahas Pasha and the whole of the Wafd party were sent by Sidky's orders on a circular tour in the desert on the occasion when they tried to travel to Alexandria to address a mob. Orders arrived for the frustrated, very much incensed and hungry politicians to be removed from the train at a wayside halt outside Cairo and to be driven back to the metropolis in closed cars. Russell knew perfectly well that they would be in a state of fury and that there was every possibility of a regrettable incident when the police arrived to remove the party, but unfortunately he was ill in bed and in no fit state to take charge of the police himself. He decided, however, to go whatever the risk to his own health and, having boarded the train and explained the object of his visit to the infuriated Nahas, he fainted from weakness.

Immediately the whole tone of the gathering changed and resentment turned to sympathy. Nahas Pasha himself supported Russell in his arms and applied smelling-salts to his nose and eventually the whole party returned to Cairo in a most friendly and amicable spirit and a very nasty situation was avoided.

Russell has achieved world-wide fame as the man who really scotched the drug evil in Egypt. Other police officers in various parts of the world have merely played with it, but Russell went at it bald-headed and very wisely tackled it at its source. He was sent to Geneva and at a meeting of the League of Nations told the assembly the stark and painful truth. He said that certain countries, which were not addicted to white drugs themselves, were producing enormous quantities of heroin and cocaine and shipping them to smaller states, regardless of the fact that they were absolutely ruining the people of these little countries. He not only named the Powers responsible but produced documentary and irrefutable evidence.

It was all very painful and regrettable, for this Police Officer did not understand or refused to indulge in the correct technique to be observed at Geneva, where the rule is that the truth should be so discreetly veiled and distorted that no one can recognize it. He was, however, quite unrepentant and irreconcilable and continued to attend at Geneva to apply his unpleasant douches of stark truth until finally the countries concerned took the matter in hand to save further unpleasantness, and the trade in white drugs was stopped.

Another official of the Egyptian service in the " Personality " class with whom I came into close contact was Dr. Ball of the Desert Survey, and it is due to Ball and his Elisha, Murray, on whom his mantle fell, that the harsh and vast deserts of Egypt are now practically all surveyed and mapped. Surveying a waterless desert under any conditions is not an easy task, but what makes the feat a definite accomplishment is the fact that the Egyptian Government themselves did not care whether the wastes were mapped or not. Ball and his small following succeeded in carrying out the work despite the Government indifference and not at its instigation or with its help. This was one of the queer anomalies of service in Egypt—one found oneself working desperately hard to accomplish some particular job of work and derived encouragement and enjoyment from the knowledge that, so far from giving satisfaction to one's employers, one was actually annoying them ! Until one has tried it, it is impossible to realize what an inciting and impelling force this is.

Ball—one must speak of him in the present tense, for he lives at Ma'adi outside Cairo on retirement—is a little man and looks the last person one would expect to be a hardy desert explorer, game to the last ounce and fit for anything. It never mattered one jot to Ball on an exploring expedition if the cars were hopelessly stuck in the sand and extraction seemed impossible, neither did he worry if water and food were running out and death from thirst seemed a possibility. Mundane matters like this were of no concern whatsoever ; but it was a very different state of affairs if anything happened to the car containing his instruments or if, when one was driving him, one changed direction so suddenly that he was unable to get his speedometer reading and bearing. The very placid little man on these occasions turned into a very good imitation of a tiger to whose posterior a red-hot iron has been applied.

Both Ball and I were on Prince Kamel el Din's first exploring expedition into the Libyan Desert in search of the missing Oasis, Zarzura, and the road to the Oasis of Kufra now in Italian Libya. I had been lured to take charge of the executive side of the expedition because I had been promised I should get either an oryx or an addax, probably both, and Ball went because he had the opportunity of putting some marks on a hitherto blank map, and one has to grasp the mentality and outlook of the born surveyor to know what this means. As a calling surveyors are filled with the same sort of proselytizing zeal that causes missionaries to figure in stewpans or adorn with their heads the gateways of Polynesian banqueting halls.

Ball is a most tolerant man; he can bear with equanimity all sorts of failings and peccadilloes on the part of his friends or his enemies, if he possesses any, but he draws the line very firmly at bad mapping. A man who goes out into the desert in a car and does some slipshod work with a pocket-compass and an uncertain speedometer and then puts the result on a map as a correct reading has in his opinion committed, not one of the Seven Deadly Sins, but the deadliest sin that any man can commit.

He had to spend the first two years after the war eliminating from the map of the Libyan Desert a vast amount of very incorrect work perpetrated by various British officers during the campaign against the Senussi. Through this he has obtained the very poorest opinion of the soldier as a topographer, though he makes an exception in the case of Major Williams, a New Zealander who served in the Light Car Patrols and whose work passed the acid test. I have heard Ball admit that if Williams had not been a soldier and a sheep farmer he might have made quite a good surveyor, and this is praise indeed.

On the expedition in question I went out ahead of the main body and worked for a month making dumps. I had no theodolite with me, which was probably just as well, for, being an amateur, I did far better with a corrected compass and a speedometer. When the Prince and Ball arrived a month later and I escorted them to the big dump some two hundred miles west of Dakhla, the Prince produced the official map, which in those days was nearly all blank paper, and asked me where we were. I put a small dot on it and said that according to my readings we were at that particular spot. Then Ball took the Prince aside and said in a voice which he thought was a whisper but, being deaf, was something in the nature of a shout, " I shouldn't pay the least attention to that; these Army men are notoriously bad at mapping and he's quite likely to be fifty miles out ! "

It was rather satisfactory after this testimonial to my topographical abilities to find I was only about *two* miles out.

During the expedition, which I described in my book, *Three Deserts*, I drove Ball in my car the whole time. It was fitted with a compass and a reliable speedometer, and as we went along he jotted down the various distances run on every bearing. The trouble was he frequently desired to stop to take a few compass shots on conspicuous hills at a moment when it was impossible for me to do so owing to the presence of soft sand. Much of the southern part of the Libyan Desert is undulating sand which has just a suspicion of a hard crust on top. A car travelling at 40 m.p.h. will skim over it in a delightful fashion ; at 30 m.p.h. the tyres will break through the crust slightly and the engine will knock, and at 20 m.p.h. the wheels will sink right in and the car will stop. The motto for drivers was, " Keep her running at all costs," as once one stopped it took a terrific amount of pushing and heart-breaking toil to get the vehicle travelling fast enough to skim along the crust again. It was therefore very difficult to reconcile the two ambitions : the driver's desire to keep travelling at speed, and the topographer's to get out at a critical moment and take a shot at some particular hill. The topographer considered the driver an inconsiderate speed-merchant and hoped he would break his neck, and the driver thought the topographer was merely being trying, as there are plenty of little hills in the Libyan waste, so why not shoot one that could be taken from hard going ?

Tempers got very short on these desert car treks, and after one of these occurrences where it had been impossible to reconcile the two schools of thought we frequently drove for hours without speaking. It was remarkable, however, how mellow we both became at the witching hour of 6 p.m. when, with cars parked and the camp made, the whisky bottle was passed round after a tiring and nerve-racking day. We became even mellower towards the end of the trip when the whisky ran out, which was not such a disaster as it sounds, for the Prince provided brandy in its place and this particular brandy happened to be Napoleon.

Ball obtained an enormous kick out of this expedition, as he was able to check the readings of a German explorer who had passed that way fifty years before. I got no kick at all, as we saw neither oryx nor addax nor in fact any living thing.

Another official who has done a vast amount of solid work in Egypt, the results of which the country is reaping now and will continue to reap for many years to come, is Mr. Brown of the Horticultural Section of the Ministry of Agriculture. Like Ball he is a fanatic, but his religion is agriculture and arboriculture and his mission in life is to better the crops and fruit of Egypt. The question whether the Egyptians wish their crops improved does not arise; as a matter of fact they do and are definitely interested, but Mr. Brown would work just as hard and unremittingly if they desired the Nile Valley to be turned into a desert.

Mr. Brown, who is known all over the country as *Abu Dign* (Father of a Beard) on account of the patriarchal growth on his chin, went to the country years before the war. In 1920, when shooting of British officials was a popular pastime with the grateful inhabitants of Egypt, Mr. Brown, who never has held and never will hold any political views, was attacked in his dog-cart and severely wounded, whilst his Egyptian *syce* (groom) was killed. Shortly after this he retired from the service and posts in his department were filled by a series of Egyptian officials who had deserved well of their country as politicians, but were not conspicuous successes as expert horticulturists. When an Egyptian takes over a post from an Englishman he at once proceeds to prove to the world how much more he knows of the work than his predecessor, and to do this everything has to be changed. In this particular branch it took the form of changing the labels on the trees, and one of the results of this was that I cherished in Sinai groves of peaches, that after years of tender attention proved to be bastard almonds and of no use to God or man, orderly rows of grape-fruit that produced fruits as big as footballs that were all rind and pith and very unpleasant rind at that, and flourishing vineyards that grew grapes recalling those eaten by the fathers in Ezekiel xviii, whereby the children's teeth were set on edge—the grapes that we grew in Sinai would have set on edge the teeth of all posterity. When this harvest began to materialize in Sinai and in parts of the Nile Valley the Egyptian Government came to the conclusion that it was time for Mr. Brown to return to the country, and about 1930 he took up his old post again, to the lasting benefit of Egypt. The first thing Mr. Brown did on his reappointment was to go out to the various Provinces to make a personal apology and endeavour to explain to exasperated *fellaheen* and Arabs that the trees which had been distributed were stock plants for grafting purposes only and should never have been issued to prospective fruit-growers. It was very difficult to explain this satisfactorily to primitive gardeners who knew nothing of grafting or its effects, and not only Mr. Brown but I also lost a considerable amount of " face " in certain parts of Sinai through this disaster which was not the fault of either of us—and it is extremely unlikely that we shall live it down in the lifetime of the present generation.

Mr. Brown is an outspoken Yorkshireman and says what he thinks on all occasions. He has never been able to grasp, in fact he has never tried very seriously, the Egyptian system by which political fervour is considered to be the best possible recommendation for a post connected with the higher forms of horticulture. Mr. Brown can get very angry, and being of large size with an enormous fan-shaped beard, he is rather terrifying when his ire is aroused; there have been several occasions when an Egyptian subordinate of his, who has been working on some particularly interesting experiment connected with grafting oranges or other fruit, has been suddenly transferred to the other end of the Nile Valley owing to his supposed political views. It has not occurred to the politically-minded ministers who rule Egypt's destiny that in horticultural experiments to remove a man with four or five years' experience from his particular job is to destroy all the evidence obtained and the results arrived at.

On these occasions Mr. Brown arises in his wrath and his anger adds six inches to his stature and volume to his voice. He goes straight to the source of the trouble—the Minister of Agriculture of the moment—and says his piece. Ministers of Agriculture change with monotonous regularity and depressing frequency, but presumably they are warned before they take over their portfolios that they will have Mr. Brown to deal with and therefore take their castigation in good part, surrendering with grace to the forces of horticulture as represented by its Director.

Some British officials in the country are suspected by the Egyptians of harbouring British Imperial views and of endeavouring, whilst serving Egypt, to assist Great Britain's political aspirations, but everyone in Egypt knows Mr. Brown. It is realized that he works for improved horticulture and that nothing else matters to him. High

Commissioners may come and High Commissioners may go; Ministries may take office and Ministries may fall, but Mr. Brown and his department go on for ever. At least one hopes so sincerely, for no one has worked so whole-heartedly and unremittingly in the Nile Valley as this fanatical horticulturist with his vast store of knowledge and experience gained by over thirty years of work in the country.

Another well-known character and definite personality who was just completing his long career in Egypt when I started my service was Colonel J. K. Watson of the 60th, known in Egypt as Watson Pasha and to all his innumerable friends as Jimmy Watson. He had come to Egypt in the first place in 1894 to serve in the Egyptian Army and acted as A.D.C. to Lord Kitchener during the campaign against the Mahdi. Later he became A.D.C. to Abbas Hilmi, the ex-Khedive, and after that was Military Attaché. It is a thousand pities that Jimmy Watson was allowed to retire from the Egyptian service in 1922, for our country lost the services of a natural diplomat who not only knew Egypt and everybody in it but had the gift also of smoothing down the prickles of disgruntled dignity, so necessary in dealing with the Orient. As a very Occidental people we are frequently unconsciously forgetful of that fragile dignity of the East and so regardless of that manipulation known to the Chinese and Japanese as face-saving, and matters might have run more smoothly in the country if occasionally some influential Egyptian had not had his corns trodden upon inadvertently by the Residency or some minor foreign deputy had not felt himself slighted over the question of his place at a State dinner.

If Jimmy Watson had been retained in the service as official " Pourer of Oil on Troubled Waters and Smoother Down of Ruffled Feathers," things might have been much easier for us during our many futile negotiations, for in Egypt as in other countries the way to agreement on knotty points is usually opened up by preliminary talks of an unofficial nature, and the various deadlocks that occurred from time to time were caused not so much by irreconcilable policies but by some minor question of hurt dignity or personal jealousy. In cases like this Jimmy would have been of the greatest value, for he had a way with him and could talk the most obstinate and disgruntled Egyptian into a sweet and sunny mood in a few moments.

CHAPTER IV

ELECTION DAY IN EGYPT

The freeman, casting with unpurchased hand
The vote that shakes the turrets of the land.
OLIVER WENDELL HOLMES.

O N the whole, politics are rather a lamentable business
as they are based on, and owe their origin to, the
party system; and though the party system may have
many advantages, there is always the drawback that its
welfare is apt to become far more important in the eyes
of the politicians than the actual good of the country.
In Great Britain politics are supposed to be more or
less clean, but during the last fifty years or so we can
look back on some fairly discreditable episodes. The
abandonment of Gordon to his fate because the Gladstone
party had been returned to power on the Liberal vote of
non-intervention in the Sudan; the Chinese slavery lie in
1906; and, in more recent times, the dangerous state
of disarmament in the country due entirely to the fear
of losing votes through the opposition raising the cry
of militarism and coming conscription. This was a
Conservative, or to be more exact a National, Government's backsliding, which was regrettable enough, but it
was completely put in the shade by the action of the Labour
Party who suddenly became pugnacious and who did their
utmost to force us into war with Italy, when, owing to
their party tactics in hanging up armaments, we were not
in a position to go to war with even a second-class power.

These are a few of the most regrettable cases of the party

ranking first and the country a bad second; and if such things can happen in Great Britain it is not a matter for wonder that more discreditable things occur in Egypt, where a democratic government elected by universal suffrage is an entirely new idea and foreign to all Oriental methods of government. Considering that over eighty per cent. of the electorate are illiterate and have no conception whatsoever of world affairs, or even the affairs of their own country, it is not remarkable that politics in Egypt are a complete farce, and that elections savour more of the pantomime than actual happenings.

As Governor of Sinai I was too fully occupied with my own elections in El Arish to study what was happening in the Nile Valley proper; but from stories that I heard from the cities and outlying districts I imagine the reactions of my own people to politics and elections were in no way remarkable and may be taken as a fair sample of the general behaviour of the Egyptians in all parts of the country.

When the announcement was made in 1922 that the Sultan was to be called King, and that there would be a freely elected Parliament of the people for the people, nobody knew quite what it was all about. One old Arab decided that it must mean that my predecessor, Parker, had been elected King of Sinai and, as he had made a very good Governor, it was only right and proper that in due course, and in strict rotation, he should be promoted to King. When, however, it came to the registration of voters, i.e. recording the names of all men over the age of twenty-one, the Beduin Arabs smiled the smile of men who recognize a trap when they see one "set openly in sight of the bird." It was all very well to talk about the free vote of the electorate, whatever that might mean, but a list of the male population with their respective ages was undoubtedly a trick, and a dirty one at that, to insert the thin end of the wedge of conscription. It was obviously a mere subterfuge to abolish the concession of exemption from military service given to the Arab race by the Khedive Mohammed Ali, and no arguments, blandishments or assurances of the absence of ulterior motives had any effect. The Arabs to a man were not going to have their names and ages registered. If it meant they lost the vote, what matter ? They had existed as a race for some two thousand years without votes and could no doubt continue to do so, and if lists of electors were a *sine qua non*, it was decided that politics were a thing to be avoided.

The townsmen of El Arish, who are not Arabs but a weird conglomeration of races, saw the matter in a totally different light, and decided that politics meant inter-family squabbles on an unprecedented and delightful scale, and very rightly detected great financial possibilities in the possession of a vote. During my spell of office in Sinai we had four elections, which were not only farcical in every way, but which upset the inhabitants of the town to such an extent that it took two years after each poll for feelings to die down, and for the community to carry on again on its normal lines.

The two candidates were heads of rival families, who had never been on the best of terms, and the advent of politics and elections gave that necessary fillip required to cause open hostility. Neither of the candidates had any policies or any views as to the government of their country whatsoever—they merely wished to join the party that was most likely to get into office, and draw the concomitant pay as Member of Parliament, and in one election both would claim to be Wafdists and in the next both Ittihadists or Liberals, the choice depending on which party seemed most likely to gain the election. This, however, had no effect on the electorate as the aim and object in view with

F.

both candidates was promotion to an easy post with £600 a year, and so the whole election relegated itself to a glorious inter-family squabble.

In two of the elections there was a quaint system of voting by thirties—that is to say, thirty men were grouped together on the list and selected their representative, and this representative recorded the vote for the candidate. This was a most unsatisfactory system and open to abuse, and I realized the rank injustice of it when swarms of incensed voters flooded my office and pointed out that the heads of their thirties had received bribes of £30 and over, but had refused to disgorge even a piastre of it to their loyal adherents who had put them in the position where wealth could be accumulated.

The real weak spot in the system, however, lay in the fact that the result of the election could be more or less determined by the officials who drew up the voters' lists of " thirties." Say, for instance, there is an electorate in a village of 1,500 which allows for fifty groups of " thirties," and also, for the sake of argument, say there are only 416 Wafdists in the village and 1,084 Ittihadists. If the election lists are drawn up with skill it can be so worked that the 416 Wafdists will be able to return a majority by the simple expedient of putting sixteen Wafdists and fourteen Ittihadists into the first twenty-six of the groups of " thirties," and massing the rest of the opposition into the remaining twenty-four. This, of course, is a very extreme case, and might cause comment even in Egypt, and the example is given to prove the general unsoundness of the method, which, so far as I could see, had nothing to recommend it beyond the fact that it caused the wildest confusion, shocking corruption and the most intense dissatisfaction. The compiling of lists was not abused quite to the extent I have quoted, but that it was abused was proved by some startling results achieved by minorities, and more definitely by the sudden affluence of clerks charged with the compilation of lists. When a clerk with a wife and six children who draws £16 a month suddenly appears in the street driving the whole family in a new Ford V8, it is fairly certain that he has been drawing something in addition to his pay.

The amusing part about elections in Sinai was the open and ingenuous view taken by one and all that a vote was a marketable commodity and nothing else. Politics were quite beyond their ken, and they were in no way interested in the machinations of either party; all they realized was the fact that they possessed a vote which, put on the market at the right moment, might be worth anything from 4s. to £2. The difficult point to decide, however, was the arrival of the right moment. This sort of thing, of course, exercises more astute brains than the fishermen and gardeners of El Arish; and one of the commonest instances of the tragedy of " what might have been " is to see the shares we sold at 7s. 3d. quoted in the market at 49s. 6d.

I once discussed politics and an impending election with a large family of fishermen on the coast of Sinai. These fishermen live their lives on the seashore in huts made of palm branches, and being almost a race apart from the inhabitants of the village, are not greatly concerned by the family squabbles of the cultivators.

" With regard to the election and our votes," said the old man who managed the affairs of the " family," which consisted of some thirty men of various degrees of relationship, " it is my opinion that it would be best for me to negotiate with the two parties, and sell them all to the highest bidder in one lot."

" No, no," protested another elder, " we will get a higher

price if we sell them separately. If you sell all, how are we to be sure of the price you obtain ? " he added darkly.

" Have you not trusted me for years with the sale of you catch in Port Said ? " exclaimed the old man indignantly, " and have not the prices I obtained been satisfactory ? If you trust me to sell a hundred okes of mullet, surely you can trust me also to dispose of a small thing like a vote to the men who will pay most for it. Selling votes is like selling fish; you must put them on the market when they are scarce and not when everyone has them for sale. My experience of the right moment to sell the family's fish will help me to know the right moment to sell the family's vote."

It was useless for me to try to point out to these keen politicians that to register one's vote was also to register one's opinion in the government of the country. This, they explained, was quite understood, but the fact remained that in their opinion whatever government was returned it would not make a vast amount of difference to fishermen who go down to the sea to fish, whereas £2 was something tangible and really did make a difference ; and there seemed to be no very convincing answer to this.

I was able to view the whole distasteful, if amusing, business of Egyptian politics and elections from a more or less detached standpoint. I had been warned by the Powers that Be to let the elections severely alone as, being an entirely Egyptian affair, it was unwise for a British official to become involved in any way. It was better to do the Pontius Pilate act with the bowl of water, and stand well to one side till the unfortunate business was over. Moreover, it is one thing to know that bribery and corruption are rampant, but quite another thing to obtain a clear case with reliable witnesses sufficiently truthful to secure a conviction. Also, when one fishes in the sea of corruption to catch small fry one may hook, inadvertently, a very large

" fish " indeed—a far bigger one than intended—and the
extraction of the hook and the return of the " fish " to its
natural element may cause both pain and embarrassment,
as the " catch " quite possibly might be much larger than
the angler himself.   Having taken satisfactory steps, therefore, to see that no rioting occurred and no heads were
broken, it was nothing to do with me if an Occidental
system of registering the free vote of an intelligent demo-
cracy became, as any fool could have foreseen, so hopelessly
orientalized as to constitute a farcical harlequinade.

On another occasion, when votes were made direct, and
not through the heads of " thirties," I had to listen to wails
from intelligent members of the electorate who complained
that the unsuccessful candidate had not paid out the five
shillings per vote promised to them by him, whereas the
elected member had faithfully fulfilled his obligations.   It
was a very nice legal point to decide whether—if bribery
constituted corruption—what exactly was the position of a
man who was bribed by both parties for the registration
of one vote.   The only conclusion I could come to was
that he was entitled to put his cross against the highest
bidder, but whether the bond he had made with the other
one still held good was beyond me.

The most humorous episode of all, however, concerned
a fat old Sheikh, who was the successful candidate at the
second election. He was returned with a thumping
majority, but before he could arrive in Cairo to take his
seat Parliament had been dissolved and he found himself
out of employment. His case was definitely a hard one,
for, as he explained to me, in the reasonable expectation of
holding his seat for two years, he had expended over a
thousand pounds in bribes, and had made, therefore, a dead
loss over the business as he had not drawn even one month's
salary.   He had a vague sort of idea that I ought to bring

pressure to bear on His Egyptian Majesty to reinstate Parliament solely on his account.

At the third election, which was held after Lord Lloyd's retirement, the whole country went solidly Wafd, but Sinai, for some purely personal reasons, returned a benign and timid old gentleman who had been accepted as the Liberal candidate. He was the only non-Wafdist member in that Parliament, and was so alarmed about his isolated position that he came to me to ask if I would mind him changing his colours. As he ingenuously explained, it meant nothing as he proposed to transfer his allegiance to the other party immediately they regained a paramount position in the country. I advised him strongly to make the necessary change. I could not see him very clearly as a Randolph Churchill leading a forlorn hope to victory, and the sooner he sought seclusion and safety in the ranks of the rabid and all-powerful party the better for him and his family.

The fourth and last election, so far as I was concerned, was Sidky Pasha's famous appeal to the voters of the country in 1931 for a mandate for his government after the Wafd had resigned in a fit of pique at the King's refusal to sign a ridiculous and vindictive Bill they had passed. The Wafd were then very strong—in fact, the country was unanimously with them—and they put forward no candidates but gave orders to their adherents to boycott the polling booths altogether. How exactly the elections were managed will never be known, but the result proved the existence of a masterpiece of organization, as Sidky obtained a mandate representing over seventy per cent. of the electorate.

During the whole of that election day in Sinai reports were coming in from Cairo and other towns of the polling results in the Nile Valley constituencies, and the figures given were incredible. Towns and districts that one knew were solidly Wafd to the last man were returning Shaabist deputies with figures which indicated that ninety per cent. of the electorate had registered their vote. Provincial Governors were telephoning to their headquarters with quite understandable self-satisfaction the wonderful results obtained in their provinces only to be informed that their opposite numbers in the next constituency had done even better.

"La-la (no, no), Saaht el Pasha, eighty per cent. is not a record—it is not even good. From Gebali near you, news has just come that they have polled ninety-five per cent. Get busy, ya Saaht el Pasha, and beat them."

It is exceedingly galling to the Egyptian nature to hear that another man has excelled him in any activity, and as the day went on the results became more and more remarkable and epoch-making. History relates that in one constituency with a particularly energetic and able staff the poll was only closed in time to prevent a return of one hundred and five per cent. not counting dead men's votes, for the election of 1931 was remarkable for the fact that every man who had died in the last five years punctiliously rose from his grave to record his vote against the Wafd party !

How this wonderful and most successful election was carried out must always remain a mystery. One may believe, if one likes, that the boycott-minded electors at the eleventh hour had a prick of conscience and flocked to the poll in a contrite spirit; or, on the other hand, one may give credence to a variety of rumours and slanderous suggestions such as the filling up of voting boxes with the requisite number of votes before they were dispatched to the constituencies. Or again, for those who do not appreciate a touch of romance, possibly the startling results were obtained by the common-or-garden method of the

Governor or Mudir backed by his police commandant and minions using their persuasive influence to obtain satisfactory results.

In Sinai our organization was not so good, as only sixteen per cent. came to the booths voluntarily, a proof that the boycott propaganda had been instilled very thoroughly. The attitude of the government at that time was that the possession of a vote made it incumbent upon the owner to use it, and that it was illegal to refuse to attend at the booth to register it. This is a very knotty point indeed, and as no such case had ever occurred in Great Britain it was quite beyond me to decide as to the legality of this attitude or otherwise. It seemed a more or less reasonable argument, however, as there is something unsavoury about an organized boycott against the government of the day, and so the police went out into the town to persuade the people to come into the booths and vote.

It was all done very pleasantly and no force or coercion was used. Voters were informed that they could place their cross against the name of any candidate they fancied, but as there was only one candidate this was not quite such a great concession as it sounded. By this means a further ten per cent. were enticed or urged into the booths, but little more could be done, as it was discovered that the remainder of the voters were hiding in the dense palm groves on the seashore.

The police went down to the beach and played hide-and-seek and cross-tag among the palm trunks and cucumber beds the whole afternoon, but though everyone enjoyed himself enormously the bag was very poor indeed and did little to pull up our average. At 5 p.m., when the booths were supposed to close, our return was merely twenty-seven per cent., which compared very unfavourably with the results obtained in the Nile Valley.

Of course, if elections are run on these lines political agents when making forecasts of returns, instead of relying on the reports of canvassers, should take into account the amount of natural cover existing in a constituency. Factors that might influence results, such as dense palm groves or thickets of sugar cane, should be considered and due allowance made for their presence. In El Arish we were very unfortunately situated with some eight miles of thick cover on both sides of the town, and therefore our return could not be expected to be so good as that of a village standing among low-growing crops, such as clover or melons.

According to the election laws, however, the officials in charge of the polling booths could keep the doors open till 7 p.m. if people were waiting outside the stations to vote. The officials in El Arish argued that voters hiding in the palm trees undoubtedly came under that category as they were certainly not waiting inside; and when the great mass of the voters returned to the town at 5.30 p.m. with self-satisfied grins on their faces they were met by the police and officials wearing still broader grins who led them, protesting feebly, to the booths. The direct result of this was a poll of something like fifty per cent., which I think was highly creditable in the circumstances.

It is not really Egypt's fault that she is saddled with a form of government entirely unsuited to the country. The suggestion that they should adopt a Parliament elected by the free vote of the people came from our own government, who fail utterly to realize and refuse to learn when faced with results that the Oriental differs from the Occidental in every way, and who believe implicitly that a healthy democratic feeling exists in the Nile Valley, as it is fondly supposed to do in Great Britain.

It is a very moot point whether Parliamentary government is really a success in Great Britain, where a very small percentage of voters are qualified to give opinons on any general or foreign policy, and where a candidate with challenging blue eyes and an ability to hold a baby the right way up can be sure of seventy-five per cent. of the female vote of any constituency. If this is the case in England, where Parliamentary government has existed for four hundred years, and where over ninety-nine per cent. of the electorate are literate, what can one expect in Egypt where Parliaments are a novelty and eighty per cent. are illiterate? The correct and most satisfactory form of government for Egypt is the old Oriental touch of the Sultan and his Viziers and advisers—it is a government that is understood and respected by the people, and so long as the house of Mohammed Ali continues to produce Monarchs of the late King's type, little harm can come to the country.

CHAPTER V

ROYAL VISITS

Kings and bears oft worry their keepers.

PROVERB.

ONE of the tasks that falls to the lot of a Governor
is the entertainment of Royalty when they enter
his Province, and the pleasure—or otherwise—of the
undertaking depends not so much on the Royalty himself
or herself, but on the immediate staff of the Monarch.

King Fuad of Egypt was a most urbane and delightful
personality to meet if one happened to be an Englishman ;
but his attitude to his own subjects always struck me as
being somewhat abrupt. He made orders to and asked
questions of his staff in a rather peremptory manner ; and
because of this the many officials who followed in his
train were in a constant state of nervousness. I do not
think I have ever seen a collection of men so excited as
the retinue that followed in King Fuad's wake, and for
some unexplained reason he always went abroad on inspection or to open institutions followed by the complete
Palace staff, all the Ministers of the government, all the
Under-Secretaries, and as many heads of departments as
could squeeze themselves into the party.

It is difficult to understand why so many unnecessary
minor officials forced themselves into these gatherings,
for they had an unhappy and undignified time when they
got there. They were pushed about by the Palace staff,
trodden on by Ministers, possibly buffeted by police, and
if by chance a royal question should be asked and it was

considered possible that some hanger-on in the rear knew the correct answer, the unfortunate man would be bundled forward by rough and willing hands, and he would arrive in the King's immediate presence in a state of speechlessness and bewilderment, this condition being further aggravated by various Ministers urging him to answer at once.

In Great Britain, although we have a far greater reverence for the Monarch than have the Egyptians, the immediate presence of Royalty does not inspire everyone with anxiety; and I can only imagine that this state of affairs is a relic of the good old days, not so very far away in Egypt, when the Sultan on all state inspections had a few heads chopped off if satisfactory answers were not forthcoming immediately. The Grand Vizier was present with a note-book while the executioner followed about twenty paces in the rear with a huge scimitar, and if the Minister of War or anybody else gave the wrong answer he had his name taken and was immediately passed down the line for decapitation.

Of course, all this has altered now; but frequently when watching the nervous crowd in His Majesty's rear I have looked to see if there was anyone present who might act as executioner. Many years ago there used to be an enormous black Major-General on the Palace staff who certainly looked the part, and though actually I never saw him carry out a decapitation I cannot imagine what else can have been his function.

The state of chaos and trepidation that ensued in His Majesty's wake caused mistakes and confusion, because unless there happened to be a British official or police officer present who would keep his head no one had the courage to tell the King what the programme was. The royal cars, the guard of honour and the assembled crowd might be waiting at the east gate of the station building in readiness for His Majesty's departure, but if King Fuad suddenly decided that he would leave by the north gate, not even the Prime Minister was man enough to put him right. With gesticulations and worried expressions they would trot along behind him, and His Majesty would enter his car that had just arrived and pulled up with a sudden jerk, and acknowledge the " present arms " of a sweating guard of honour who performed the movement as they doubled into position through a scrambling crowd. I rather suspect that His late Majesty took a puckish delight in these fiascos, and believe that he derived a vast amount of amusement from the terrified demeanour of his staff and followers.

As the direct antithesis of this I may mention the departure of the Princess Royal of Great Britain, when she came from Palestine to Kantara by rail on her journey to England after a visit to Egypt and the Holy Land. The P. & O. ship on which she was to sail was scheduled to arrive at Kantara on the Suez Canal at 5 p.m., and was to tie up temporarily until Her Royal Highness had embarked. Lord Lloyd, the High Commissioner, was to arrive from Cairo by rail at 5.15 p.m., and the train from Palestine was due at 5.25 p.m. There was very little margin here for delay, and if it had been an Egyptian show everything, the ship included, would have had to be in position twenty-four hours in advance.

I had a Camel Corps guard of honour at Kantara, and about 4.30 p.m. my Egyptian officers started to panic and rush around.

" What are we to do, Sare? The ship is not arrived. Lord Lloyd is not here, and if Her Royal Majesty arrives what shall we do with her? "

At 4.35 p.m. a cloud of smoke to the south denoted the progress of the P. & O. mail-boat up the Canal; at

5.10 p.m. another cloud of smoke a little farther west marked the arrival of Lord Lloyd's train; and at 5.20 p.m. everything was in position according to plan. The Princess Royal descended from her carriage at the exact spot indicated, and having shaken hands with all the Egyptian officers—a charming touch that our Royalty never forget— went aboard her ship. As my senior officer said, wiping away streams of quite unnecessary perspiration, "I had no idea it could be done so quietly."

There was only one untoward episode in this arrival of the Princess Royal in Sinai, and that was the fact that her train was carrying an enormous amount of hashish— the contraband drug of Egypt. No blame whatsoever attaches to Her Royal Highness for this, as it is an old Palestinian and Sinaitic custom for trains carrying personages to be heavily laden with contraband. The motives that dictate this delicate attention are easily understandable, for the smugglers hold the view that in the general excitement inspection will be cursory or overlooked entirely. Lord Lloyd, when High Commissioner, returning to Cairo from a visit to Sinai, carried even more of the drug in his special train than did the Princess Royal; and it is believed that when King Fuad returned from El Arish he took with him sufficient hashish to supply all Egypt for six months. Unfortunately we were unable to check the figures and work out a priority table, for though the Princess Royal's and Lord Lloyd's consignments were captured at Kantara, King Fuad's lot got through, and we only heard of it by rumour; but it was sufficient to put the Arab camel-runners out of business for half a year.

During my service in Egypt I had the pleasure of meeting King Fuad several times, and the impression one obtained was that he disliked the feverish adulation and subservience of his retinue, and was glad to talk naturally to someone who was not going to grab his arm, try to kiss his hand, or dive to the ground to press feverish lips on his boot. He had several kingly gifts, one being the ability to remember names and faces which he amplified by being able to recall the particular hobbies in which one happened to be interested. In my case he always brought the topic round to ornithology or fruit-growing, and on both of these subjects he was extremely well informed. In fact he was a man of very wide knowledge indeed, and undoubtedly knew far more of Egypt and its people than many of the Ministers who served him.

My interviews with him were merely the routine audiences that one is granted after receiving an Egyptian decoration, and at different times during my service I was awarded three. He also sent for me for a special interview during the locust invasion of Sinai, because he required the fullest and latest information on the matter, and did not put much faith in the official reports rendered to him. On this occasion I found him not only extremely knowledgeable, but most sympathetic and understanding about the difficulties of the campaign. In this respect he differed entirely from his Ministers, for there was no need to explain to him that the question of supplying water to the locust-fighters in the sands of the desert was a matter of some difficulty, or that a heavily laden lorry travelling over rough and rocky country would not maintain the same mileage per hour as it would on a first-class macadam road.

The last interview I had with him was on the occasion of the publication of my book on Sinai. This was brought out by Blackwoods for the ordinary British public, and so far as I could see there was no harm in it, and nothing to hurt Egyptian susceptibilities, which are as tender as the new skin which grows over a bad wound; but my

Egyptian friends, when they saw it, gave a gasp of horror:
" It has no frontispiece of the King," they said in hushed
voices. Apparently I had dropped a brick of no ordinary
proportions, for in the Nile Valley it is understood that
every book published has the King's portrait as a frontispiece and it is dedicated to him as a matter of course.
This had never occurred to me, for I am certain our King
George would be most harassed and perplexed if every
one of the 16,000 books published annually in this country
were dedicated to him.

I knew that I was expected to present the King with
a copy personally—this is regarded as a *sine qua non* in
Egypt—but realizing the grave omission I had made over
the frontispiece I decided to do nothing about it. Then
I heard by the usual roundabout method that he had
commented on the fact that no copy had been given to
him, and so something had to be done about it. I often
wonder now if the King really gave utterance to all the
little speeches with which he was credited. I was always
hearing the remark that I must do this or that " because
the King wishes it," and as some of the things I was
expected to do were extremely unsound I strongly suspect
that most of these hints emanated from his staff or his
Ministers.

However, as it had been explained to me that I must
present him with a copy of my book, I took one to a
binder in Cairo and had a most royal cover in white
parchment picked out in green and gold fixed on to it.
The result was wrapped in cellophane with a green ribbon
round it, and when I went to fetch it I induced the book-
binder to put a second cellophane wrapper to it and a
second green ribbon, and this I tied with a special and
intricate sailor's knot I had learned in my youth.

I then went forth with the book in my hand, and in

due course was ushered into the Royal presence. His Majesty took the volume with some gracious words of thanks, and after fumbling with the knot for some minutes managed to get the first cellophane cover off. He seemed somewhat surprised to find there was a second cellophane cover and a second ribbon to untie, and put it down to recover his breath. I at once engaged him in conversation about desert partridges, a favourite topic of his, and the book was pushed to one side to enable him to discuss the matter fully. When the subject had been flogged to death, he put out his hand to take the book again ; but I at once returned to the charge—on this occasion about bustard and their hawking with peregrine falcons. By the time this fascinating subject had been adequately discussed my interview was at an end, and I left the audience chamber with the book lying on the desk still firmly tied with its green ribbon, and sincerely hope it has remained in that condition until to-day, so that the King never realized that I had omitted to include his portrait. Here again, however, I wonder if the King really cared a scrap whether his portrait appeared or not. In all probability it was only another of those manifestations of servility to royalty on which his staff insisted.

In my administration we had as Director-General a nice old retired Major-General from the Egyptian Army, who was what was known as a " King's Man." That is to say, he took no part in any of the various political moves and intrigues of that time but nailed his colours firmly to the Royal mast.

On one occasion the Director-General, who was something of a sycophant, rather overstepped the limit in his desire to please, and this occurred during the visit of King Fuad to the Oasis of Siwa. This Oasis lies in the heart of the Libyan Desert, and a rest-house to accommodate the King on his journey was built half-way on the route across the sand and gravel plain. Egyptians are past masters at the art of decoration and embellishment, and do it very cleverly as a rule; but the Director-General overdid it. He had three thirty-foot date-palm trees shifted from the sea coast at enormous expense and planted in a graceful group in front of the rest-house. The weather at the time was particularly hot, and when His Majesty arrived about seven days later on his visit the unfortunate trees were plainly advertising the fact that they had no roots, and were merely stuck in the sand for effect.

The King was an arborist of no mean order, and the effect these unhappy dying trees had on him was most unfortunate. It was obvious at a glance that they had been shifted recently, equally obvious that palms of that size cannot be transplanted, and still more obvious that no date palm or any other growth could survive in that stark desert. His Majesty took it as a definite insult to his intelligence that anyone should have thought that they would pass with him as growing trees.

" Who did that ? " he roared in an angry voice. " Who is the person responsible for that ? "

" What, your Majesty ? " asked the Director-General in a small trembling voice.

" Those date palms—who did it ? "

" I don't know," replied the Director-General with admirable presence of mind; " I will make inquiries." And he spent the evening ladling out twenty-piastre pieces to all the car-drivers, exhorting them, if inquiries were made, to profess profound ignorance on all topics connected with date palms.

King Fuad's visit to El Arish followed his trip to Siwa and I had therefore the benefit of knowing what to expect, namely, that His Majesty was no trouble whatsoever, but that the retinue surging in his wake rather like football enthusiasts fighting their way to a Cup Final would successfully defeat all my efforts to run the show on orderly lines.

The King and party were arriving by train, and I was much exercised in my mind as to how I was going to deposit some forty attendants into ten cars in the very circumscribed area at El Arish station, knowing full well that immediately His Majesty had driven off there would be an attempt on the part of all his followers to scramble into the first motor. The officer in charge of the cars on these occasions is in a most invidious position, as if he attempts to use force, and nothing else is of any avail, he may find that he has torn the coat-tails off his own Minister, and that his future has gone into the limbo of the melting-pot. I, therefore, arranged for His Majesty to inspect the Camel Corps guard of honour on foot and then to enter his car at the far end of the line; and whilst he was doing this I hoped that my Staff Officer would succeed in persuading the Ministers and officials to enter their conveyances with due deference to seniority.

Unfortunately the idea of the guard inspection was rejected, and instead the King was put hurriedly into his car and driven off. Immediately there was chaos, and everybody present was imbued with one idea; to get into the nearest car and follow post-haste after His Majesty. Those who got in first shouted to the driver to start, and the vehicle jumped into motion, upsetting those who were scrambling on to the running-board. The next four cars were treated in the same fashion, and the drivers themselves, being infected by the excitement and panic, banged in their clutches and leapt off as if they were striving to beat a record on Daytona beach. In three minutes it was all over, and my unfortunate Staff Officer, with his tarbush battered in, stood in the midst of four unwanted cars and watched the wild career of the other six, loaded well over the Plimsoll mark, tearing madly up the road through a dense crowd of yelling Arabs, who put the finishing touches to one of the most hectic moments of my life.

To make the situation worse, my Arabs in accordance with time-honoured custom raced alongside the cars mounted on horses or wildly careering camels and, yelling their war-cries, fired off rifles in the air. The King enjoyed the show thoroughly; but the Ministers and his staff were in a state of extreme trepidation because they thought His Majesty might be murdered by these wild men whilst they were in charge of his person. The programme had, of course, to be carried out, but the King was rushed from one spot to another and finally put into his car and driven back to the station amid another yelling crowd some two hours before the special train was scheduled to start. A very intriguing spectacle at the conclusion of that never-to-be-forgotten day was three high functionaries gesticulating and arguing with a black-faced engine-driver as to the possibilities of starting a train without a head of steam.

The most amusing scene, however, occurred prior to this when, in a big reception tent in the village square, His Majesty presented robes of honour and swords to the paramount Sheikhs of Sinai. I should here explain that three days prior to the visit, when I had all my arrangements cut and dried, the Director-General, on his own responsibility and without the cognizance of my headquarters, had sent down a senior Egyptian officer to assist me in my work. I cannot say that the services of this officer were of any great value to me, as I had my own staff who were quite capable of doing all that was required, but the Egyptian official mind is addicted to the practice of detailing two men to do one job. Also the Director-General made the fatal mistake of communicating direct with his representative without reference to my office. I had been asked officially to send in a list of paramount Sheikhs who were to receive robes, and I gave the names of the nine who were of suitable importance, and who I had arranged should be present. Unfortunately the Director-General communicated direct with his man and asked him to render a return of Sheikhs also. He obtained his information from a clerk in my office without reference to me, and sent in a list of thirty-seven, which included every Sheikh and sub-Sheikh in Sinai, the greater number of whom were quite unfit to receive a robe of honour or anything else connected with that quality; and who, living some two hundred miles away in the south of the Peninsula, were not able to be present at the ceremony.

When the Director-General asked if the Sheikhs were all ready to be received by King Fuad, and heard that instead of the thirty-seven for whom robes had been provided, there were in fact only nine, he lost his head completely. Apparently it would give very grave offence in high circles if, after the provision of thirty-seven robes, only nine recipients were present to receive them, therefore twenty-eight more " Sheikhs " had to be found at once, and here the Sinai Police, thoroughly appreciating the Gilbertian situation, rose to the occasion with that vigour and initiative they display invariably in awkward and unforeseen contingencies. If His Majesty required twenty-eight " Sheikhs " at short notice, twenty-eight " sheikhs " there would be. " Wallahi " (By God) and every townsman who in any way resembled an Arab, and who looked as if he might fill the part, was given a quick " wash and brush up," fitted with an Arab shawl and head-dress from stores, and sent up to answer his name as Sheikh Fulani Fulani (what's his name) of the So-and-So tribe.

The second visit—which took place in Southern Sinai—was on a very much smaller scale, and was only remarkable for one amusing incident. The Royal yacht, with its attendant escort of Coastguard cruisers, was lying off the quay at Abu Zeneima when I saw approaching a boat filled with queer-looking *effendis*. *Effendi* is a title coinciding, I suppose, with that large class in Great Britain which, with a fine disregard of Debrett, styles itself Esquire, and really means an individual of the middle-class who wears European clothes, and does not soil his hands with manual labour. These particular *effendis*, instead of being on the small side with indifferent physiques, were all hefty, brawny men with large-sized hands and truly terrific feet. There was something definitely un-usual about the party, for the fact that they were something else disguised as *effendis* was as obvious as the sun in the sky, and as one has to be responsible for the safety of the Monarch when he visits one's Province, I called out to ask who they were.

"We are Secret Police," they yelled at the tops of their voices for the benefit of the assembled crowd, and as everybody heard, except Atrash, the stone-deaf fisher-man of Abu Zeneima, there was no need for anyone to worry further about their identity. I discovered later in the day that their rôle was not quite so secret and intriguing as their designation suggested, for I noticed that their duty consisted solely of gathering together parties of the assembled crowd, and leading and inspiring the requisite shouts and loyal cries that the occasion demanded—and they did this extremely well. • It struck me that they were a very remarkable and worthy body of men, but I could not see any valid reason why they should be called secret police—" claque " seemed to me a more suitable description.

King Fuad, I believe, desired to see the Monastery of St. Catherine in Southern Sinai, or at least I was told repeatedly that he wished to do so; but whether the wish emanated from the Royal mouth or from one of his advisers, I never discovered. I rather suspected that there was some ulterior motive in this, for though the Egyptian Director-General of our Department was merely a figurehead as far as administration went, he had very strong views on religion—and in short was a Mohammedan fanatic.

He had visited the Monastery of St. Catherine himself, and was horrified to find this little stronghold of Christianity in the midst of a Muslim desert. What worried him above all things was the very doubtful Mohammedan orthodoxy of the Gebaliya tribesmen who serve the monks. They are the descendants of Wallachian slaves who were sent there by Justinian in the sixth century, and were, of course, originally Christian; but living outside the walls of the convent fortress they found it very dangerous in the past to profess the Christian faith, and so became Mohammedan and adopted Beduin mode of life. They, however, are still fully aware of their origin, and look to the Monastery for their living and continued existence, and I imagine their adherence to the Mohammedan faith is to say the least rather shadowy. Anyway, the Director-General discovered that they did not know the Mohammedan prayers, and that their religious training was practically non-existent. On his return to Cairo he therefore made great efforts to introduce a Muslim atmosphere at the Monastery. He desired to open up an eleventh-century mosque inside the convent walls that had been built as a gesture during a fanatical period, and which had never been used for worship; he tried to persuade me to establish a police post there; and he made every effort to have a Muslim *fiki* (religious teacher) posted to the place.

As I was serving a Mohammedan government my position was a very difficult one; but I was not going to be party to any interference with the sanctity of this lonely little outpost of Christianity in the mountains, where the monks had been allowed to carry on their devotions through sixteen troublous centuries. The opening of the mosque, which abutted on the Church of St. Helena built in A.D. 342, would have been regarded by the Brotherhood as a deadly affront and sacrilege of the worst variety. Police in my eyes are only a painful necessity, and one does not post them where they are not required. If an area can be run peaceably without police it is madness to maintain a post, as the saying " Satan finds some mischief still for idle hands to do " applies more to police than to any other class. My Sinai constables were the most excellent fellows, and if there was any work to do they did it with zest; but if there was no work to do they invariably made it, and policemen making work is a very regrettable business. As for the *fiki*, this was unthinkable, for *fikis* as a class are steeped in religious intolerance. They are the youthful, fanatical and ignorant product of the El Azhar Mosque in Cairo, and if there is anything in existence that will destroy harmony and create discord quicker than the average *fiki* it has escaped my notice in fifty-eight years of a varied existence.

I maintained therefore an attitude of resilient obstruction, so that the mosque was not opened, the police post never materialized, and the *Fiki* remained but a figment of the brain. The Director-General sensed this resistance and, thinking that the King, as a Mohammedan, would see things from his point of view, was very probably the instigation of the proposed visit. If this was the case it was, of course, a forlorn hope, for King Fuad, though a Mohammedan, was a broad-minded man, and would have been the last to take any steps to interfere with the monks and their tiny outpost in the desert, for never at any time in the history of the Convent had they engaged in proselytism.

However, it was conveyed to me that King Fuad desired to visit the Monastery, and I was asked to draw up a programme and make the necessary arrangements. The stories I had heard of the trip to Siwa filled me with alarm and despondency, for if regrettable episodes and hitches had occurred on the good hard going of the Libyan Desert, what would be the results of an attempt to ascend the craggy mountains of Sinai?

There is no real road to the Monastery, and the track to it for a hundred miles or so winds up the bed of the Wadis Feiran and Sheikh. The surface of these wadis is either fine shingle or sand, but floods in the winter-time leave a slight deposit of clay which binds this loose material together sufficiently for the first car to travel with ease at the rate of forty miles an hour. The following car, finding the fragile surface broken, can only do twenty miles an hour, and the third—if it carries on in the same tracks—will probably stick in the sand and require pushing. By selecting a new line of country over an unbroken surface, some five or six cars can make the journey in comfort and return, but the drivers must be men who understand thoroughly the desert and desert motoring.

His Majesty's advisers were so imbued with the idea of regal splendour and dignity that a convenient patrol of some half-dozen cars to carry the King and his immediate

retinue was unthinkable, and so far as I could see, he was
to be accompanied by the whole Ministry and their secretaries, most of the Palace staff, a special guard of honour
from the Bodyguard and a small army of cooks, *sofragis*
(waiters) and coffee-makers. One way and another, the
cars would number between forty and fifty, most of them
driven by chauffeurs who had never seen the desert in
their lives, and the proposed trip had all the ingredients
of a first-class disaster.

I drew up an estimate for the road at a figure that I
hoped would scotch the proposal, but unfortunately the
sum was approved instantly by Finance, and I had to go
ahead with the preparations for the trip, which I felt
convinced would go down to posterity as the biggest
royal disaster since King John's unfortunate experience
in the Wash. I spent thousands on smoothing and repair-
ing the road to Abu Zeneima, half-way between Suez
and the Monastery, and made it more or less possible.
Another £5,000 was spent on making a by-pass between
the shore and the cliffs at Abu Zeneima itself; but there
was definitely nothing that one could do to the hundred
miles of fine gravel bed in the narrow valley that led to
the Monastery. It was either a question of a fifty-pound
job, consisting of clearing away a few boulders and bushes
and making the track straight, or a first-class tarred road
with innumerable culverts, bridges and embankments that
would have cost a quarter of a million. The latter, of
course, was impossible; and so I cleared the track as
best I could and hoped that not more than half the cars
would stick and be left behind. A vain hope because,
from my experience of Royal trips, I knew that even if
only two cars stuck they would inevitably be carrying the
King's special food and his personal clothing, owing to
the fact that highly excited officials changed the loads at

122

every halting-place without informing anyone of their actions.

When all was ready I notified Headquarters with gloomy forebodings, and then, luckily, a hitch occurred because apparently I had quite overlooked the Sheikhs' tombs on the route and the visit had to be delayed while these were put in proper order.

Dotted about over the deserts in the mid-East are round mosque-like buildings of uncertain age that have been erected in the past over the grave of some devout Sheikh. No one really has the foggiest idea who these Sheikhs were, though every Arab you ask will tell you his name and the full details of his life, and every Arab will give you a totally different name and a totally different biography. There happened to be three on His Majesty's route, all in a lamentable state of disrepair; and it was just possible that the King would notice their existence. One was the tomb of Abu Zeneima, of whom nothing whatsoever was known; the second, a particularly dirty one that had been used as a latrine by generations of Arabs, was erected, apparently, over the body of fifteen different Sheikhs—had I asked more than fifteen people the number would have been increased in the same ratio; and the third was the tomb of Nebi Saleh. Nebi Saleh apparently was a nebulous prophet who lived before Mohammed, and he died all over the place. There are as many tombs to Nebi Saleh in the mid-East as there are houses in England in which Queen Elizabeth slept. In fact almost every other tomb you come to belongs to Nebi Saleh, who must have held the record for burials and resurrections.

Not only had these three tombs to be put in a proper state of repair; but a life history of the Sheikh had to be worked up for His Majesty's benefit, and this was difficult as probably King Fuad knew far more about the movements of the old Mohammedan patriarchs than I could possibly work up in a short month with nothing but the vaguest hearsay evidence on which to go.

However, in due course the tombs were whitewashed, repainted and put in a decent state of repair, and at last everything was ready for the much-dreaded visit. It was scheduled to start on the 1st November, and on the 30th October I went to Suez with my fleet of cars to meet the enormous entourage of King Fuad that was coming from Cairo—many of which would probably remain stuck in the fine gravel of Southern Sinai for months to come. Nothing, so far as I could see, could possibly avert the disaster, and then the weather, which throughout my life has treated me with special contempt, came to my rescue. On the evening of the 30th it blew hard and hot from the south, banking up clouds on the northern horizon; and on the 31st the wind changed, the clouds opened and torrents of water poured down on the desert's dusty face. Never in the lifetime of living man had there been such a storm in southern Sinai; and twelve hours later when the thunder ceased rumbling and the clouds rolled away disclosing a brightly shining sun not a vestige remained of my road to the Monastery. The level stretch to Abu Zeneima was scored out twelve feet deep in fifty different places, the by-pass had gone into the sea, and the hundred-mile track up the gravel wadi was a boulder-strewn gorge up which a camel could hardly pick his way.

The King's visit was postponed indefinitely, and then ensued a series of political upheavals of such a serious nature that they prevented his leaving the capital for any length of time. About this time also his health began to fail and one of his medical advisers informed me that he had no intention whatsoever of allowing the King to visit

Mount Sinai as he feared the effect of the great altitude on his heart, and so one way and another the expedition, which had hung over me like a nightmare for some five years, never materialized.

CHAPTER VI

ARABS, CAMELS AND MELONS

Do not wonder if the common people speak more truly than those of higher rank; for they speak with more safety.   BACON.

I AM sometimes taken to task as a man who has " let the side down " in that having been an Arab administrator for eighteen years, I have had the bad taste to come home and explode romantic myths by criticizing the Arab race.   It is a recognized trait of the Englishman after serving with or administering an Asiatic or African people for some years to become in course of time so attached to his subordinates that he can see nothing but good in them. The Indian Army officer maintains that there is nothing in all the world to compare with his Ghurkas, the West Coast man puts his Hausa far up the scale as a first-class soldier and desirable citizen, whilst the Sudan I.C.S. and Defence Force naturally swear by the Sudanese; and, as this country is inhabited by many different peoples, the Sudan is divided against itself with those who champion the Dinka, the Shaqi and the Nuah, and argue their respective merits.

This in itself is a most excellent thing, as it makes for successful administration and popularity and there is no great harm done if ex-Indian officers and Sudan officials sing the praises of Ghurkas and Dinkas for the rest of their lives.   In the case of the Arab, however, things are different because the Arab and his future constitute a difficult problem with which we have to deal in several of our dependencies and commitments and it is essential that the question is studied without bias or regard to false values, and here the Arab administrator is liable to prove a too enthusiastic propagandist and an unreliable guide. Such is the natural and intriguing charm of the Arab people that the man who has lived too long among them is apt to become so enthralled by the race that he sees everything from an entirely Arab point of view, and he gives vent to his feelings and opinions so vehemently in the Press and on the lecture platform that the people of this country and the United States have come to believe that the Arab is a paragon of all the virtues—a blend in fact of Richard Cœur de Lion and Saladin with the acquired wisdom and restraint of Mr. Asquith thrown in.

My criticism of the Arab people is not very drastic, however, and I think the most I have ever said is that there is not much real romance or chivalry in their general make-up, that they are not the first-class fighting race they are popularly supposed to be, and that they have no marked inclination for hard work. This distaste for manual labour is not due entirely to a natural aversion to hard labour, but more particularly because to be a cultivator is to lose caste in the eyes of the Beduin. He has for some three thousand years or more been a nomad breeder of camels and in Beduin eyes one was slightly low in the social scale if one descended to such plebeian beasts as sheep. Farming the land, ploughing the soil and harvesting the crops was and still is regarded as a degrading and menial task, and the Arab for generations has looked down on the occupation in much the same way as our Trade Unionists regard domestic service. The name *fellah* (cultivator) is a term of reproach and the Beduin has as much contempt for the tiller of the soil as he has for the cultivator's camel which he calls a " bean-fed pig."

Actually I like the Arabs, and if I had my life to live

over again I would still choose the job of administering these people, for they have many sterling and lovable qualities, and I have been happier among the Arabs than with any other race. It annoys me, however, to read and hear the silly and sickly adulation of this very ordinary but hardy nomad people, and to have to wade through books written by what I call the "professional travel-monger" where the praises of very rapacious and very artful Arab tribesmen are sung in no uncertain strain and who are endowed with every good quality that human nature can show. Actually, of course, the "travel-monger" has come into contact with only the worst characters of the tribes—the dragoman class—who are incidentally the most plausible and winning of the race. Every nation possesses the type; here in England we produce men with such charm of manner and such wonderful plausibility that they can roam the country in a car and persuade the inmates of rural rectories, rich widows, and even the retired official from the Orient to sell their sound holdings in government stock to enable them to acquire shares in a silver mine in Mexico, not quoted in the market but which will shortly pay a dividend of 25 per cent.

If poor old humdrum England can produce cavaliers of this type it is not remarkable that the East, the home of romance, can find some picturesquely clad paragons of plausibility also, and when I use the word "romance" I do so in the sense given in the dictionary: "A fictitious narrative which passes beyond the limits of real life." The most uneducated Arab can be most wonderfully convincing and persuasive when his statements are based upon a firm foundation of mendacity and roguery.

As an instance of this I might mention an American missionary who came to El Arish with the idea of Christian proselytism among the Arabs. There were innumerable objections to this sort of thing, the chief of which is that the Egyptian Government is a Mohammedan one, and though quite tolerant does not look kindly upon attempts to divorce people from the faith of their forefathers and of the State if there is any risk of it leading to a breach of the peace. Another objection is that in the whole history of missionary work in this part of the world no real conversion of a good Mohammedan into a good Christian has ever been made, nor is ever likely to be made.

The missionary came to me and explained the object of his visit. He said he wished to build a small church and to start active work in the village. When I explained that there was not the slightest prospect of any result he disagreed with me.

"I have been staying for the last few days," he explained, "with a very devout and good man who is most interested in the life of Our Lord and who has given me to understand that after teaching he would be prepared to accept Christianity. That is proof of what I can do."

I was amazed, for the village is fanatically Mohammedan, and asked the name of the man in question.

"Ahmed el Khraith," he said, "and he is a splendid specimen of an upright Arab."

I rang the bell and told the orderly to ask my sub-Governor to come in. He was an Egyptian and a very clever one who understood the hearts of the people and I explained to him that I wanted him to tell the missionary the sort of man Ahmed el Khraith was.

"He is the biggest rogue in the village," said the sub-Governor with conviction. "I have known him for ten years and he has never told the truth yet. He has been at the bottom of every fraud we have had in this Province and he has been in prison for almost every form of crime."

F

" But why did he show this interest in Christianity ? " asked the missionary. " He seemed most devout and eager to learn."

" You are talking of building a church," said the sub-Governor. " Among other activities, Ahmed el Khraith is a building contractor and a very dishonest one. He thinks he will get the contract for building the church."

This missionary, who spoke Arabic fluently, had been working in the mid-east for some five years, and if he could be so completely taken in by a real rogue it is small wonder that " travel-mongers," who make a very short stay and who know very little of the language, are deceived to an even greater extent and ultimately return to their homes and their writing-desks in the firm belief that they have seen the innermost souls of that charming and ingenuous people, the Arab of the desert.

There was a book on the desert published recently describing the trials and hardships of a travelling journalist. He wore Arab dress whilst in the desert and it was his contention that by doing so he passed as an Arab and was admitted to their inner circles, and so came to know them thoroughly. This I have no doubt was implicitly believed by many of his readers, for the book was a success and sold in large numbers.

The truth of the matter is, however, that no European by dressing as a Beduin and speaking the language ungrammatically and with a marked accent can possibly pass as an Arab or anything resembling one. This procedure merely has the effect of rousing the genuine Arabs' suspicions and causing them to be more secretive and untruthful than would normally be the case. Their natural conclusion is that this weird European passing himself off as an Arab is undoubtedly a government spy prying into matters that are better kept secret, and in all their dealings with him they are very much on their guard and also very hostile. This particular journalist was eventually murdered by the Arabs in a well-policed area where Europeans are respected, and it is safe to assume that if he had been dressed as an ordinary traveller and not rigged out in fancy costume such a regrettable occurrence would never have happened.

A few years ago in El Arish I received an excited telephone message from a frontier police post saying that a very suspicious-looking man—obviously up to no good —had crossed into Sinai.

" He is dressed as an Arab," said the *Hakimdar* (noncommissioned officer in charge of the post), " and he has a beard, but he is not an Arab. Perhaps he is English, or maybe a Jew. I am having him followed."

During the course of the day and the next night the telephone was busy with messages from all posts leading to the frontier, and one of my Arabs on secret service work rode in hurriedly to report the movements of a mysterious person who was without doubt a smuggler.

The following day the individual arrived, a very pale-faced young Englishman with a most unnatural-looking black bristly beard—the result of a month's neglect of a razor. He was wearing full Arab dress and looked as if he were bound for a Chelsea Arts Ball. In other words, his appearance proclaimed in large advertisement type that he was a European masquerading as an Arab. It appeared he was an antiquarian looking for digging sites, and when I asked him why he was dressed like that he said he had done it because he thought he would attract less attention.

" Attract less attention ! " I said. " It may interest you to know that the telephone went immediately you crossed the frontier and has been ringing ever since. If the police hadn't been so interested in your movements

ARABS, CAMELS AND MELONS

because they thought you were a bad hat you might quite
likely have had your throat cut by the Arabs as being a
person of no known nationality and therefore of no
account. If you'd come here wearing shirt and shorts
with a topee no one would have become excited, and you
would have been treated with respect, but in fancy kit like
that you ran a definite risk."

These remarks on the futility of dressing in Arab clothes
do not apply to such well-known characters and travellers
as St. John Philby, for instance. Philby when on a journey
wears the national kit because he has adopted the Mohammedan religion, but there is no attempt at disguise in his
case for his name is so well known among the Beduin
that such a proceeding would be useless. Philby has
spent the greater part of a lifetime in Arabia and is therefore
in an entirely different category from the ordinary traveller
whose name carries no weight in the tents of the nomad.

After reading some of these books of travel in Arab
countries I feel so entirely inadequate and prosy when I
attempt to write one myself, for I cannot offer as fare to
my readers anything half so attractive and exciting. Although I have lived eighteen years alone among the
Beduin, I have no hairbreadth escapes to relate, my car was
never held up by bandits, and the only time my life was
really in danger during this period was when I had come
in from the desert with its savage "sheeks" and happened
to meet a very nasty crowd of Alexandrian dockers who
were demonstrating in the slums of the city. I have not
mentioned this as it seems such a lamentable confession
of failure to admit that one has not had a single real adventure
in the desert from the race that for the last twenty years
has provided material for so much wonderful fiction and
still more wonderful travel books.

The behaviour of Arabs in Sinai, Southern Palestine

and Trans-Jordan towards travellers can only be described as exemplary. Not only is there never a case of interference of any kind but they are unfailingly polite and helpful, and last but not least scrupulously honest. Everything that falls from passing cars—and with inexperienced drivers this is a daily occurrence—is invariably brought in to the nearest police post by Arabs, which is very remarkable considering that in nine cases out of ten the article that most frequently drops from cars is a warm woollen rug, worth a king's ransom to a thinly clad and shivering Arab in winter.

I have known gangs of Beduin, who have come in from their grazing flocks, sweat and strain pushing an embedded car out of sand and then, when they had it finally on the move, wave their hands, smile with a flash of white teeth, and walk back to their animals without a thought of any monetary reward. On these occasions, I may say, the travellers have never failed to stop at the first police post and leave a sum of money to be distributed among their helpers, the identification of whom was no easy matter.

There was the case of a very fat American who stuck in the sand for a whole day during a terrible heat-wave and who was very nearly at the last gasp when two undersized Arabs appeared and after a great struggle managed to push the car on to firm ground and safety. His gratitude took the form of £50, for he confidently believed he had been saved from certain death, and perhaps he was right, and the extraordinary part of the whole business was the difficulty I experienced, when I had traced his benefactors, in forcing them to take the money. When one considers the natural avarice of the race, it is very difficult to understand this attitude, but it is based apparently on the old nomad idea of desert hospitality and the rendering of help to those in need. In their eyes they had merely done that which they were compelled to do by the unwritten law of the wilderness.

This attitude of being helpful and hospitable to all passing motorists is the more remarkable when one considers that the advent of the car and lorry has altered the life of the Beduin to a very great extent and has deprived him of one of his means of livelihood. Travellers, both merchants and tourists, now do all their journeyings by car or taxi instead of by the more expensive method of hiring camels, both riding and baggage, from the Beduin and paying moreover a *Khuwa* (goodwill money) to the Sheikh conducting the party. Lorries now exist in most Arab villages for the transport of merchandise, and the result is that the camel is losing his position in the desert, causing a fall in price and lowering of the standard of the animal. If another Great War should occur, the whole of the mid-east would be combed out for camels and the supply would be absolutely inadequate to the demand, for, despite the improvement in motor transport, the camel as a beast of burden is by no means an anachronism in wartime, as there is still much work that he can perform efficiently that no mechanized vehicle can do. This the Italians discovered to their cost in Abyssinia, and but for the ridiculous and ineffective sanctions the Arabs of Arabia and Sinai might have had a good year with their livestock.

The other side of the picture, a more amusing one, of being helpful to stranded motorists was provided by a labour gang of mine who were working on the road at Mitla Pass just east of Suez. The Mitla Pass is a small gap in the Sinai hills twenty-five miles from the Suez Canal, and its natural difficulties are added to by the fact that all the sand-dunes in the area converge on the spot. For some years about a mile of the road was constructed of wire netting that was laid on scrub and desert grass ; this served its purpose fairly well provided one did not swerve off into the sand and provided also that no car with a low clearance ripped up about thirty yards of wire netting. Once a motor had gone off the track it took a fairly large party of men to get it back.

My labour gang were at work putting in stone and bitumen at the worst part, and, to enable cars to pass during construction, they had made a small divergence, and this divergence, I noticed, led into the very softest sand that nothing could possible negotiate. It was Easter-time and the big annual exodus of Cairenes to Palestine was taking place with cars passing every half-hour or so, and every one stuck with the greatest regularity and had to be pushed out by an enthusiastic and happy crowd of workmen singing " Oh, haily O." The labourers, however, were not Arabs but Arishia from El Arish, gentlemen with very keen financial brains, and I heard afterwards that the divergence had been mapped out by sand experts and that the takings during the holiday season had worked out at roughly five shillings per head per day !

The Beduin Arab is essentially a man who, to quote the Wessex expression, " keeps hisself to hisself," and normally he has not the slightest desire to mix with Europeans or adopt any of their customs. He is entirely satisfied with his isolated nomad existence and does not yearn for the fleshpots of civilization, fearing he might become so entangled with possessions that his ordinary care-free, brink-of-starvation existence would be interfered with.

There are, however, exceptions—perhaps one should say temporary exceptions—and once when visiting an Arab encampment in the heart of Sinai I was amazed to meet a quite ordinary Beduin wearing the usual Arab kit who spoke English fluently but with a marked American accent. It appeared that as a boy at the end of the war he had been employed by one of the travel-agent firms at Kantara as a messenger and, having a quicker brain than the average Egyptian lads serving with the firm, had risen in the business till finally he had gone to America with some tourist who had taken a fancy to him. After ten years in New York, during which he followed various occupations, the old nomad urge had come upon him again and he had exchanged his trilby hat and lounge suit, and possibly his " Tuxedo " also for the *galabeyah* of the Beduin, and there he was back again living the extremely hard and penurious existence of the Arab in a harsh and waterless desert and apparently perfectly happy.

During the war a considerable number of boys from the Arab tribes were employed temporarily in the Royal Engineer workshops at Amria. They learned carpentering and blacksmith's work with amazing ease, becoming quite expert in a year and receiving rates of pay that meant unlimited wealth to a nomad, but none of them stayed the course. Invariably, after eighteen months or two years, these budding craftsmen would disappear from their benches without previous warning and would later be discovered tending a flock of sheep in the desert for which they were being paid, if they were lucky enough to extort their wages at all, of the rate of £1 a year instead of the £6 a month they had been receiving as workmen.

To the Arab, civilization is hateful because it means he must live in a house and is not free to wander at his will ; it necessitates also adherence to a time-table and, except on the question of prayers, there is no such thing as time to a Beduin, and even in his devotions he is fairly lax ; and last but not least he might become so soft and dependent that he could not set forth on a month's journey in the clothes he stands up in and nothing else. The average Beduin, if the occasion arises, will cheerfully start on a journey across the desert without carrying even water or food, a change of clothing, or notifying his relatives of his departure. He does not even trouble to fill his tobacco pouch; he hopes he will meet people by the wayside who will provide him with his wants, and if they do not materialize, going without water or food for a day or two will not worry him unduly. When a race has perfected absolute freedom in this fashion one can more or less understand the mentality that causes them to struggle against all temptation to fetter it in any way.

We ourselves have been so hopelessly tied up by the bonds of civilization from birth that this type of freedom is beyond our ken and moreover would not attract us if it meant going without our daily bath and only eating a meal when some passing wayfarer provided the food. Nevertheless, I have felt sometimes a sneaking longing to be as free as an Arab and to be able to "walk out" on the bonds of our rather intricate existence.

One meets from time to time along the desert tracks that cross Sinai and northern Arabia a small figure trudging steadily along—and the Arab on the move approximates very closely to four miles an hour—and finds that it is a Beduin on a hundred-mile walk to fetch a goat or attend a Court. He is wearing a tattered cotton shirt and drawers, a black goat's-hair *abaya*, or cloak, a leather belt supports his big curved sword, and slung around his neck on a thong of leather is his *kees*, or purse, in which he carries his flint, steel and tinder, and his documents or *hojas* (land deeds). These papers, black with dirt and creased with much folding, usually consist of a few *shehadas*, or chits, from various officials whom he has assisted from time to time as a guide or camel-man, and his land deed proving his right by inheritance to some stretch of rather hopeless desert. If he is a very provident man he may have tied up in one corner of his *abaya* a flat slab of native bread or a couple of pounds of barley-flour, but this is very far from being the rule as normally the Arab takes the road with nothing at all if he travels on foot, and such a thing as a supply of water in a goatskin bag is almost as unusual as a top-hat.

When one realizes what a fortnight away from home means to us, one understands why the Arab fights so hard against the comforts and adjuncts of civilization to which we are such slaves. We have to pack our kit with many changes of raiment—the black suit for dinner, flannels in case there is tennis, breeches and boots as we may be called upon to ride, plus-fours and the golf-bag, as there is sure to be golf. Arrangements have to be made for the cat and a temporary home found for the dog; the servants have to be parked out on board wages; and last but not least voluble instructions given to the gardener, none of which he will be able to carry out owing to the weather.

Nothing of this sort ever worries the Arab. He has no cat and his dog is not the sort of canine autocrat we suffer so gladly, for he trots at master's heels all day and apparently can exist on nothing. Another great asset about the Arab's existence is the fact that there is no need to shut up the house and find a caretaker while he is away on business with his family, as there is an age-old desert custom by which a man may pack up his tent, his cooking pots and plough, and even his store of dates and flour, and place them in the vicinity of some Sheikh's tomb until his return. This system of furniture depository has much to recommend it as no charge is made for storage and no roaming Beduin would dare to raid the kit for fear of reprisals from the *Afrit* that haunts all tombs. Frequently also I have seen household gear of this description stowed away under some rock where there is no guardian angel or devil to protect it, and it is an understood thing in the Beduin world that, though theft is not by any means unknown, the pilfering of another man's hoard in his absence is definitely "not done."

The average Beduin of Sinai is not a big man, for the extremely poor and meagre food he eats has caused him to be "very small, very spare and sadly shrivelled—poor over-roasted snipe," to quote Kinglake. There is, however, in the north of the Peninsula a tribe called the Bayyadin, who are one and all huge, brawny men averaging over six feet and who, unlike the ordinary Beduin, manage to grow big and bushy beards. I have never discovered the origin of this tribe, but I have an idea that they may possibly be descended from some foreign legionaries of the Roman Army. I have no proof of this whatsoever, but the fact remains that they are most certainly not pure-bred Arab or Egyptian, and their fine features and striking good looks suggest European, almost Anglo-Saxon, stock. In fact, one of the Sheikhs was so like my father-in-law that my wife always made a great fuss of him, which was to be regretted as his handsome face and fine features were the best part of him; in every other respect he was undesirable, a fomenter of trouble and strife, and something of a bully and braggart. In addition to their vast frames and patriarchal beards they had one and all very deep resonant voices and from my office chair I always knew when the Bayyadin were concerned in a case in the Court near by owing to the terrific volume of sound that almost made the earth shake.

Beyond admiring them as magnificent specimens of manhood I had not very much use for them as they bullied the other tribes, were constantly quarrelling among themselves, and were addicted to smuggling, but they had their uses on account of their nuisance- and shop-window values. If some distinguished visitor came to El Arish and looked forward to seeing a real desert " Sheek " in flowing robes I guarded against disappointment by always inviting half a dozen Bayyadin Sheikhs to morning coffee on the verandah, and the visitor would go away with an exaggerated opinion of the Arab race that would last him or her a lifetime and which nothing would ever shake.

Then again it was often necessary in the interests of one's job to remind those who controlled things and pulled strings in Cairo and London that Sinai *was* important and that its Arabs were a factor to be considered and who required some administering. The peculiarity about the Arab is that he avoids well-recognized roads and all the haunts of semi-civilization, so that it is possible to cross Sinai in a car and see perhaps only half a dozen Beduin. This absence of the right sort of Arab was a very bad advertisement for the Province, especially if one were trying for an increase in the police force or, more mundanely, for an increase of pay for oneself; therefore when a *Hess Kebir* (Big Noise) was visiting Sinai to see things for himself the landscape was always well decorated with Bayyadin and a dozen of the biggest, noisiest and most savage-looking were introduced personally. This always had the desired effect and the visitor would go away shaking his head and saying, " A nasty problem those Arabs if anything went wrong with things and one lost control with the Suez Canal so close." Of course one never volunteered the statement on these occasions that the Bayyadin numbered only four hundred at most; one spoke of them as if they covered the desert's dusty face like locusts.

The Bayyadin's finest show occurred at Kantara during

the visit of the Egyptian Prime Minister. He had been
in Palestine to meet the High Commissioner of that
country and was returning by train, which meant that he
would arrive at Kantara, the terminus of the railway, on
the Suez Canal, which is the Bayyadin country.

My Mamour (Egyptian officer) at Kantara, who ran a
very excellent and smart show, was always most incensed
when a notable or Royalty arrived at his station because
the Egyptian Governor of Port Said, who was very much
his senior, would cross over the Canal into his territory
and "steal his thunder." In the East meeting Kings,
High Commissioners and Prime Ministers is the salt of
life, as, besides the honour and glory of greeting the great, the
hope is always harboured that a first-class guard of honour
and a good show generally may be favourably remembered
when promotions and decorations are being considered. I
received an S. O. S. message on this occasion from my
officer asking me to come down personally on the train
to save the situation, and by reason of my seniority to short-
head the Governor of Port Said if he tried an invasion.

As my unhappy representative had suffered badly in
the past and lost "face" in consequence, I travelled down
on the train to see fair play and ensure that the Prime
Minister was introduced to my officer as commanding
the station, duly inspected the guard of honour, and met
the assembled Arabs. Unfortunately the Prime Minister
and I were so busy discussing some problem that I did not
notice we had arrived in Kantara until the train had stopped.
The Prime Minister stepped out and was immediately
greeted by the Governor of Port Said and his assembled
officials, who, elbowing my Mamour on one side, hustled
His Excellency into a launch and rushed him over to the
western side of the Canal without allowing him to inspect
a very creditable guard of honour that had been waiting

for two hours or shake hands with the assembled Sheikhs and Arabs who had been in position for three days.

Personally I was not very much upset at this, for Prime Ministers are so very ephemeral in Egypt and after " one crowded hour of glorious life " are so often relegated to the dust from which they may not rise again, but my hard-working and altogether admirable officer was heart-broken and in tears. " It is not fair, Sare," he sobbed ; " he always does this in my command and blackens my face among my people."

On the other side of the Canal in his own territory the Governor of Port Said had erected a huge " fantasia " tent and here a state tea-party was held for the Prime Minister whilst he awaited the Cairo train. There were several hundred of the " best people " from Port Said at the feast and one and all were clad in their natty European lounge suits and wearing horn-rimmed spectacles and new scarlet tarbushes. I sat on one side of the Prime Minister and the Governor of Port Said on the other, and shortly after the tea-party started I broke it to His Excellency that he had hurt the feelings of my Mamour at Kantara.

" He has been working very hard to arrange things for you," I said, " but you were led straight to the launch and were not allowed to greet all the Sinai Arabs who have been invited to meet you."

The Egyptian is naturally polite and a stickler for correct formality on all occasions, and this particular Prime Minister was always most punctilious about greeting the people who assembled to meet him.

" I am deeply grieved," he said. " Please bring your officer to meet me and tell all the Arabs to come in and have tea with me."

I passed the word and when my Mamour arrived said behind my hand, " Let loose the Bayyadin."

Two or three minutes later the fly of the great tent bulged in all directions and fifty or sixty enormous bearded men stalked in with their hands on the silver-encrusted hilts of their great curved swords. Their behaviour and bearing were most correct and punctilious so far as His Excellency was concerned, but as for the assembled guests they simply did not exist. With a booming of their great voices they came forward in a surging mass of silken garments, sweeping the other partakers of the feast away from the table to the floor, and bowed over the hand of the Prime Minister who, rather staggered by their magnificence and warlike appearance, waved them to seats. Actually every seat was occupied, but this was no deterrent to the lordly sons of the desert who, being invited to sit, did so by casually tipping the occupants from their chairs as if they were flies or some other negligible vermin. From this moment the Bayyadin held the centre of the stage, talking loudly of Sinai and the loyalty of their mighty tribe, and when the much-impressed Prime Minister left by train half an hour later on the Nile Valley line a search had to be made for the Governor of Port Said, who had been lost in the crush and buried beneath the voluminous robes of the Sheikhs of the desert.

"After this, Sare," said my Mamour, gleefully, as I boarded the night train for El Arish, " I shall not complain so much of the troubles the Bayyadin cause, for, *Wallahi!* they have their uses."

Every Arab tribe has its mark or crest, in Arabic *wasm*, and this is used chiefly for the branding of animals, though one will also see these symbols roughly hacked out on a conspicuous rock in the desert to notify that the country surrounding belongs to a certain tribe. The marking of animals, particularly camels, is most necessary in the

Beduin world for if the grazing is suitable animals are left entirely to their own resources and devices, and they may be at large with no herdsman in charge for several months at a stretch. Rustlers, or animal thieves, are not unknown in the Beduin world, though, considering the opportunities, they are not nearly so common as one might imagine, and therefore a satisfactory brand must be put on the camel at an early age to assist in identification. The marks are of various types—circles, crosses, pothooks and hangers—and they are always placed on the same part of the animal. That is to say, one tribe will brand a pothook on the upper part of the off foreleg, another will use a circle on the near hind, and so on. The reason for this is that if a camel-thief wishes to fake a pothook so that it looks like a circle he may be clever enough to achieve something good enough to pass muster, but what he cannot do is to obliterate the pothook from the off foreleg and transfer it to the near hind. The Beduin appears to lead a most haphazard, careless life, leaving everything to chance, but when one comes to inquire into it more closely it is not quite so casual as at first sight it appears and he has customs and laws and observances which seem to guard against most eventualities.

The thing that used to cause me more amazement than anything was the cheerfulness with which an Arab would set forth to look for his camels in the desert after they had been left to graze of their own sweet will for four months or more. He had turned them loose possibly at Kuntilla on the Palestine border, but there was not the slightest reason why he should find them in the vicinity of that place or even within a hundred and fifty miles of it. In search of the very sparse herbage or edible scrub bushes on which they feed they might have wandered north-west as far as the Suez Canal, again they might have turned on their tracks and gone into the Dead Sea depression, or it was quite possible they had gone southwards into the maze of deep granite gorges at the apex of the Peninsula.

It rather suggests a race with untold leisure and to whom time means absolutely nothing when one sees a little Arab with no kit or supplies of any description setting forth to comb out an area about the size of Scotland for six camels worth possibly £25. Actually it is not nearly so hopeless and difficult as it sounds, for our little primitive man can recognize at a glance the tracks of all those six camels and can, moreover, put a fairly accurate date on each track. This appears to be so incredible that few people will believe it, but when one comes to think of it we ourselves have so perfected the art of reading type that any one of us can open the morning paper and in less than fifteen seconds take in all the headings so that we know the morning's news all over the world from London to Tokio. As the Arab has spent just as much time studying his reading primer, the sand of the desert, and matriculated in the art, it is not very remarkable that he can distinguish between the tracks of his own camels and those of others, and that he can estimate the age of those blurred marks. After all, he has specialized in one subject and has not been compelled, as we have, to waste his time following after false gods such as algebra and Euclid.

Also there is another factor, and that is the daily news of the desert. At first glance these wildernesses appear to be absolutely devoid of life of any kind, but the impression I have obtained is that it is impossible to walk a yard in any direction without one's movements being noticed by someone. It is not a question of secret service or anything of that description, but is based on the fact that the Arab is an inquisitive man by nature. So little occurs in the desert to distract his attention or occupy his mind that he makes an indelible mental note of anything he happens to see and, having exceptional eyesight, there is little that escapes him, whilst being free from worries of any kind he has a wonderfully retentive memory.

One may ask a passing Arab if he has seen a certain man of a certain tribe and he will answer at once that the individual in question passed that way eight months ago with two camels and three goats and his *sitt* (wife). He may not have seen the man himself, but he has heard the news round the camp fire and made a note of it in his subconscious mind. If by any chance, however, the man about whom one is inquiring should happen to be a malefactor or wanted by the police for some misdemeanour it is quite a different state of affairs—not a soul has seen him or even heard of him, and in fact one feels that to suggest such a thing is lacking in taste and decent feeling. I do not know whether this is due to a wish to protect a brother-Arab, or an instinctive desire not to be mixed up in anything of a police-court nature for fear of repercussions. I rather suspect the latter reason.

The question of *wasms* was one that caused me much trouble in Sinai, for on the recognition of these depended the payment of Customs dues when animals crossed the Suez Canal into Egypt proper. Owing to the fact that the Sinai–Palestine frontier is situated in a rolling plain of sandy country no attempt is made to place a Customs barrier in such an unsuitable spot, and the inspection and payment of dues takes place 130 miles west on the Suez Canal. This forms a most effective and economical obstacle to free trade, but the drawback to it is that one has to make certain provisions for legitimate Sinai products and to enable the Sinai people to send their goods and animals to the nearest market without having to pay duty on them.

There was a constant war of wits between the officials of the Customs Administration and my Arabs over the question of what were Sinai products and what were not, and if Customs made many pettifogging and troublesome regulations to avoid a little mild smuggling, the people of Sinai always seemed to have a trump up their sleeve with which to take the last trick.   There was, for instance, the question of water melons which are grown in enormous numbers on about five miles of sandy country on the Sinai side of the frontier and for ten miles on the other side. The Customs Administration got all hot and worked up over these melons, for they suggested, and rightly, that a considerable proportion of those exported to Egypt proper came from Palestine.   My attitude was, that if for the sake of economy and their own convenience they had their Customs barrier 130 miles within the boundaries of their country, they should not penalize the unfortunate inhabitants in consequence, and therefore that they should not charge dues on all the melons that crossed the Canal, which was the remedy they suggested.   Eventually they arrived at what they considered was a water-tight arrangement and so long as they were satisfied all was well.

The land of the Sinai cultivators was inspected by officials prior to the harvest, the growing melons actually counted on the plants, and the owner was then given a permit to export that number of melons and no more. The cost of making the inspection and numeration was more than double the amount collected in dues, but the really humorous part about the whole business was that the inspectors, not being agriculturists, were in the hands of the cultivators and were made to count every melon they saw from those twice the size of a football to little globes rather smaller than marbles.   Anyone with experience of melons knows that, though ten or more fruits may

form on a plant, only two or at most three come to maturity
and that the small button-sized ones wither and fall away.
This careful inspection and enumeration therefore left the
Sinai man with a very comfortable margin for a little mild
smuggling, and the fact that there have been no complaints
whatsoever suggests that the system is giving complete
satisfaction to both parties.

Over the question of camels and *wasm* marks things were
not so satisfactory as the trade is a very big one and the
dues payable on an animal considerable. The system in
force when I first went to Sinai was that camels were
inspected by a Board consisting of an Egyptian officer and
two Sheikhs, all of whom were expert on Arab *wasms* and
could recognize them at a glance. On the result of their
inspection depended the fact whether the camel-merchant
paid 12s. on the animal or took it across to the Cairo
market free gratis. This was " money for jam " and too
good to be true.

In one year I discovered Sinai had exported over one
hundred thousand camels of home production whilst all
Arabia and Syria could only account for a paltry forty
thousand. Either little barren Sinai was the greatest camel-
producing country in the world or there was something
radically wrong, and the fact that the three members of the
Board were one and all men of very considerable wealth
rather pointed to the latter explanation. Many years later,
when all three members of this redoubtable Board were
dead, I heard the explanation, which was very simple and
very much what I had expected; the camel-merchants,
having agreed to a figure, or to be more exact the bribe,
handed over their animals to the Sawarka Arabs of northern
Sinai, who were experts at the obliteration of old *wasms*
and the creation of new ones. After ten days' treatment
the camels with " old " Sawarka brands on them were

paraded before the Board and duly certified as of Sinai origin. What I never managed to discover was the fee paid by the camel-merchant to the Board and the *wasm* fakers, but, as the Oriental is a hard man at a bargain, I estimate that it cost him half the sum he would have to pay in Customs dues. So this happy little Board of experts was making something like £30,000 a year out of their activities and the Government were losing £60,000, for it transpired eventually that Sinai's export of legitimate Sinai camels was to all intents and purposes *nil*.

I tried various devices to counteract the malpractices of this Board and, failing conspicuously, I formed another Board with another officer and other Sheikhs only to discover that the mantle of Elijah had fallen upon Elisha and that Sinai was producing even more camels than usual and Arabia less. In the end I persuaded the Government to remit the annual head tax on camels in Sinai and in return to charge Customs dues on all animals, whatever their origin, when they crossed the Canal to Egypt proper for sale in the markets. This pleased everybody except the plutocrats of the Board; it saved me the trouble of trying to grind half a crown per head for every camel the Arabs owned and which I was seldom able to collect, it gave the Arabs a sense of freedom from Government interference, and it brought some £60,000 into the coffers of the Government in lieu of a very problematical £2,000 animal tax.

After this everything went smoothly for some ten or twelve years until the malpractices of the all-powerful and corrupt Board had become such ancient history that I imagined everybody had forgotten how things were done in the good old days. Then one year, whilst I was on leave in England, the Egyptian Government fell out with the Hedjaz over some economic question and as a reprisal double Customs dues were inflicted on all Arabian products.

To discriminate between Hedjaz camels and those of other countries the Customs Administration had the entirely original idea of appointing a Board of three officials to examine *wasms* and decide on the nationality of the animals. This Board was in existence for only a short three weeks before I succeeded in getting it suppressed, but the period was quite long enough as two of the members, minor officials on £200 a year, immediately blossomed forth with new Ford V8 cars, but the fact that the third, a member of my own Administration, could only manage a Baby Austin rankled somewhat with me as it suggested our Department was not quite on an equal footing with others or that we had provided the weakest member of a very far-seeing and redoubtable team.

When an Arab Court is sitting to assess the compensation payable in a case of assault one may obtain a totally false impression of the Beduin's reaction to bodily pain, for the injured man will be assisted into the room groaning piteously and will shriek loudly when his wound, probably nothing more than a trifling bruise, is examined. This, of course, is mere play-acting, which is the keynote of most Beduin cases, and is done solely for the sake of enlisting sympathy and increasing the damages.

Actually the Arab is the most stoical creature and shows a disregard of physical agony that is remarkable. I have seen men with the most ghastly unhealed wounds walking about and leading their ordinary life as if they were suffering from nothing more than a superficial cut, and one can only imagine dimly the agonies they undergo from their teeth. The Beduin as a young man has a most amazing array of regular milk-white teeth, but they deteriorate rapidly. Those autocrats of the tilted chair whom we visit so often din into our ears, when our mouths are filled with swabs and the drill is whirring merrily so that we cannot argue,

that all our dental troubles are caused by leading an unnatural life, using the wrong sort of toothbrush, and eating
the wrong sort of food. If we were more primitive and
lived more like the savages all dentists would go out of
business. This theory, however, is proved to be a fallacy
in the case of that very primitive creature, the Beduin, for
he has far more trouble with his teeth than the most self-
indulgent and *foie-gras*-complexed stockbroker or chocolate-
eating, meringue-minded female. The average Beduin of
forty has a mouth consisting of gaps and unsightly brown
stumps, and it is obvious that he must have suffered agonies
from abscesses and all the other horrors of neglected teeth.

As an instance of their contempt for pain and wounds I
recall the episode of a Mezeina Arab of South Sinai who,
as a side-line, earned a little money by collecting wild
animals for the Cairo Zoological Gardens. I never discovered the methods he employed in trapping them, but
he succeeded in obtaining for me a whole family of hyrax,
the coneys of the Bible, several young ibex and a variety
of foxes. The Director of the Zoo particularly wanted a
specimen of the Sinai leopard, which is not very plentiful,
and I offered the Arab £10 if he could obtain a pair of cubs.
£10 is a very large sum to an Arab, but, as the leopard is
very scarce and not exactly amenable to reason when found,
I imagined that the catching of two cubs would be no easy
matter.

Some months later I met my friend with a group of
Arabs in front of the office at Tor and asked him if he had
managed to get the cubs. For some unexplained reason
this constituted the best joke in the Peninsula since Aaron's
rod turned into a serpent, and the whole party rocked with
merriment, the wild-beast-catcher laughing louder than
anyone.

" No, he hasn't got the cubs," gasped one man between

gales of laughter, " but he got more than he bargained for. Look at his hand."

The Arab held out a right hand mangled out of all recognition with three fingers missing, and at sight of it there were renewed roars of merriment.

" He thought he had found the leopard's lair," went on the first man, " and put his hand in the rocks to pull out the cubs, but it wasn't a leopard's lair at all; it was a hyæna's and the hyæna was at home ; and that's what she did to his hand."

Although I have a fairly keen sense of humour I failed utterly to see the point of this particular joke which was too subtle for my Western mind. I therefore paid over the £10, cubs or no cubs, feeling that I was responsible for the accident, and considered it a very poor compensation for the loss of a right hand.

Those who have read Doughty's classic *Arabia Deserta* will recall frequent mentions of a queer nomad race who were not Beduin Arab stock and who were called the Solluba. Doughty met parties of them on many occasions during his wanderings and relates of them that they are a nomad people who live by hunting, veterinary work and the tinkering of pots and pans for the Beduin.

Nothing whatsoever is known of the origin of these Solluba, or Nawah as they are called in Palestine and Egypt, but there seems little doubt that they are an Eastern branch of that queer and unaccountable race, the Gipsies. Making allowances for difference of climate and surroundings, their methods of life are almost precisely the same as those of our gipsies in England. The Solluba live to a great extent on the gazelle, hares and jerboa rats of the desert, whilst our gipsies with their brown lurcher dogs do much the same in England with the hedgehog of our countryside taking the place of the jerboa.

Tinkering of pots and pans is common to both races, but it is over the doctoring and faking of animals that the similarity is most marked. It is a recognized fact in the British Isles that our gipsies have a mysterious gift with horse-flesh, so that some worn-out old crock, bought at a fair at ten shillings a hoof, is sold a few months later as a perfectly sound animal in the pink of condition. In a very short time the horse cracks up again with all its disabilities and diseases in an aggravated form, but long before this occurs the vendors are three counties away looking for further bargains and mugs to whom they can sell them.

The Solluba of the desert, as Doughty relates, have the same extraordinary gift with horses, donkeys and camels, but the Beduin like the British farmer is very suspicious of anything that emanates from a Solluba encampment, for the filing of teeth to hide the correct age and all the other devices of the expert horse-coper are known to them. Another charge that is made against this race is the mysterious disappearance of chickens that seems to coincide with their arrival in the vicinity of Arab encampments, and the English poultry-farmer also complains of losses when gipsy vans are in evidence.

It is, however, among the womenfolk that the resemblance is most marked, for the Solluba woman, unlike the retiring Arab female, is a brazen creature with flashing black eyes and striking good looks which she sets off by huge ear-rings and cheap jewellery. Her features, as a rule, are very similar to those of the English gipsy girl, and there is usually some hint of the Tartar in the slanting angle of the eyes and the height of the cheek-bones.

She is a professional singer and dancer, being taught by her mother from her earliest youth, and with the menfolk beating the *taboor* (drum) and twanging the *kamanga* (zither) she gives turns at the Beduin encampments for

which the " hat " is passed round afterwards. The con-
tributions are usually in kind rather than coin and take the
form of corn, olives and coffee beans. When they become
old and lacking in charm and allure, fortune-telling takes
the place of dancing and in every Solluba encampment
there are wizened old hags who, when their palms are
crossed with silver, will give one glimpses into the future
where lovely girls and fast-riding camels play a prominent
part.

The Solluba speak Arabic but, like our Romanies in
England, also have their own language which they use
among themselves only ; it is disappointing if one tries to
link up the two races to find that there is apparently no
similarity between the two vernaculars. One point, however, they have in common is the fact that it is an entirely
original language and almost impossible to arrive at a
derivation of any of the words used.

The policemen of the East have much the same opinion
of the Solluba as have our constables of the gipsies—in
other words, they prefer their room to their company.
In return the Solluba have little use for the forces of law
and order and the appearance of a uniform is usually the
signal for a quiet fading away into the desert wastes. It
is this natural aversion to officialdom that hampers one in
one's efforts to discover the origin of this queer people,
for they are naturally on their guard when interrogated in
any way. A harmless question such as " Where did your
people come from originally ? " is immediately considered
to be the beginning of a cross-examination concerning a
shady camel deal at the last camping-ground, and the
Solluba become mute or evasive as the result.

The Arabs believe the Solluba are the descendants of
the *Asakir el Seleeb* (Crusaders), but there is no proof
whatsoever of this contention, and in the absence of other

evidence it seems certain that these queer people owe their origin to the same mysterious stock that first made its appearance in Europe in the fourteenth century, and these forerunners of the present-day gipsy are considered to have been of Hindu origin, not Egyptian or Tartar stock as was the common belief until recently.

CHAPTER VII

BANDITS, BRIGANDS AND BAD MEN

Now Barabbas was a robber.

JOHN xviii. 40.

IN European countries the great drawback to being a
brigand is that one has of necessity to lead a rough
life in the mountains or forests far away from all the
amenities of ordinary civilization, but if the Arab of the
deserts decides to take up banditry as a profession it in no
way interferes with his normal existence. "And he will
be a wild man; his hand will be against every man and
every man's hand against him," was the summing up of
the nomad Beduin in Genesis, and the passage of time has
done little to alter the Arab's mode of life or his general
outlook. If he is a man of peace he of necessity leads a
hard life far away from civilization, existing on the
barest and most meagre foodstuffs, so that if he should by
force of circumstances become a bandit "on the run" it
makes no very great difference to his normal existence.
He has no house and no possessions that can be estreated;
he has no home life in the sense that we understand it and
continued separation from his wife and family means
nothing to him. Moreover, his small family, being of the
same fibre as himself, it is quite possible for the bandit to
transport to live with him in the back blocks of the
wilderness, knowing that if a police raid should take place
his wife and family would be immune from interference.
This being the case, it is remarkable that the calling does
not attract more adherents and that there are so few brigands

and highwaymen in Sinai, South Palestine and the Libyan Desert.

My first experience of bandits occurred in early 1919 when I was commandant of the Amria area in the Western Desert. Amria lies some twenty-five miles from Alexandria on the western side of the Mariut Lake, and to the south-east is the province of Behera, a stretch of the Nile Valley that had more or less recently come into the irrigated area through the construction of the Nubaria Canal. Prior to the arrival of the water supply this semi-desert area had been occupied by the Aulad Ali Arabs of the Libyan Desert, who used it as grazing land and, though the Egyptian Government would have preferred to hand the newly irrigated area over to Nile Valley *fellaheen*, who are the finest and hardest-working cultivators in the world, the difficulty of getting rid of the nomad squatters was such that they adopted the line of least resistance, and allowed the Aulad Ali to settle down on the soil. In consequence the Arab portion of the Behera is not cultivated with the same degree of efficiency as the rest of the Nile Valley, and for many years the villages on the extreme west along the Nubaria Canal were notorious for harbouring all the bad men of the country. Nevertheless, the Arab has settled down on the soil and given up his nomad habits, so that probably in another fifty years it will be difficult to distinguish between these settled Beduin and the ordinary *fellah* of Egypt.

In 1919 Egypt was suffering from the aftermath of the war and there was much lawlessness in the Behera owing to the fact that no British inspector existed to tighten up public security. Most of these officials had gone off to the war in 1914 and as few came back there was some difficulty about filling their vacant posts. There were many " wanted " men on the official police list of Behera and the Western Desert and among them was one Ibn Suliman, who had committed a particularly atrocious murder in the vicinity of Amria prior to the war. After a quarrel with a neighbour he had not only murdered his actual opponent but had wiped out the whole family, including the wife, two children and old father. Justice in Egypt is rather like the mills of God and grinds slowly but not so effectively, with the result that Ibn Suliman was still at large and on the " wanted " list when I took over at Amria in 1918.

One day when things seemed particularly humdrum and dull an Arab came in with information that Ibn Suliman was living peacefully in a village just over the Nubaria Canal. I had never heard of Ibn Suliman, but upon looking up his record I decided he was well worth arresting as the reward for his capture dead or alive was £500. I therefore set off in two cars on what I realize now was a very ill-advised and haphazard show, for I took only two of my own police with me, I neglected to inform the authorities of the Behera province that I proposed to make an arrest in their territory—and in Egypt we are very touchy about poaching on the preserves of others—and I carried out the raid with both the police and myself disguised as peaceful *fellaheen*. It is my opinion that no policeman whatever his nationality can really disguise himself. The London constable when equipped in white tie and tails for a raid on a night club rather creates the effect of an elephant endeavouring to hide his figure in silk pyjamas, whilst the average Egyptian policeman when he tries to look like a harmless villager merely succeeds in giving a first-class representation of a big-footed cut-throat of the very worst variety.

We travelled by night and arrived at a Behera police station on the Nubaria Canal in the very early hours of the morning and here I, very improperly, turned out the ten men of the post and ordered them to put on plain clothes. Then, with the whole party wearing the long cotton *galabeyahs* of the *fellah* topped by very incongruous tarbushes and carrying rifles, we descended upon the village of Ibn Suliman. We were a weird and ominous-looking gang, and though we might have been mistaken for almost anything there could have been no doubt whatsoever on one point—we were definitely *not* peaceful inhabitants going about their lawful occasions, which was the impression we wished to give.

The village was the usual collection of one-storeyed mud-brick houses with the pink-and-white semi-modern villa of the Sheikh standing in the centre, and on all sides were the deep and wide water channels of the Nile Valley irrigation system and dense patches of *durra* (maize) and sugar cane. We came down the centre street in the pale light of early dawn and the first person to see us was the old *ghaffir*, or night-watchman. It must have been the first occasion on record of a Nile Valley night-watchman being awake and on duty before sunrise. He had had to deal with many cut-throats and members of the underworld in his time, and there was no doubt whatsoever in his mind as to what we were. Our appearance proclaimed our nefarious calling and he promptly opened fire on us with a double-barrelled shotgun—and small blame to him. We were all well peppered with small shot and after this I am not very clear as to what happened exactly. Every door in the village opened and men and women poured out into the street in a state of terror, the women keening shrilly whilst the men at once plunged into the depths of the sugar cane and maize and were lost to sight immediately. My scratch police force, being very vague as to the object of the raid, opened fire on all and sundry with their rifles, but luckily they were one and all extremely bad shots and no one was hit.

It appeared that the village was under the impression that this was a raid on the part of the authorities to obtain recruits for the Egyptian Labour Corps, for, though this very useful and efficient force was supposed to be a volunteer organization, it is a regrettable fact that during the latter stages of the war local authorities obtained their quota of recruits by press-gang methods. The police thought rather naturally that every man who tried to evade arrest must be the much-wanted Ibn Suliman for whom £500 was payable alive or dead and therefore plastered every flying figure with bullets. The Sheikh of the town, who eventually turned out rubbing the sleep from ophthalmic eyes, having been assured that I was not an Arab cut-throat but a British official in disguise, asked what it was all about. When he grasped the fact that all we wanted was Ibn Suliman he seemed mightily relieved and pointed to a tall figure making away rapidly down a canal path. " There he goes," he said, " and we shall be glad to be rid of him."

Unfortunately all the police were crashing about in the sugar cane and *durra* plots playing a game of cross-tag with the peaceful and very frightened inhabitants, so I set off alone after Suliman and a long stern chase it was. I was greatly hampered at first by my long skirts, to which I was unaccustomed, so proceeded to tear strips off the garment as I ran until finally I was clad in a neck-band only from which hung long streamers of cotton cloth. Luckily Ibn Suliman, though exceedingly good at a sprint, was not in the Marathon class and after a half a mile I began to gain on him until I was near enough to send a revolver-shot buzzing over his head. This had the effect of putting him into top gear again, but a second shot that kicked up the dust near his feet brought him to a standstill and he turned to await my arrival. He was well above the normal Arab height, standing some six foot two in his sandals and, judging by the expression on his face, capable of any form of murder at any time of the day, so that I was very glad I still had four cartridges in my revolver. I was so completely blown by my run that a child of five could have knocked me on my back, therefore I sat gasping for breath on a tussock of sword-grass and shoved my revolver into the pit of Ibn Suliman's stomach and there we remained for a very trying and nervous quarter of an hour until my police arrived to inquire ingenuously what I had against the large Arab with the revolver-barrel in his abdomen!

Ibn Suliman was tried later in an Alexandrian Court and got off with an extremely light sentence; the effect of time on murder is much the same as that on wine, it has a most mellowing and softening effect, and the story of a ruthless killing as recounted by witnesses some ten years after the event is shorn of all its horrors and gruesome details, making it sound quite a normal and almost righteous proceeding. That side of the question did not concern the police unduly, but the failure to pay any reward under some purely Egyptian statute of limitations rankled very deeply and became one of those undying things about which in the East one writes a letter every six months, and which forms the subject of personal complaints till the sands of the desert grow cold and the hair of one's head turns grey. I think I had my last complaint on the subject about a month before I left Egypt for good.

Whilst I was in the Oases of the Southern Desert I was free from all worries in connection with crime and bandits, for the inhabitants are a most peaceful and peace-loving community. This is a definite drawback in some ways as, if one's department is not too generously treated over the payment of casual labour and the employment of sweepers, it is very difficult to run a satisfactory show without that very useful and never-failing concomitant of public works, a nicely filled prison of minor malefactors. I often smile when I think of one day in El Arish in Sinai when a land-ownership case that had caused great excitement in the village was being tried. Four very large and quarrelsome families were concerned, feelings ran high and the police were anticipating trouble. At the time we were engaged on bridge-building on one of the desert roads and funds to pay masons and labourers were getting low and this was common knowledge. When judgment in the case was announced and the general free fight we expected took place the police sailed into the *mêlée*, passing the combatants down a queue and sending them flying through the doors of the prison which had opened up in anticipation of a good haul. All went well till the enthusiastic prison sergeant in charge of labour was heard shouting: " Arrest the masons and workmen, you fools ! Fishermen are no use to us," and this very apt and wise remark—which was meant only for the police on duty—had a most chilling and depressing effect on a really delightful family fight and the combatants faded away like snowflakes in the sun.

In Kharga and Dakhla the inhabitants used to bicker occasionally over the question of irrigation water, but their noisy squabbling in high-pitched voices always reminded me of the little chattering fights you see in a canary's cage and were quite as harmless. The cultivators carried always in their belts small curved sickles which they used for cutting the *bersim* (native clover) or corn, and these were capable of inflicting a nasty wound. They invariably drew these when a quarrel was in progress and waved them in the air at each other, but not once during my two years' stay in the Oases did I hear of an actual blow being struck.

There was one squabble that went on in front of my house for three days when two respectable middle-aged gentlemen with some grievance about flowing water shrieked insults and accusations at each other all the hours of daylight. From time to time one of them would work himself up into a spasm of rage and, drawing his sickle, would plunge furiously through the clover at his opponent with the weapon lifted. I would watch the scene anxiously from the window, hoping against hope for a blow and a few occupants in my deserted prison, but I was doomed to disappointment for the descending sickle always stopped a few inches short of the other man's head and the long-expected cut was never delivered.

We did have one murderer at Kharga, but only one, and he worked in the house and was an intimate friend of the family. The story of his crime was that he had an argument with a plate-layer on the railway line as to whether he should get out of his compartment to have a drink at a wayside engine tank or not. The plate-layer thought not and tried to enforce his views, and the "murderer," whilst trying to descend, either threw from the carriage or dropped inadvertently a small sack of flour he was carrying. It landed on the unfortunate plate-layer's head and neatly broke his neck, hence a trial on the capital charge and the title of murderer. One of the most poignant and harrowing scenes I have ever witnessed was when this very charming criminal completed his sentence and in his "going-away" clothes came to say good-bye to my wife and the servants. I have never seen so many tears, masculine and feminine, shed in my life and I was seriously afraid that another plate-player would have his neck broken by a sack of flour to enable our delightful friend to serve a second sentence in our house.

When I arrived at El Arish after two years in the Oases I found a very different state of affairs, for the Eastern Beduin is a quarrelsome and hot-headed man and shoots or stabs on the slightest provocation. There was also the contraband trade in hashish in which almost every Arab engaged when not occupied with his harvest, and so we had seldom less than sixty occupants of our prison.

For some unexplained reason the Arab prisoner always appears to be a most charming individual when serving his sentence and meeting them constantly in my garden I made many warm friends. One of them, a fisherman by profession, used to go down to the shore with me every morning early in the car to set and haul a big trammel net I had. Whilst I was bathing he would haul the net and re-set it and we would then return to breakfast in the car, which I stopped at the prison gate for my partner to descend and start his day's work.

There were also two prisoners—smugglers serving three-year sentences—who were put in charge of a big nursery garden. Here we grew from seed olives, lemons, guavas, and apricots, grafting them with fruiting stock when they were a year old. The two men became the most enthusiastic and useful gardeners, and frequently I would find them hard at work grafting lemons with orange stock or watering plants hours after the time for cessation of prison work and without warders or escort of any kind. The prison sergeant, who was a man of considerable understanding and common sense, made it his business to study the characters of all his convicts, and when he found a man who was unlikely to try to escape, and who could perform useful work, the greatest latitude was allowed him. On the credit side was the fact that the government had the benefit of much skilled and valuable labour performed by men who were willing and doing their best, and the convict himself was moderately happy and therefore not deteriorating in character.   On the debit side was the fact that he had far more freedom than is supposed to be allowed a prisoner and there is no doubt that one of the restrictions that should go with convict life—deprivation of tobacco—did not apply to these prisoners who worked without warders.   I frequently saw, or failed to see, a cloud of cigarette smoke floating away from the vicinity of a busy prisoner's head.

On one occasion when I had arrived back in El Arish after three months' leave in England I found, stuck up in conspicuous places in my garden, small pieces of wood split at the top to hold a sheet of paper.   They looked like miniature notices of the " Keep off the grass " order and written on the paper in Arabic was :

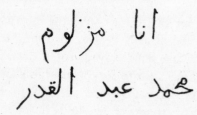

" *Ana maẓloom.*"   ("*I am unjustly treated.*")
MOHAMMED ABD EL QADR.

After I had seen these mysterious notices appearing on my lawn and flower-beds for three consecutive days I asked my old gardener who Abdel Qadr was.   He said he was one of the prisoners working in the garden and that, like a good many of them, he thought he had been unjustly treated as his sentence was too heavy.   It transpired that he had been given three years for what Nasr, the gardener, said was rape.

Of course, rape is a very serious crime, but clear and definite cases are rare, very rare indeed, and when I made inquiries at the office I was by no means satisfied as to Abdel Qadr's guilt. He had been *sofragi*, or footman, in the house of one of the senior Egyptian officers of the province and had been caught in the maid's bedroom. Looking at it from a purely British point of view, it seemed to me that if every footman in England's smiling land who paid a visit to a housemaid's bedroom were to be given three years' hard labour there would be a need for a vast increase in our existing prison accommodation. The sentence seemed to me to err on the side of severity, and I said so.

" But, Sare," explained the judicial officer who had tried the case, " it is a very bad thing for the officer's honour that this should happen to his maidservant in his house. His face would be shamed before all men and he would be degraded."

I pointed out that if this were the case a good many members of the British peerage had had their honour besmirched in the same way at some time during their lives, but had managed to survive the blow and hold their heads up. As the maidservant was well over the age of consent and just as willing as Barkis is supposed to have been, I gave orders for the release of the adulterer, for he had already served two months of his sentence, which I considered ample punishment for a slight mistake over bedroom doors.

In the East the truth always comes to the surface in course of time, though its upward action may be tardy. About a month later when I was crossing the desert in a car alone but for my Sudanese driver, he told me the true story of Abdel Qadr and the bedroom.

" He really deserved the three years," said the driver,

166

" but not for the charge on which he was tried. He was not found in the maid's bedroom ; he was in the bedroom of the *wife* of the officer, but the charge was made out that it was the maid and not the wife to save the officer's honour."

This I discovered later was the accepted method of dealing with such cases in Egypt, and owing to the seclusion in which many wives have to exist and a shortage in the eunuch market, adultery with men-servants is not entirely unknown. It is, however, impossible to tolerate a system of justice by which a man is tried and found guilty of an offence he has not committed, and is then given the sentence he would have received if he had been charged with his actual misdemeanour.

When I first came to Sinai there was a gang of bandits on the Palestine frontier organized by two Arabs of the Terrabin tribe, Abu Seneima and Eid es Sani, but as they confined their activities to the Palestine side I was not actively concerned with them until one of my own Arabs joined them. This man, Abu Mahdi, who belonged to the Sawarka tribe of northern Sinai, lost a lawsuit over a question of land ownership and turned bandit in consequence.

This case was one of those in which it was quite impossible to arrive at the real truth ; Abu Mahdi had nothing to produce in Court beyond his own statement, whilst his opponents, some non-Arab inhabitants of El Arish, possessed legal documents that could not be disputed. Abu Mahdi's statement, which I have now every reason to believe was true, was that he had mortgaged his land for £14 in 1913. When he tried to pay off the mortgage in 1921 the temporary holder of the land produced a deed o sale signed by Abu Mahdi showing that he had sold his land outright in 1913 for £140. Although it was a miscarriage of justice, it was quite unavoidable as, with the evidence produced, judgment would have been given against Abu Mahdi in any court in the world; but to guard against any further exploitation of the Arabs of this nature I passed a Province Order that no deeds concerning the transfer of land would be recognized in future unless copies of the documents were lodged in the government archives and both parties were present to hear the deed read over to them. One of the results was that a crop of amateur forgers came into being and altered the dates on deeds to a period prior to this Province Order, and until one man did two years' imprisonment for his clever penmanship nobody saw anything very wrong with the device.

Abu Mahdi was so incensed over losing the case and his land that he turned bandit and joined the gang of Abu Seneima and Eid es Sani, who were only too glad to welcome a new recruit. Almost immediately they all started to raid the settled cultivators in northern Sinai and specialized on the family who had acquired Abu Mahdi's land. These people were marked down for constant attention, and every time they travelled with goods for the supply of their stores at Rafa or El Arish a galloping party of bandits would swoop down on them in the open desert, relieve them of their camels and baggage and most of their clothes, and leave them to walk back to the nearest village.

When not on the raid, the gang lived in one of the deserted precipitous valleys that wind down to the Dead Sea south of Beersheba, and as they resided fifty miles away from the nearest police post they invariably received early information of any patrol setting forth to surround their hiding-place. Moreover, most of these deep valleys leading to the Dead Sea depression from the Trans-Jordan hills have a small stream of water in them, so that whenever one hiding-place became too well known to the police they moved to another offering equal advantages. When setting out on a raid they travelled quickly and by night, avoiding all well-known tracks, and were thus able to be on their raiding area in the vicinity of Rafa and Khan Yunis on the Palestine border before either the inhabitants or the police had any warning of their arrival. They then held up all the passing caravans, relieving the merchants of their goods and animals and, before the police could get a strong patrol ready to cope with them, they made off again with their loot southwards to their haunts in the mountains. Here they remained quietly until the forces of law and order, tired of searching an empty desert, called off their patrols and then, immediately the coast was clear, up came the bandits again for another raid.

Their activities always took place in that open cultivated area on the Sinai–Palestine coast where there is constant camel traffic between the towns of El Arish and Gaza, and the reason for this was that the people settled in this area are not of Beduin Arab stock. They belong to that type of *fellah* or cultivator that claim Arab nationality but who are actually the descendants of the ancient Philistine or Jebusite who occupied this part of the world prior to the coming of Moses. There is an age-old hostility and vendetta between " the desert and the sown " because, according to the lordly nomad, the cultivator of the soil who lives in a house is his natural prey—his milch-cow as it were. From time immemorial the Beduin has regarded it as his absolute birthright to raid the villages on the desert's edge and to levy blackmail on the inhabitants, and one of his great objections to any form of *Hakooma* (Government) is that it takes steps to prevent him exercising these rights. Owing to the existing controversy between the settled Arab and the Jew in Palestine, this old enmity has been lost sight of, but in Sinai and Trans-Jordan it still exists and it only needs a weakening of the governments concerned for the Beduin to attempt to exercise again his old privilege of levying toll on all those people foolish enough to toil the day long in the fields in the degrading pursuit of agriculture. Actually, he might not find this so easy as he imagines, for the *fellah* has realized of late that he is not quite so helpless as the nomad imagines, and, moreover, Beduin stock has slumped somewhat of recent years owing to the employment of motor-cars and aeroplanes.

The bandits employed their cut-and-run tactics with marked success for some two years, and then one day a mounted patrol of Palestine police operating on the Sinai frontier surprised both Eid es Sani and Abu Seneima in an Arab encampment and arrested them. Unfortunately they were too far away from their police post to reach it before dark and they therefore camped in the desert with their prisoners tied up.

During the night some members of the gang, who had escaped capture, succeeded in enlisting the services of a large body of armed Beduin from the surrounding encampments and at dawn an attack was made upon the police. The fight lasted for several hours, both sides firing at each other from the slight cover provided by scrub bushes, but the police were hopelessly outnumbered, and when six out of the seven had been either killed or wounded, the sole survivor managed to get away to warn the police outpost at Auja.

Immediately the men could be assembled a large punitive force of Palestine Police was sent out from Beersheba and Auja, and I was asked to assist by seeing that nobody escaped over the Sinai border. To do this I sent all the Sudanese Camel Corps and Sinai Police available and had a cordon of patrols along the frontier just in time to turn back to the retribution awaiting them a general exodus of the Terrabin tribe into Sinai territory. With the light-hearted irresponsibility of the Arab race, and their natural instinct to side against the forces of law and order, they had joined in a massacre of the police without considering the results; then, realizing the folly of their action, they hoped to escape the punishment awaiting them by crossing over and joining the Sinai section of their tribe, where they would as a matter of course become peaceful inhabitants entirely ignorant of anything that had occurred over the frontier.

When the police patrols, searching for the dead bodies of their companions, entered the undulating sand country on the border and started to interrogate the tribesmen they encountered the blandest and most sublime ignorance of anything untoward having occurred.

" Police ! " exclaimed the Arabs; " we have seen no police before you came, and as for bandits and fighting, *wallahi !* we have not heard of either."

There is nothing so entirely innocent and convincing as the Beduin's profession of knowing absolutely nothing of a murder when he is caught more or less red-handed after committing the crime, but the officer in charge knew how to deal with a situation of this description. A few hefty cuts with a riding-whip on the bare buttocks of some of the more convincing of those who had neither seen nor heard anything had the effect of loosening tongues, and the patrol was led to the spot where the six missing men were lying. Although some of them had been only wounded at the end of the fight, they had all been finished off by sword-cuts or bullets at close range, and the police were in a dangerous frame of mind when, after burying their comrades, they set out to arrest the murderers. As the result of the drastic action taken then, Abu Mahdi, who had not been present at the fight, came in to surrender to the Sinai police before it was too late. Abu Seneima and the rest of the gang were either hanged or sent to penal servitude, and there remained only Eid es Sani at large.

A few months later he was reported at an Arab encampment near Beersheba, and a British warrant-officer of the Palestine Police at once set off in a car with a few men to try and effect his arrest. As they drew near the encampment they saw Eid es Sani's white Arab mare standing by a tent and at the same moment Eid es Sani dashed out and began to mount. The warrant-officer knew the mare by repute as the bandit had escaped from patrols on several occasions owing to the speed and endurance of this animal, and he realized that once Eid es Sani was mounted he could easily outstrip the car in the heavy sand country. He took a shot at the mare and brought her down, whereupon Eid es Sani dived in behind a large boulder and opened fire. The warrant-officer did the same and for ten minutes or more the sniping battle continued. Then the policeman pushed up his helmet on a bit of stick and held it out on the right side of his rock while he crouched down on the left. Eid es Sani was taken in by the trick; he exposed his head to take a carefully aimed shot at the helmet and next moment the policeman's bullet took him fair and square between the eyes. This brought an end to all banditry in the southern area of Palestine and the warrant-officer was decorated for his gallantry, but, as he said afterwards, "It was all spoilt for me by having to shoot that lovely mare, but I had no alternative."

There was another bandit about at this time who worked on his own in the Hebron district. His reputation as a ruthless killer was such that, even if he held up a caravan with five or six men in attendance they were so terrified that they never by any chance offered any resistance, which was all the more remarkable as this particular bandit often shot down his victims for amusement after he had robbed them.

His tactics were the same as those employed by Abu Seneima's gang and he lived usually in one of the deep gorges east of Beersheba, coming up periodically to raid the Hebron merchants. The police had followed him upon many occasions after his robberies, but always he had a clear start from his pursuers and had got away easily. Then one day news was brought to the police post that he was out on the raid again and the Arab officer in charge on this occasion used Arab cunning. He did not go in the direction of the raids that had been committed, but instead rode with his patrol as hard as he could towards a certain pass in the mountains that this bandit always took.

On arrival there, and finding no recent camel tracks, he posted his men among the rocks and waited. In two hours' time along came the bandit sitting easily on his fast-trotting camel and wearing on his face an expression of contentment and "something attempted something done." In the narrowest part of the pass six rifles went off simultaneously and the bad man dropped from his camel very dead indeed with six holes in his body and head. The sequel to this was that the Ministry of Justice in Palestine wished to try the police for wilful murder, as on their own showing they had made no attempt to take the man alive, and the Police Commandant had the fight of his life to save them!

There is a good old custom adopted by many Eastern police forces that this Arab officer had neglected to observe, and that is, when hunting for bad men who shoot on sight, invariably to fire off the murderer's rifle after his death if he has neglected to do so himself. An eye-witness's account is then given of resisting arrest and no awkward questions are asked.

It is always so difficult to reconcile the point of view of a British judge, imbued with all the traditions of British justice and the principle of the Habeas Corpus Act, with that of an Arab policeman who takes his life in his hands every time he goes out to make an arrest. The policeman knows perfectly well that Mohammed What's-His-Name is a bandit with a dozen killings to his credit or debit and he has no intention of being the thirteenth if he can help it, while the British judge maintains that all men are innocent until they are proved guilty in a properly constituted court. Moreover, British laws of evidence are so hard and fast and so very uncompromising that often a bad man with a terrible record escapes scot-free when he is tried because it is impossible to produce the right sort of evidence to secure a conviction. If this occurs the unfortunate policeman, who effected the arrest, realizes that he is due for a bullet in the back at the first opportunity. This being the case, one must remember that one cannot make omelettes without breaking eggs, and when a real *budmash* meets his end it is as well not to ask too many questions. The correct thing to do is to get the Secret Service money out of the safe at once and show that bandit-removal, unlike virtue, needs a reward. When one has had the peace and progress of one's Province disturbed for years, one's inhabitants raided, terrorized and murdered every month, and one's own reputation tarnished by one's inability to cope with the activities of a bloodthirsty bandit, one does not exactly stand upon ceremony or inquire too closely when an energetic policeman puts paid to his account and omits to add " E. & O.E."

CHAPTER VIII

BLACK TIES AND BROWN FACES

Costly thy habit as thy purse can buy
But not expressed in fancy; rich not gaudy;
For the apparel oft proclaims the man.

SHAKESPEARE.

THE pioneer in the wilderness and the frontiersman at the back of beyond are frequently held up to ridicule by journalists and artists for committing what is considered by them to be the height of absurdity—dressing for dinner when alone in the bush or desert ! There is something about the proceeding that seems so entirely ridiculous and unnecessary, and the feeling is probably dictated by the fact that when they themselves go on a fortnight's holiday in a cruising yacht or caravan a pair of grey flannel slacks and a zip-fastener shirt appear to be adequate for all occasions. They forget, however, that one cannot go on being a bush-shirted backwoodsman for ever and that the state of general sloppiness that makes a holiday so attractive should not be extended in perpetuity. As a man who has perpetrated this particular form of idiocy, snobbery, " Old School Tie-ism " or what you will, of dressing for dinner in the desert for eighteen years, I think it necessary therefore to make some form of apology or explanation for this extraordinary and stupid behaviour.

When one first takes up one's post in a lonely bungalow a hundred miles or more from any form of civilization, the first and natural reaction to solitude and boredom is to become slack. The early morning ride for exercise when

A Desert Dinner Party.   " Now, Carruthers . . . no cheating "

taken alone becomes deadly monotonous and it is easier to stay in bed reading if there is no other man to drag one out ; meals when eaten in solitude are tedious and seem far too lengthy, and the ordinary decencies of life appear at first to be unnecessary and hardly worth while. One thing leads to another until at the end of three or four months the exile—if he happens to be the sort of man who should be trusted to fill a post of this description—suddenly and with consternation awakes to the fact that he has slipped a long way down the path that leads to complete disintegration of character and that the end will be " going native " or taking to drink.

It is essential if a man lives alone that he should exercise some discipline with himself, and this is more particularly the case if he is working among Beduin Arabs than with other nationalities. These queer attractive, but haphazard, people possess such natural charm and have so many engaging qualities that it is very easy in course of time eventually to drift unconsciously into their mode of life and to see everything from their point of view, and as this point of view dates back to the tenth century, if not earlier, it hardly fits in with modern conditions or with the objects of the administration that employs the official.

I am not certain if one can call the character of the average Beduin a strong and compelling one, but the fact remains that in nine cases out of ten he leaves a far more indelible mark on his administrator than his administrator leaves on him. At the conclusion of fifteen years' service or so the official leaves the people in his area precisely the same as he found them ; he may have improved their conditions, he may have brought some measure of prosperity, and he has probably given the under-dog a chance, but in every other respect they are exactly as they were before. The same cannot be said of the administrator himself, for no matter how he may have fought against it, the Arab has stamped him with the Beduin hall-mark and he will find for the rest of his life that this queer nomad outlook will persist in all things. I have been conscious of this fact for many years, but it was brought home forcibly to me the other day when a candid friend said : " Why is it that all people who have lived among the Arabs for a long time are slightly ' gaga ' ? "

It may be argued that the wearing of a black tie at night is a queer and petty method of fighting against this Beduin bewitchment, but it is a gesture, a definite stand in fact, against the very natural desire to let all unnecessary details and routine go by the board. There is something so entirely British about the proceeding that unconsciously one regains every evening something of the Occident that has been lost or Orientalized during the day. Moreover, hygiene demands after twelve hours of burning sun and considerable heat in a dusty country that some sort of toilet is made in the evening even if only for the sake of comfort and personal cleanliness. This being the case, there is no reason why one should not put on the correct dress for the occasion and make one's solitary dinner something of a function. There is no necessity to wear that abomination of civilization the boiled shirt or a stiff collar—in any case they are unobtainable—but as one must bathe and change one may as well don a soft white shirt and collar and slip on an aged dinner jacket, or in hot weather a white drill imitation of the garment, for after all there is nothing so comfortable and easy as this particular cut.

There is one other point to be taken into consideration, and this is the question of the domestic staff and their reaction to " going native." The servants one has in the East are most excellent in every way and are quite prepared to keep up the standard of life wherever one happens to be, but if Master goes slack it is a most excellent excuse for this slackness extending to the kitchen. The Berberine is a very good mimic and if encouraged in any way will introduce some special ideas of his own, and his conception of going back to nature may extend far beyond anything his master contemplated. During my first six months in the desert I made the mistake that so many tyros make and decided that a four-course dinner when most of the dishes were tinned was a bore and a burden, and I gradually cut them out until finally my evening meal consisted of one dish which was very badly cooked and then literally slung on to the table by a dirty, half-naked *sofragi* (waiter) who immediately departed and left me to fetch the necessary knives, forks and spoons. When I realized the depths to which I had descended it was far too late to re-establish the decencies of life with those particular servants and I was forced to discharge them and obtain others.

With the Berberine apparently there are no half-measures ; you either live up to the standard of the Ingleezi or you do not, and if you do not you are obviously a man of no account and anything is good enough for you and this information is passed on to the police and other subordinates. For the sake of one's staff and one's own credit, therefore, it is essential to make the evening meal a real dinner, for the Berberine is a creature of routine and does everything by " rote."

From time to time, too, one's desert home is invaded by people from the civilization beyond and it is the exile's particular form of conceit to endeavour to show these passers-by that, despite the difficulties and isolation, he can put a dinner on the table that even a *gourmet* will not despise. No matter how well trained one's servants may be, a month of haphazard waiting at table serving scratch meals is quite sufficient for them to forget completely the routine of an ordinary dinner, and one's guests will have whisky poured into their sherry glasses with the soup course, soda water squirted into port, and other enormities will occur giving definite proof to the visitors that this is the first time in one's life one has attempted to give a dinner-party.

This striving at a high standard of civilization—one might say luxury—in the back-blocks may sound very silly and futile to the ordinary denizen of the city, but there is a good deal more in it than a mere desire for display. Insistence on brightly burnished buttons seemed very unnecessary and stupid in Flanders rest-camps behind the line, but it was those Divisions where highly polished accoutrements were *de rigueur* that invariably made the best show in the attack and holding the line in retreat. In the same way the administrator in a lonely post who tries to live up to the standard to which he is accustomed is generally a better man at his job than his opposite number who disregards the ordinary decencies of life.

We ourselves used to experience a considerable amount of childish pleasure from our guests' surprise at finding that our standard of living in Sinai was quite the equal of that in Cairo, and in some ways better, for our coast provided an unlimited supply of excellent fish and our garden a variety of English vegetables. Most people seemed to imagine that we lived in a bell tent, dining every night from a tin of bully beef, and visitors would come to stay with the idea that they were going right back to nature in its most primitive form. There was one lady tourist, who had an introduction to us and who came to stay bringing with her a large packing-case filled with tins of sardines, salmon and " bully " which she thought would be welcome to desert housekeepers. We happened to be very well situated at the time with both the garden and the sea coast in full bearing and she dined the first night on mushroom soup from our mushroom bed, cray fish *à la Americaine* from the Gulf of Akaba, saddle of desert lamb from our flock, asparagus from the garden and an oyster savoury provided by the Faroan oyster beds. She rang the bell that night and when the *sofragi* arrived bribed him to dispose of the case of tinned foods she had been thoughtful enough to bring and to say nothing about it. He carried out the first part of the instructions to the letter but failed lamentably over the second part.

" Going native " and taking to drink are not the only risks run by the exile if he does not keep a tight rein on himself. There is the danger, a very real one, of becoming peculiar. Insanity is perhaps too harsh a word for it and the French describe it more aptly as the *cafard*—a cockroach state of mind caused by solitude, sand and sun. *Cafard* takes various forms and the commonest one in the French Foreign Legion is to take a rifle and a handful of ammunition and run " amok " shooting at everybody in sight, or occasionally a Legionnaire will strike out into the Saharan wastes without water or supplies in the vain hope of escaping. With the Englishman it usually takes a much milder and more phlegmatic form and a sure sign that the British official in the open spaces has " gone queer " is when it becomes evident from his dispatches and telegrams that in his opinion his small bit of territory at the back of beyond has become the centre of the universe, and his favourite black sheikh or chief ranks second only to George VI of England. This is a very certain indication that all is not well and the situation can be eased up if taken in time by extended leave in the United Kingdom or transfer to a more populated centre where the patient will be able to regain his sense of perspective before the malady becomes acute and permanent.

In my own administration we had several mild cases of *cafard*, and when one sees the ghastly arid spots in which some of our officials had to live alone it was small wonder that from time to time some of the poor exiles went queer. Once Sollum, a small post on the Libyan shore, suddenly became of world-wide importance, second only to London and Paris, and on another occasion Siwa Oasis with its degenerate inhabitants came well into the limelight as a factor in international affairs. A variety of the usual theme was provided by a solitary Camel Corps officer in Central Sinai, who telephoned to say that the surrounding mountains were marching in on his post steadily and that it was becoming increasingly difficult to breathe in the confined atmosphere.

A more advanced case occurred in the Sudan many years ago when an administrative official, who was normal in every other respect, used to sing or whistle on odd occasions the old musical refrain that goes " la tiddley la da," whereupon his servants, staff and police were trained to come in immediately with the concluding " pom-pom." This official used to go to his office every morning on his bicycle, and on his return would dismount at the garden gate and send the bicycle flying down the slope to the tune of " la tiddley la da," on hearing which a waiting servant would dash out of the door, catch the machine as it arrived and hold it at arm's length with a triumphant " pom-pom." This official, it may be mentioned, lost his taste for music entirely after a short spell in a station where there was a certain amount of company and social life. Cartoonists and journalists therefore should not be too hard on the solitary exile if his temporary mental aberration takes no worse form than putting on a black tie and a white shirt for dinner every night; after all he is only striving and making a gesture to maintain his sanity.

A factor that in some areas tends to lead towards one form of insanity, megalomania, is the Arab's natural, almost unconscious, gift for flattery. They have a wonderful and most disarming flair for making an administrator think that he is easily the cleverest and most far-seeing official serving in the Empire, a blend in fact of Cromer, Kitchener and Cecil Rhodes. There is no question of vulgar flattery and fawning adulation at which the Egyptian dragoman is such a past-master; it is something far subtler. The Arab is at all times a perfect gentleman and this flattery he instils comes out apparently quite naturally, inadvertently as it were, and is on that account all the more convincing. It is administered in very small doses, for flattery like strychnine is a dangerous if stimulating drug and an overdose is fatal. The net result, however, over a term of years, is very invigorating, so that the most modest official is apt to get a very exaggerated idea of his capabilities and general ability.

The administrator, during the whole period of his service from the day he takes over as a young and impressionable district officer until he clears up his desk on his departure as a retiring governor, will hear the following remarks made to him apparently in deepest sincerity. They will not be all made at one sitting neither will they be contributed by one man only, but at every interview with every Arab in his area he will at some stage of the conversation hear something of this nature all retailed in Bimbashi, or the easily-understood and ungrammatical variety of Arabic.

" Saahtak tifham kull shay quies. Wallahi (hand placed over the heart and the eyes rolled devoutly upwards) ana gool kull el nas daiman, mafish wahed zai Sahhtak abidan. Yani, kan fi mufftisheen hena gabl saahtak. Zoobat quieseen wa shutar kamman, walakin mush zai Saahtak."

("Your Excellency understands everything so clearly. By God, I am always telling the people that there has never been anyone like Your Excellency—never. I mean to say, there have been other inspectors here before your Excellency—good officers and clever into the bargain— but not like Your Excellency.")

"El balad de kan mush mabsut min zeman. El nas kan mazloomeen wa fakireen. Dilwaqti—wa de el hakika dururi—(another appeal to the Deity) mafish haga fil balad *abidan*. Kull el nas—el meshaikh, el nas kubar wa el nas soggahayareen-mabsutin khalis min Saahtak."

("This town used to be very unhappy long ago. The people were unjustly treated and very poor. Now—and this is the truth—there is nothing wrong in the town *whatever*. Everybody—the sheikhs, the notables and the small fry—are happy, very happy under your rule, Your Excellency.")

"Genabak tikallim Araby quies khalis. Wallahi, ana aref. Genabak, yani, tikallim zai wahed Masri tammam. Lemma ana isma Genabak tikallim Arabi aftikir—wa de el hakika—aftikir huwa wahed min el orban nasuhum."

("Your Honour speaks Arabic very well. By God, I know, you speak like an Egyptian exactly. When I hear Your Honour speaking I think—and this is the truth —that he is one of the Arabs themselves.")

"Lemma Saahtak tegoom lil London ala agazah, wallahi, el nas mazloomen gowi, gowi. Walla wahed auz estanna fil balad, kullu auz yemoot. El shoogl el bolis mush quies, el Mamour battal khalis, fi hookum mush dogri fill qaddiyah wa kull shay zai zift. Ana mush fahim ezzai.

Lemma Saahtak terga hena bad el agazah, wallahi, kull es zoobat masrieen illi amal shoogl battal khaifeen khalis wa nas farhan. Wallahi, makanshi wahed zai Saahtak ABIDAN."

("When Your Honour goes to London on leave, by God, everybody is unhappy, very unhappy. Nobody wants to stay in the town—everybody wants to die. The police are very bad, the Mamour is worse, there are bad judgments given in the Courts, and everything is like pitch. I don't know how to describe it. When Your Honour comes back from leave everything is all right again. The Egyptian officers who have been acting badly are very frightened and all the people are happy. By God, there has never been anyone like Your Honour— NEVER.")

One cannot help thinking of the well-worn saying, "You may take in some people all the time and all the people some of the time, but you cannot take in all the people all the time," and if this is the considered opinion of some 45,000 inhabitants with whom one has been working over a term of years, it is only reasonable to come to the conclusion that there must be something in it.

For all this I give the Arab the highest marks, for he plays the right cards and plays them, moreover, with the most consummate skill, so that if there is such a thing as an Arab-Jew or an Arab-Assyrian or an Arab-Anything-Else problem the British officials on the spot are almost invariably pro-Arab to a marked and most disconcerting degree and continue as such long after retirement has come to stultify and warp their activities.

It is to the skilful application of the right sort of flattery that the Arab owes most of his adherents and by means of it has won to his cause Englishmen and women who are almost prepared to die for it, and this amuses the Arab intensely, for the whole history of the race proves that he is first and foremost an individualist always ready to sink nationalism for the sake of personal advantage. The extraordinary part about it is that, though the Arab may impress the average Briton with his personality and create a lasting effect on his views, his own interest in any particular administrator or pro-Consul is entirely ephemeral.

There was a belief, not only in England but also in the United States, that Lawrence had only to return to Arabia for the whole population to arise as one man to follow him in any enterprise. It is therefore something of a disappointment to find to-day, except for a few big Sheikhs who were constantly in his company, that Lawrence is forgotten by the great majority of the Beduin of the desert.

There is no intention here to belittle in any way the great work that Lawrence performed in 1917 and 1918 or to deny that during the revolt his name carried the greatest weight. The fact remains that he is remembered by us far more clearly than he is by the people to whom he devoted the best of his life.

This may be due to some extent to the fact that though epoch-making events occurred during Lawrence's control of affairs in Arabia the period he spent actually among the Arabs was a comparatively short one. To an age-old people living in an age-old desert, where no sudden changes ever take place, new ideas, new conceptions and new personalities are not grasped and understood with the same celerity as is the case with other and more impressionable races. Lawrence's meteoric career with the Arabs of northern Arabia started late in 1916 and to all intents and purposes ended with the armistice—and two years is a very short period with a race that thinks in centuries.

The remark applies to nearly all the Englishmen who have served the Arabs; while they were working among the tribes their names were household or rather tent-hold words, but three or four years after retirement or death it is as if they had never existed. Among the large number of officials who have served the Arabs, there are only a few exceptions to this rule of forgetfulness and oblivion, and one is Palmer, who carried out a certain amount of exploration in Sinai and Southern Palestine, and who was murdered in 1882 by the Beduin on account of the gold he was carrying for the purchase of camels during the Arabi rebellion. In Palmer's case I rather suspect that his name is fixed in Arab memory more on account of his murder and the reprisals which followed it than for any lasting impression he himself made.

In a different category entirely comes Colonel A. C. Parker, known among the Arabs as " Barkal," who retired in 1923 after thirteen years as Governor of Sinai, and who died in 1936. Unless one knew Parker intimately one did not realize that he was a great personality; he had an essentially quiet, almost retiring manner and the only unusual thing about him was a rather disconcerting and very direct stare that came into his eyes when he was listening to an explanation. His face then became absolutely immobile without a trace of expression on it, and it was this character-istic that completely defeated the voluble Beduin, for they obtained the impression that Parker was reading their thoughts and they all believed he possessed psychic powers. Parker, it may be remembered, was a nephew of Kitchener, and this disconcerting stare was apparently a family characteristic. There are many soldiers living to-day who will admit to having the " fear of God " put into them by one cold look from Kitchener of Khartum.

I can vouch for the effect this hypnotic stare had on a defendant or litigant as my first meeting with Parker took place when he was acting as military administrator of the

Frontiers Administration. The occasion was not a very happy one, as I had been called in to Cairo to explain the reason why one of my cars with two policemen had run amok in Alexandria on a day of riot and had killed upwards of twenty people without being invited to do so. This episode I relate in my book, *Three Deserts*, and I was perfectly satisfied in my own mind that the fault, if fault there was, was not of my making. During the whole interview Parker said nothing but sat watching me with an unwinking stare and at no time did the slightest expression cross his face to indicate that I had scored a point or otherwise. The effect it had on me was definitely disconcerting and I began to feel sure that my arguments were not so convincing as I had previously thought them and that the story was not meeting with the reception it deserved.

I have seen litigants arise in an Arab Court and proceed to address the gathering with a wonderful flow of language and still more wonderful story. The Arab is a first-class natural orator and the most convincing producer of fiction which is so well recounted that it sounds like the truth. The witness when Parker was holding a Court would start off in great style and never hesitate for a word at first, and all the while Parker would sit there immobile with his eyes fixed on the speaker. After a time the orator would begin to feel the hypnotism of the stare and lose the gist of his story and the ready flow of language, then he would begin to stammer and hunt for words until he finally broke down altogether. On one occasion I heard a Sheikh say weakly after recounting a most thrilling story, " All my words were lies ; it did not happen in that way at all. I will now tell the truth which Barkal already knows ! "

Another reason why Parker is remembered in Sinai and Southern Palestine is that he obtained for the Beduin the recognition of their laws and customs by the Government of Egypt. As is well known, the Arab code of law differs entirely from that of any other race, for it recognizes tribal and not individual responsibility, and compensation in money or animals, not death or imprisonment, is payable for all crimes from murder or assault to wife- or camel-theft. Previous to Parker's governorship in Sinai an attempt had been made to control the Beduin by the application of the ordinary laws of Egypt, and this not only incensed the Arabs but proved to be entirely ineffectual and useless. Parker saw clearly that if ever the Arabs were to be controlled and administered it must be by their own laws which they themselves would see enforced and not by an ordinance which was both foreign and distasteful to them. In 1911, after a lengthy struggle with the legal pundits in Cairo, he succeeded in obtaining for the Beduin a Khedivial decree by which the Arab law should be applied to all the desert provinces " save in so far as the same should be contrary to equity or good conscience."

This law which was first recognized in Sinai was later adopted for the Beduin areas of Palestine after much argument and shocks to the legal mind, and also in Trans-Jordan, where, prior to the British Mandate, Ottoman law had functioned or not functioned as the case might be. The Arabs of the desert have never forgotten that it was " Barkal " who first obtained for them this concession and they are duly grateful, though actually from a purely Beduin point of view it is somewhat of a double-edged weapon, for, though it gives them the right to try and give judgment in their own cases in their own way, it is also used by the police forces of the countries concerned, who conveniently remember when there is trouble that Beduin law recognizes tribal and not individual responsibility.

There are two Englishmen serving in Trans-Jordan at the present time who probably will be remembered by the

Arabs after they have retired from active work in the mid-East, and the reason in their case is that they have given up so many years of their lives in the Arab service endeavouring to arrive at some state of harmony in the northern part of Arabia, thereby fixing themselves indelibly on the memory of the Beduin. Both these men have been factors in the ordinary life of the nomad Arab and at his desert law-courts since the days of the war and their task has been to arrive at a workable form of tribal peace to replace that which had been upset not only by hostilities but by the new boundaries and sub-divisions of this part of the Arab peninsula. They are Colonel Peake Pasha of the Arab Legion and his second-in-command, Major Glubb, who previously served for many years in Iraq and who received recently the Lawrence Memorial Medal for his work among the tribes.

Peake Pasha, or Beake, as he is called by the Arabs, there being no " p " in the Arabic alphabet, formed the Arab Legion and for sixteen years from his head-quarters in Amman has been responsible for the general public security in the state of Trans-Jordan. In the old days it was probably one of the most lawless countries in the world, and unless a traveller was adequately guaranteed by Sheikhs and watched over by Turkish police he ran something more than an ordinary chance of having his throat cut whilst on a visit to Petra. For the last seven or eight years car-loads of tourists have been travelling backwards and forwards all over Trans-Jordan in perfect safety, and as a large number of these were dressed up in Arab fancy dress, presumably to amuse the Arabs or confuse them, it says something for Peake's administration that there was never a case of interference or robbery despite the episodes recounted in Mr. Carl Raswan's *Escape from Baghdad.*

In raising, recruiting and inspecting his Arab force

Peake came in contact constantly with all the Sheikhs and their families, and as for eighteen years, with his red-and-white Arab shawl over a pair of particularly British blue eyes, he has been a regular feature at all tribal gatherings, it is probable that the proverbial short memory of the Beduin will not apply in his case and that "Beake" will be remembered as one of the Ingleezi who made modern Trans-Jordan.

Peake obtained a considerable amount of fame and credit among his Arabs by taking up flying during the latter part of his time in Trans-Jordan and travelling by air in his own machine to his various police posts in the desert. The Trans-Jordan Beduin were very proud of the fact that their British officer had his own aeroplane and, what was more to the point, flew it himself. They "rubbed it in" rather that one had not achieved such distinction oneself. Whenever one stopped the car in Trans-Jordan after Peake had obtained his aeroplane the following conversation, or something like it, would take place:

"Yes, Beake was here five days ago. He came in a *tiyara* (aeroplane). His *own* aeroplane; not one belonging to the *Hakooma* (Government). And he flew it himself. Wallahi, I have seen many *zubat* (officers) flying aeroplanes, but never one who flew as Beake Pasha. Is *Saahtak* (Your Excellency) going to get one?"

Actually, of course, as Peake took up flying after he had reached the age of forty, he was, though quite a reliable pilot, hardly in what one might call the Schneider Cup class, despite the fact that much of his tuition was given him by none other than Roger Atcherley, who is, or used to be, the finest pilot in the Royal Air Force. There is a very good story of this tuition as one day when up for instruction in the machine, which was fitted with dual control, the joy-stick suddenly came away from its fittings in Atcherley's hands, and the machine was out of control. Atcherley turned round and, to call Peake's attention to the mishap as a signal for him to take charge, waved the detached joy-stick in his face. Peake for some reason did not recognize it as the all-important joy-stick, and, thinking that Atcherley was merely making a gesture of *joie de vivre*, waved his hand cheerily in reply, and at that moment the machine crashed. Atcherley escaped unhurt and Peake got off with a damaged rib, but the aeroplane caught fire and was destroyed.

Shortly after this, when Peake had obtained another machine and was still more or less in the pupil class, I went over to stay with him. When I arrived at his house in Amman I found a note from him saying that he had had to go to Zerka but would be back at 6 p.m. His servants brought in drinks and at that moment I heard the faint drone of an aeroplane. I looked out of the window and saw a small machine about four thousand feet up. As I watched it it dropped like a stone straight towards the village of Amman. About two hundred feet from the roofs of the houses, when it looked as if there were going to be a disaster, it suddenly flattened out, shot along the line of the main street, then made a sharp turn to the left, standing vertically in the air as it did so, and swung quietly along to the aerodrome, where it made a perfect landing. A most spectacular and masterly, albeit dangerous, exhibition of stunt flying.

" See that aeroplane," said Peake's safragi delightedly. " That's the Pasha's aeroplane, and what is more, he was flying it himself ! " And if there was one thing that was certain in this world it was the fact that Peake was not flying that machine otherwise he would have buried himself six foot deep in the main street of Amman.

Glubb, who is known among the Beduin of northern

Arab sheikhs at coffee
Magnificent specimens of manhood—Sheikhs of the Bayyadin tribe

[See page 96]

Feriq Peake Pasha, C.B.E., Commanding the Arab Legion of Trans-Jordan

[*See page* 191]

Arabia as *Abu Henaik*, is the official peacemaker and negotiator for the big raiding tribes of the Iraq, Trans-Jordan and Saudi Arabia. His task has been a most difficult one, for not only has he had to cope with age-old enmities between tribes that have been mutually hostile since the earliest days, but also he has had to deal with new and unforeseen troubles owing to the divisions in tribal areas and unnatural frontiers demarcated by that creator of unnatural frontiers, the Peace of Versailles.

Glubb has been singled out by the Arabs for a nickname, and there is no more certain method of ensuring that a man goes down to posterity. *Abu Henaik* means "Father of Chins," and is accounted for by the fact that Glubb sustained a nasty wound during the war which smashed in one side of his jaw. Possibly some of the wiser and more important Sheikhs know that his name is Glubb, but normally one is met by a blank stare of wonder if one asks after Major Glubb, to be followed by a spreading grin and a flash of white teeth when one mentions Abu Henaik :

"Abu Henaik—of course, everyone knows him. Why did you not say so before?"

Glubb's task of official peacemaker takes him into the heart of the Beduin country and here for weeks, sometimes for months, living among the Arab folk he waits patiently, interviewing, pleading and arguing, until finally the various apparently insuperable difficulties and personal jealousies are overcome and a pact is agreed to. Of course, like the "Gentlemen's Agreements" made in Europe nowadays, these pacts are sometimes broken, but the Arab does it in a rather more gentlemanly and less flagrant manner than that adopted by the more civilized and advanced nations.

All this requires, together with an intimate knowledge of Beduin life, Beduin history and Beduin law, a great strength of purpose, a sense of humour, and, last but not least, much patience. Litigation is the breath of life to an Arab, and he is not only loath to arrive at an agreement before he has had a good run for his money but he regards a willingness to come to terms quickly as a sign of weakness. In Arab Courts one finishes the day of ceaseless talk and boring argument with all the major issues settled and complete agreement in sight only to find on the morrow that there has been an absolute disruption and reversal of opinion during the night and that one is back again where one started. Glubb's tact and gift of long-suffering patience have enabled him to win through when all question of agreement seemed impossible, and as Arabia's peace-maker he will probably be remembered as a power in the land for many years to come.

CHAPTER IX

THREE FISHERS

Of all the world's enjoyments
That ever valued were,
There's none of our employments
With fishing can compare.　　　DURFEY.

THERE is a very strong resemblance in character and
outlook on life generally between fishermen the
world over, and perhaps it would not be stretching a point
too far to say that the Arab fishermen of Sinai have more
in common with their opposite numbers in Cornwall and
Dorset than they have with the men of their own tribes
who live an ordinary Beduin life, grazing a flock of sheep
and goats and growing an odd patch of barley.

One peculiarity above all others that they share with
their colleagues of Great Britain is their rooted objection
to selling a small quantity of fish to a resident in the district.
It appears to be the unwritten law that fish must never
be sold locally, but must be immediately packed in ice
to spoil its flavour and shipped to some central market
from which it can be returned to its place of origin for
distribution the following day to the consumer.

Before the war we lived on Chesil Beach, near Wey-
mouth, where enormous hauls of mackerel are caught
during the spring and summer, but if one desired really
fresh mackerel for breakfast it was necessary to visit the
beach shortly after dawn and beg for them with the air of a
suppliant at double their market value ; otherwise by the
inexorable law of the fishing fraternity one could only

obtain them the following morning after they had made a trip to London and back, and the mackerel is essentially a fish that should travel direct from the sea to the frying-pan.

The fishermen of Sinai in the same way preferred to sell the whole of their fish at a very cut price indeed to a local contractor and had a marked disinclination to dispose of a shilling's worth on the beach to our servants, even though, when the haul was a poor one, the few selected specimens required for the household might yield more in cash than the bulk of the catch. This was all the more remarkable as until quite recently the local fishermen regarded soles as being worthless and even *haram* (forbidden), whilst prawns were called contemptuously *barghut* (fleas), both these delicacies being picked up with the weed and thrown back into the sea; and our servants, acting on instructions, invariably bought this "offal" when available.

If a man is brought up to sea fishing from his youth he obtains what one might call a fisherman's outlook on life and his mind is occupied so constantly with the weather, the state of tides, movements of shoals and, most important perhaps of all, the fluctuations of the fish market, that as a class he has very little time to worry unduly about world affairs, politics, or even religion. Fishermen, as a rule, take their religion seriously, but the calling seldom produces fanatics or those troublesome puritans who are unable to live comfortably and at ease on account of the worry they experience over the deplorable state of other people's souls. This type, not unknown in Great Britain, is all too common in the mid-East and an administrator who serves in a Mohammedan country will find much of his time employed in stultifying the evil work and underhand actions of some hypocritical interfering puritan, who has never heard of the parable of the mote and the beam.

A considerable number of the population of Sinai are fishermen and they are men of all types : the hefty semi-Arabs who work in the vicinity of El Arish ; the conglomeration of all races hailing from Port Said and Suez ; and the real Beduin with his small cast net and trot line of fifty hooks or so. They are one and all extremely likeable personalities and, being addicted to a little mild smuggling of hashish when opportunity offered, I frequently had members of the fraternity serving sentences in El Arish, where I got to know them intimately. I never regarded a convicted smuggler as a criminal because I have that feeling of " There but for the grace of God walks myself," and one can be very tolerant of a misdemeanour that one might commit oneself if times were hard and the prospect of a successful run looked good. I should certainly not experience that feeling of loss of caste after an act of smuggling that would inevitably follow a theft or picking up a discard in a poker hand.

The fishermen who operate along the northern coast of Sinai all hail nominally from the town of El Arish, and are of the same mixed breed, in which the basic stock was probably Arab, but which has been mingled during the last two thousand years with Roman, Greek, Crusader, French and Turkish blood. They are, however, a race apart and all members of the fishing families follow their father's calling and never by any chance take up agriculture or shop-keeping.

The leading family is the Bardawil, who claim descent from Baldwin, the Crusader King of Jerusalem, and, as a large number of them have reddish hair and blue eyes with short straight noses, there is no reason why they should not be distant cousins of the late Premier of England. The theory is their forebears were the small Crusader garrison who held the post of Filusiat at the eastern end of the Bardawil Lake, and that when the Saracen revival swept eastward this small community were cut off from Palestine. Then by force of circumstances they had to settle down and eke out a living at fishing, embracing as a matter of course the Mohammedan faith.

Nothing remains of Filusiat now except the walls of the Crusader outpost built up on the ruins of a Roman fort, a red heap of detritus accumulated by the various garrisons, and an early Christian church the floor of which is flush with the surface of the lake and is inundated in winter. This is interesting because the black mud of this part of the Bardawil lagoon suggests that at some time the level of the coast lay much lower than it does at present, and that the waters of the Nile flowed into the lake from the Pelusium branch, whilst the site of the church, which dates probably from the very early days of Christianity, proves that when it was built the position was several feet higher than it is at the present time. This bears out Sir Flinders Petrie's theory that the coastline of Egypt started to sink about the first century A.D. and during the following twelve hundred years subsided to a maximum of forty-one feet. It then began to rise again, so that at the present time it is now twenty-three feet lower than it was when the sinkage started at the dawn of Christianity. If this theory is correct the church must have been built some considerable time before the subsidence reached its maximum, for the Romans would not have erected it, so that its floor-level was flush with a sea marsh as it is at the present time.

Filusiat derives its name from the Arabic word *filus* (money), and the reason for this is that if one scratches for a few minutes in the heap of rubbish that lies amid the ruined stone walls one will almost invariably detect in the light dust a hint of coppery-green and unearth a

Roman *dinar* so corroded by salt as to be completely worthless and undecipherable. I have never heard any explanation of this great mass of copper money and can only conclude that the Cohort who were stationed in the place in the late A.D.'s received their pay in coins of the lowest denomination and for some unexplained reason lacked needles and thread with which to sew up the holes in their pockets. The fact remains that, though there are ruined Roman villages the whole length of the northern coast of Sinai, Filusiat is certainly more fruitful of coins than any other site in which I have scratched for *antikas*.

The Bardawil family lives in palm-reed huts on the shore of the Bardawil lagoon, and, as fishermen go in the mid-East, is fairly up to date. Their boats, which are *felucca*-rigged, i.e. one lateen sail on a long gaff rigged to a fairly short mast, are strong and well made and their seine nets, trammels and long trot lines are kept in an excellent state of repair. In this respect they are very much in advance of their poorer relations the fishermen of Beduin strain, who ply their trade in Southern Sinai, and whose boats and gear rather suggest that they had obtained their requirements from some wealthier fisherman's rubbish-heap.

The commonest fish on the north Sinai coast is the ubiquitous grey mullet, a fish that though it is quite common in the waters of Great Britain has never been appreciated properly by housewives, so that fishmongers rarely stock it, and fishermen in consequence do not go out of their way to catch it. Mullet having figured on our own breakfast and dinner table for a matter of a hundred days out of every three hundred and sixty-five for fourteen years, I may possibly have acquired a taste for it and am biased in its favour instead of nauseated by it. In my humble opinion it is a very first-class fish indeed, blending the flavour of the herring and the mackerel with the faintest hint of the trout, and containing just sufficient natural oil to make it attractive whether split and fried or served boiled with a sharp sauce.

The mullet is a haunter of estuaries and brackish water and will make his way into every lagoon or river's mouth into which he can find an opening. The big Bardawil Lake, which is some thirty miles long and seven miles wide, is in reality a vast clay-pan separated from the Mediterranean by a narrow strip of sand some two hundred yards wide. In the ordinary course of events it floods with sea water whenever the waves are big enough to break through the sand belt to the pan beyond and the fishermen, realizing that on these occasions the mullet swarm in millions to the newly formed lagoon, now keep a channel permanently open for the benefit of this fish.

The mullet enter the lagoon in October and November as slim fish about herring size, and they feed and wax exceeding fat on a green scum that forms on the bed of the lake, so that by the following May they are all averaging from two to two and a half pounds and are full of roe. At the same time the water of the lake with approaching summer becomes unpleasantly warm and very salt from evaporation, and this is the signal for the mullet to make their way to the open sea.

They find, however, their way barred by a permanent net across the opening and, as the mullet can jump like a steeplechaser, a second net is stretched horizontally on a platform at the top of the perpendicular net. The mullet making their way to the sea cruise up and down the barrier for a few minutes searching for an opening and then, finding their way closed completely, take a leap that neatly clears the top of the net but which lands them flapping and gasping on to the platform. Hundreds of

thousands of fish are taken in one day at this permanent
barrier, and the profits from the haul are very considerable
as the roe is turned into a form of caviare which sells at
2s. 6d. per pound in Cairo and the cities as it is firmly
believed to have aphrodisiacal properties and anything
of this nature is worth untold gold in the Orient. The
remainder of the fish is turned into *fessikh* ; that is to say,
it is pressed into barrels with a certain amount of salt,
sufficient to keep the contents from disintegrating entirely
but insufficient to stop putrefaction setting in to a certain
extent. The stench from barrels of *fessikh* has to be smelt
to be believed, and as it is exceedingly popular with all
classes in Egypt one can usually detect its presence on every
railway station in the Nile Valley, particularly Luxor,
where one arrives in the early morning not feeling one's
best after a long night in the train, and the smell of *fessikh*
before breakfast has a most alarming effect on the stomach.

When the mullet are not on the outward run the Bardawil family catch them by the ordinary method of a seine
net which is drawn round the shoals, but the net also has
a platform which is supported on the surface of the water
by light bamboo rods. The ordinary seine net would not
be of the slightest use for mullet, as if a shoal of several
thousands were encircled and there was no platform every
single fish would escape by jumping.

I discovered this little idiosyncrasy for myself some
years ago in Ireland when living on a small tidal river.
During a very high spring tide a huge shoal of big mullet
came right up the stream to a spot where at low water there
was normally only a trickle two inches deep. I fixed a
tennis net firmly across the stream below the shoal of fish
and weighted it down at the bottom with boulders. I
fondly imagined I had caught the whole shoal, but when
the tide turned, after a few minutes' splashing in front of

the barrier, a fine Grand National-class mullet soared over the top to safety, and in a moment was followed by the remainder of the party, so that all I obtained for my trouble was one small fish that had become entangled in the meshes.

In the spring a very large number of sand sharks migrate to the eastern end of the Mediterranean and the Bardawils catch them by long lines of unbaited hooks laid along the surface of the sand in a depth of about fifteen fathoms. Apparently these sand sharks, nosing along the bottom, transfix themselves on the hooks and catches of twenty to fifty running from three to five feet are common. The skin, fins, etc., and all other distinguishing marks are then removed and the carcasses sent to Cairo where they are sold as *samakh*, i.e. just plain " fish " with no pretentious name. This recalls the story of a hostess at a dinner-party in Cairo, who, when complimented upon the excellence of the fish and asked its name, replied, " I think it is a kind of fish called *samakh* (fish)."

At El Arish we occasionally had a very delicious silvery fish, but we could never let it figure on the menu when guests were present as they invariably commented on it and asked its name. This made things awkward, for it was called *myass*, and it was very difficult to pronounce the word without giving offence.

The most attractive form of fishing, however, is that which is carried out by means of the cast net and, considering how popular and efficient it is in the East, it is somewhat remarkable that it has never been taken up by fishermen in England. This net is made in the shape of an umbrella, that is to say, it is perfectly round when stretched on the ground. The throw cord is attached to the centre and from it radiate draw-strings fixed to the edges of the net which act like the ribs of an umbrella.

All around the net are small lead weights enabling the thrower to cast it a considerable distance, and carrying the net rapidly to the bottom, thus imprisoning the fish.

To cast the net properly requires a considerable amount of skill and, though I have practised for hours, I have never been able to shoot it out so that it falls into the water in a perfect circle or anything approaching it. One of the men in my regiment who was a Poole fisherman in civil life, became most expert with this net, and when he was demobilized at the end of the war took two home with him as he said he would find it most useful in Poole harbour for obtaining bait for his lobster and crab pots.

To make a cast the net is lifted by the centre and folded neatly across the right forearm, with the weighted fringe hanging down about eighteen inches, while the cord is held in the left hand. The cast is made by a swinging movement of the right shoulder and arm and the net should shoot out to the extent of the cord, open like an umbrella and drop on to the surface of the water immediately over the fish. The draw cord is then pulled steadily, which has the effect of bringing in to the centre the outer circumference of the net with its lead weights, and the fish is caught in the meshes. It is difficult to say when the cast net was first invented, but there is probably little doubt that when Jesus found Peter and his brother Andrew fishing in the Sea of Galilee and called upon them to follow Him they were throwing precisely the same sort of cast net as is in general use to-day.

The cast-net man " fishes the rise " like a dry-fly purist. That is to say, there is no question of " chuck and chance it," and when one sees a cast-net fisherman running and crouching on the sandy shore as if he were an ibex-hunter making a stalk he is actually watching the movements of a fine two-pound mullet or small tunny, which to the ordinary observer is quite invisible. Most fish swim quite close to the surface, and apparently in certain lights the fisherman can see the fish as they are lifted slightly by the small uncrested and unruffled wavelets that are usual at dawn before the breeze gets up. I have occasionally just been able to catch a glimpse of them myself, but the skilled cast-net man apparently never loses sight of his fish and will follow a big fellow for a mile or more until it loses its sense of caution and comes in close enough to allow of a throw. It is a most fascinating and graceful form of fishing and one that would make a most attractive film.

The Beduin fishermen in the south of Sinai are just as expert with the cast net as their more enlightened colleagues in the north, and I have seen them with one throw catch over a thousand small red mullet that for some unexplained reason go by the name of Ibrahim Pasha. This is the same fish as is known in the Mediterranean as the *baboonia*, and he affects a long barbel-like moustache. I imagine that when Ibrahim Pasha invaded the Hedjaz via Akaba and Sinai in the middle of the nineteenth century the local Arabs were greatly struck by the enormous Turkish moustache he wore and nicknamed the fish after him.

There is a queer little edible crab that is fairly common on the north Sinai coast, and he is unlike the ordinary crab of British waters in that he lives on a sandy coast and when taken from the water dies within two minutes. He is blue in colour and considerably nicer to eat than the English variety, being, in fact, quite a delicacy.

It was never easy to obtain these crabs as the fishermen did not worry about them and the cook did not encourage them to do so as dressing crabs for the table, particularly small ones, is a lengthy and tedious proceeding. I finally worked up a most excellent *liaison* with two small boys, the sons of a fisherman, who made a considerable amount of pocket-money by bringing in large quantities of crabs almost every day. Then after a month the *liaison* broke down as *liaisons* have a habit of doing in Egypt and no more crabs arrived. The cook, when appealed to, said that the boys had not brought them as they were no longer obtainable and out of season, but when I met the lads themselves some time later I heard quite a different story, for crabs were apparently still plentiful.

" But we did not bring them to the house any more," they said, " because the cook called us sons of a depraved dog, drove us away, and said he would beat us if we brought the accursed things to your Excellency again."

The truth in the East resides consistently at the bottom of a well, but sooner or later something occurs that stirs it up and brings it to the surface to the discomfort of the unwary liar.

A thing that will strike the casual observer in connection with Sinai fishermen both on the Mediterranean and the southern coasts is the very considerable number of them who lack one or two fingers of the right hand and in some cases the whole arm, together with an empty eye-socket and facial scars. These disfigurements are the result of bombing, an illegal form of fishing that the Beduin learned from British troops during the war and which appealed instantly to the Arab mentality as being an extremely rapid, efficacious and labour-saving method of obtaining a large amount of fish with very little trouble. " The evil that men do, lives after them ; the good is oft interred with their bones," is particularly true of the British soldier in Egypt, for, though the Oriental might have learned much of lasting good from this very sterling specimen of humanity, it is a lamentable fact that the only British habit or custom the Arab acquired from him during four years of war was the knack of bombing shoals of fish with the Mills' ready-made article, or, failing that, an amateur contrivance of explosive wrapped in newspaper and fitted with a piece of time-fuse. Any form of explosive will serve the purpose for to the Beduin there is no difference between gelignite, T.N.T., or blasting powder—the fact that a handful of the first two will blow a man to scraps and the third merely give him an invigorating shock is such a slight difference that it is hardly worth taking into account.

Bombing is certainly a most effective method of obtaining fish as a well-placed bomb in a shoal of mullet or the little blue and red herring of the Gulf of Akaba will produce a boatload of fish with no greater effort than the labour of ladling them on board, but like all easy things in this world it has its drawbacks. One is that a bomb destroys all marine life within a radius of the explosion—spawn, fry, and the minute organisms of the sea that provide larger species with their foodstuffs—and in course of time excessive bombing scares fish away. This is noticeable at Akaba, where the fishermen possess practically no tackle of any kind, their gear consisting solely of a dozen home-made bombs rolled up overnight for the day's work, and for ten miles in the vicinity of this post fish are exceedingly scarce, whereas ten or twelve years ago this part of the Gulf was literally teeming and it would be no exaggeration to use the Irish ghillie's description and say " they were shoulthering each other out of the wather."

To obtain the necessary explosive the fishermen have recourse to the various ammunition dumps both British and Turkish that existed and still exist in all parts of Sinai. In theory these have all been destroyed and cleared up many years ago, but actually a very large number of shells still remain buried in the sand on the sites of the old dumps, quite sufficient to supply the Beduin fishermen for many years to come. Their method of extracting the powder is both haphazard and risky; they hammer off the nose-cap of the shell with a mattock. If the nose-cap happens to be "alive" or of the percussion variety, there is an immediate vacancy in a fishing syndicate and a weeping widow, backed up by close relatives, will come into the Governorate at El Arish with a sad story of an unsuspecting shepherd, who lit a fire in the desert to cook his food, when suddenly a shell under the sand exploded and blew him into the middle of the hereafter, and what about compensation from the *Hakooma* (Government) who is responsible?

One day whilst sitting in my office at El Arish on a peaceful sunny morning there was a most colossal explosion, far greater than anything I had heard during the war. Both the windows of the room crumpled into fragments and the entire population of the town, some ten or eleven thousand, started to race towards the spot where the bang had occurred. I followed and found about a hundred yards from my office a hole in the ground some ten feet deep, a dead camel, and a crowd of small boys bringing in fragments of a man on bits of stick, which the Government doctor, a well-known jig-saw addict, was trying to fit together.

It appeared that a fisherman had discovered in the sand outside his house one of the twelve-inch shells fired by our naval guns at El Arish during the occupation of the town by the Turks. It was an outsize in shells and contained enough explosive to provide bombs for a whole season's fishing, so the discoverer cocked it at an angle on a stone, sat astride it and proceeded to hack off the nose-cap. It was a percussion shell, as he discovered after the third blow, but the information came too late for it to be of any use to him in this world, and unfortunately his ghastly fate was no deterrent to other seekers after illicit explosives for quite a heavy mortality by shells among the fisherfolk continued with, to use a recognized *cliché*, monotonous regularity during my service in Sinai. After every fatality the Government took steps to clean up still more thoroughly the various ammunition dumps, but sufficient shells always remained in the sand to enable a percentage of the fishing fraternity to commit suicide, and the extraordinary part about the whole business was that no one was more surprised than these amateur " breakers down " of ammunition when a shell exploded.

The missing fingers, eyes, and other maimings that are so frequent are due not to shell-bursts, but to the premature explosions of bombs in the hand. The Arab bomb is a small quantity of blasting powder, gelignite, T.N.T., or dynamite—they are all the same, so why worry—rolled tightly in a wad of paper and tied with string to a medium-sized stone. About three inches of time-fuse is inserted— any sort of time-fuse will do as like the explosive they must *ipso facto* be all the same and of similar timing—and the fisherman with a lighted cigarette either walks along the shore or is rowed in a boat until he spots a shoal of fish. The fuse is then ignited by the cigarette-end and the angler " fishing the rise " throws it when he thinks he has left just sufficient time for the bomb to arrive at its destination and sink a matter of three feet into the water. Owing to the fact that there are quick- and slow-burning fuses, and also because Arabs as a race are notoriously bad judges of time, accidents are frequent; hence the fact that a considerable percentage of Sinai and Trans-Jordan fishermen are deficient of a finger or two and occasionally, as I have said, an arm or an eye. Bombing is, of course, prohibited and the penalty for the use of explosives is very heavy, but this does not deter the Arab in the slightest

degree, as he regards it merely as unwarrantable interference with a perfectly legitimate and sound method
of obtaining fish with the minimum of effort.

The fishermen of north Sinai, and those that hail from
Port Said and Suez, were one and all keen business men,
and so long as there was a marketable and catchable
fish in the seas they had very little time for frivolities and
side lines such as taking rod anglers out for a few hours'
doubtful and to them entirely ridiculous sport. "Life is
real ! life is earnest !" was their motto, although they had
never heard of Longfellow. It was amongst the more
haphazard Beduin in the south that one met the definite
characters, men with the most inefficient gear and casual
outlook on life, but good sportsmen withal, and possessing
a far finer and closer knowledge of the ways of fish and
freaks of the weather than their more mercenary and opulent
brothers of the calling who dwelt in the north.

Doughty and other writers on the Arab race dismiss the
fishermen with scorn and contempt as being "fish eaters"
and therefore quite beyond the pale, and there is no getting
away from the fact that hobnobbing with low, no-account
fellows who use a net and frequent seashores does cause one
to lose caste with those noble scions of the tribes who live
by camel-herding. I had many warm friends among the
fishermen and I am afraid that this little weakness of mine
was commented upon severely by the more exclusive
county families of the Peninsula. It was regarded as a
very queer kink in my character that I should find anything
attractive in fishermen, and that I should actually take part
in the degrading business myself was a matter that should
be hushed up at all costs.

One of the most attractive of these Beduin, who live on
the shores of the Gulf of Akaba, and who as a result have
more or less lost touch with the tribes to which they belong,

was Radwan. Nominally Radwan belonged to the How-ietat tribe of Trans-Jordan, who formed the spear-head of Lawrence's Arab force, but personally I think there was some doubt about his ancestry and I imagine he was really descended from the Maghrabis (Moorish soldiery), who garrisoned the forts on the old pilgrim road to Mecca.

Radwan was my original ghillie and, though he did not belong to Sinai, I was able to see quite a lot of him and take advantage of his services owing to a slight disagreement with the police of Akaba over the question of a *nabbut* (staff) applied to somebody's head, which made his residence abroad advisable for some time. I never discovered exactly what the truth of the incident was, as being a representative of law and order myself, and one in whose hands lay powers of extradition, Radwan preferred not to discuss the episode, but his abridged version when pressed to explain matters gave one an uncomfortable feeling that in this world the upright and godly are frequently mis-judged and that men of character when they are innocent prefer to suffer in silence. Radwan was the best man at telling a story I have ever met, and the intense gravity of his expression and the sadness of his eyes when recounting the tale entirely obliterated any suspicions as to his veracity that might have been aroused by the other and entirely different version of the occurrence as told by my *Hakimdar* (N.C.O. in charge).

Radwan when I first met him in 1922 was very " small beer " indeed, as his gear consisted of a cast net, some rusty hooks attached to a frayed line and a dug-out canoe. The canoe carried a sail which bore what one imagined was the sail-maker's mark—a broad arrow with the letters G.S. Only the initiated realized it was not a real Ratsey and recognized it for what it was, a portion of an Army bell tent. The mast of the canoe was another and more obvious tent product, namely, the bamboo pole of an E.P., while the halliard block was supplied by J. & P. Coats, a large-sized cotton-reel. The world war, which spelt ruin and disaster to so many nations, was to the Arabs a sort of super and benignant Marks & Spencer where everything was free, and this century will be old indeed when the last of the supplies obtained finally disintegrate.

Personally I did not like the look of the canoe at all and felt far from happy when I got into it, for to describe it as cranky was deliberately to understate its behaviour. Its natural instability was such that a man with fatty degeneration of the heart, or any disease that would in the slightest degree affect his normal balance, could never maintain his equilibrium in it, and as a matter of fact no one suffering from heart trouble in any form should have ever attempted a voyage in it.

My first and only trip unfortunately coincided with the monthly inspection visit of a large man-eating shark who makes a patrol of the harbour of Akaba every thirty days or so. His big, dirty beige-coloured fin kept skimming past our little craft, very silently and very ominously, and in consequence I could not give my undivided attention to the work in hand—trolling for barracouta.

With the idea of starting a little light, chatty conversation to take my mind off large-sized fish, I asked Radwan if he had owned the canoe for a long time.

He shook his head, accompanying the action with the characteristic Arab click of the tongue against the teeth.

" No, Effendim, only three months," he said, adding as an afterthought, " I bought it from Ahmed, or rather Ahmed's wife."

" Why ? " I asked. " Had Ahmed given up fishing ? "

" Yes," said Radwan sadly. " He gave it up entirely."

"And what did he do instead—shop-keeping, camel-breeding, or gardening?"

"None of them, Effendim," replied Radwan. "He didn't do anything."

"What happened?" I pursued. "Was he in prison?"

"No," said Radwan, "he wasn't in prison, for he was a good man and in with the police. He was dead," he added sadly.

"Poor chap," I murmured sympathetically. "I suppose he died from that influenza you had here last winter?"

"No, Effendim, he was quite happy and healthy before he died. I myself spoke to him that morning and inquired after his health and he said, 'Thanks be to God, the Merciful and Compassionate, it is good.'"

"Then how did he die?" I demanded.

Radwan raised his head and pointed to the fin which was then very close to the canoe—much too close, in fact.

"*He* had him," he said calmly. "He knows this canoe as well as I do, for he has had three from it in five years."

And it was at this moment that I discovered it was long past lunch-time and gave the order to 'bout ship and make for the shore as quickly as possible.

In those days Radwan was a complete novice as regards trolling for big-game fish, which he regarded as an entirely asinine proceeding, so much so that when he discovered I meant to continue to fly in the face of all the best Arab traditions his countenance wore an expression of intense gloom and utter boredom. The Beduin Arab has a fixed idea in his head that the Englishman comes from a country where there are neither horses nor cattle nor chickens, nor in fact anything that runs or flies, neither has he seen the sea before nor anything that swims in it. The English are a great race and can provide wise and just rulers; they can also make and drive cars, construct steamships, and fly in aeroplanes, but it is always a surprise to the Arab, a matter for mirth, in fact, that one of this nationality should pretend to know something about hatching chickens, the doctoring of horses, or, *mirabile dictu*, the ways of fish and how to catch them. I had badly blotted my copy-book in trying to catch fish by the laborious method of trolling a dead bait behind a moving boat, an idiotic performance, as it meant, if there were no wind, that some unfortunate Arab would have to row. Lastly, the crowning folly, I had brought with me a cage, a form of trap, into which the *bint el roban* (the daughter of the pilot, or, to be more exact, the crayfish or langouste) would walk, when anyone in his senses knew that the only method of catching this queer crustacean was by looking for him with a flare by night and planting a bare foot on his spiny shell when detected.

When I caught my first barracouta on a trolled dead bait Radwan was interested, but affected to regard the occurrence as one of those flukes that happen occasionally to very innocent and guileless beginners, and it was not until my fourth fish had been well and truly gaffed that he began to admit that there were possibly matters concerning fish that the Englishman understood. This question of a reel, for instance, that looked entirely fanciful, not to say " sissy," had something to recommend it, for it saved labour, and that is always attractive to the Beduin, and it was over the reel that Radwan, still practically a novice at the art of ghillying, rose to his greatest heights and increased my respect for a race that affects as a form of pose to be stupid and out of date and yet can show great acumen and wonderful initiative on occasions.

It was a warm, stuffy evening and the last day of my stay at Taba on the Gulf of Akaba. Queer little gusts of hot wind were coming down the mountain gorges, ruffling the surface of the sea spasmodically and just filling the flapping sail for a minute or less, and so we were proceeding slowly, almost lethargically, under man-power provided by Radwan's nephews. He himself sat in the stern holding the tiller and telling me of wondrous catches obtained before the war, and at his feet dozed my Aberdeen terrier, a mad keen fisherman, but even his canine enthusiasm had become dulled by the unnatural and uneventful calm of the evening. I was holding the rod limply across my knees, and had been doing so for such a considerable period without any response that I had quite forgotten I was fishing when suddenly, like a bomb exploding, a whole lot of things happened at one and the same moment. In the first place, I received a most terrific punch in the short ribs from the butt of the rod which was jerked forward nearly out of my hands; Radwan fell off his seat; the Scottie jumped excitedly at the thwart to see what was the cause of the disturbance; and the reel, after one agonizing and despairing shriek, threw in its hand completely and fell on the burden boards of the boat in two pieces—one, the outer shell with handle attached; and two, the actual drum with the line coiled on it—while a third portion, the completely useless casing, remained attached to the rod. To make a long story short, I had been taken by the father and mother of all the big fish in the Gulf of Akaba, and he had come and gone!

Then suddenly the drum that was lying on the deck started to jump and tumble like a decapitated chicken and Radwan and I realized that a miracle had happened; despite the disaster to the reel the fish was still on. This is where Radwan gave definite proof that the Beduin are a race that will show extraordinary initiative when faced with eventualities, for, though he had only made the acquaintance of a reel two days previously, he did that which would never have occurred to me, and I doubt if any Scottish or Irish ghillie would have risen to the occasion in like manner. Catching the detached drum between the soles of his bare feet, he righted it and allowed it to spin round with just the right amount of check applied and with his two hands playing the part of rings, and very efficient and sensitive rings too, he paid out the line to me and the rod which I was still holding helplessly in my hands.

" *Istaghal!* " (" Get to work ! ") he shouted fiercely, bringing me to my senses with a jerk ; and then occurred a most epic battle with the unknown monster.

The fish took Radwan's reel out till the soles of his feet must have been raw and the drum was nearly empty. Then as the boys brought the boat round and we followed in his wake Radwan began to regain line, drawing it in with one hand and spinning the reel neatly with the other. Wild rushes occurred from time to time and the drum was nearly wrenched from its fleshy bearings, but Radwan kept his head and his feet, in no way assisted by the Scottie's desire to help. Meanwhile all that I, the angler, had to do was to maintain an upright rod, hope for the best, and leave every-thing to a better man than myself. The minutes went past slowly till the last rays of the sun on the tops of the Hedjaz mountains died away, and still we zigzagged about the darkening gulf in the wake of the fish, with Radwan hauling and letting go alternately and I sitting on the thwart with the upright rod like a statue of some angling notable of the past.

The end of the story is unfortunately distressing and almost heart-breaking, for after an hour and a quarter of this unequal struggle we had got eventually to the stage when it was merely a question of bringing the tired monster to the surface to apply the gaff when disaster occurred. The fish, absolutely dead beat, was lying some five fathoms below the boat and was being raised gradually to the surface by slow heaves on my part and a steady strain on Radwan's, when suddenly there came that devastating feeling of nothingness. The line coiled limply in Radwan's hand and the rod straightened itself in an aggressive manner in mine ; the strain was gone and with it the fish. Most annoying of all was the fact that as we had never seen it we had not the faintest idea of its species, so one mystery of the gulf has never been revealed.

The largest fish I ever caught in these waters was a barracouta of fifty pounds, which I killed in twenty minutes and, judging by the length of time I played this giant and his great strength and endurance, he must have been twice the size and certainly not a barracouta, as he never showed once during the struggle.

I shall never forget poor Radwan's grief at this untimely end to his protracted struggle, and the trouble is that with the Mohammedan boatman one cannot apply the universal salve that will remove all trace of heartburnings and memories of disasters if the ghillie happens to be Irish or Scottish. A stiff tot of whisky is no good to a devout Muslim, and so I did the next best thing—I purchased the fattest sheep from a neighbouring flock. Actually its fatness was merely a matter of comparison, but we sat over it at the camp fire saying, as anglers do, " Now if I had only——" till Venus in pursuit of the waxing moon had crept well up the zenith of the sky.

Radwan has now risen to great eminence in Akaba and as boatman to Excellencies and the Great is a man to whom even camel-herders look up. He has, however, never forgotten that fight when he acted as bearings to my reel, and I believe that the story he now recounts almost passes the ordinary and generous scope allowed to anglers who lose fish. He has entirely recanted his original views about trolling, but he won hands down over the futility of the lobster-pot, for never at any time did it produce even the smallest crab !

*   *   *   *   *

Some forty miles south of Akaba on the Sinai coast there is a place marked on the Ordnance atlases as Wasit, which appears to be a very suitable name for a spot that has definitely no present and apparently no future. There is a ruined fort there, but the town merely consists of huts constructed from palm branches in which live fishermen of the Mezeina tribe in Sinai. The Mezeina are descended from the oldest and most aristocratic of the tribes in the Yemen and claim that they came over from Arabia with the Conquest, for in the Arab world this " coming over with the Conqueror " business is just as acute as it is with us. The Mezeina, now the poorest of the poor, are very conscious of their origin, and when you discover them plying the degrading trade of fishermen they do not fail to remind you, like the proverbial landlady, that " I was not brought up to this sort of thing at all and merely do it to oblige."

One of this kidney was Sulieman, who, when I first met him, was crouching along on the seashore carrying a cast net at the ready and wearing cotton drawers only. I was in need of a guide to show the way across a difficult pass in the mountains behind and Sulieman at once volunteered his services.

" I am a herder of camels and not a fisherman," he said, with a touch of hauteur, and then with the air of a retired Colonel discovered fishing the rise for trout in his spare time : "I only do this sort of thing to amuse myself and to get an odd fish for a meal occasionally."

The skill with which he neatly flung his net over a huge shoal of red mullet, and the business acumen he displayed later when disposing of the catch, rather belied his amateur status, however, and he was, as I discovered, one of the cleverest and most knowledgeable fishermen of the gulf. In employing him, however, as a ghillie, it was always a matter of honour as between gentlemen to adopt the attitude that he was the merest tyro giving me a hand for the sake of the sport and the emolument he received later for his services was, of course, merely the tips to be handed over to those common Arabs who had assisted with bait and other matters. Knowing Sulieman, I think it extremely doubtful if the poor fellows ever saw a piastre of the money.

On the strength of Sulieman's knowledge of the country generally, his skill as a fisherman and boatman, and his undoubted personality, I had appointed him as *ghaffir* (watchman) on the western shores of the Gulf of Akaba, and this little touch of authority constituted him a very present menace indeed. There is always a grave risk in the police that the bestowal of an unpaid lance-corporal's stripe on an Arab private may create something of the Major-General class with rather more than his authority and powers, and to take a wild Beduin fisherman and suddenly turn him into a government watchman was asking for trouble, and I obtained it very quickly. The first party of Hedjaz fishermen who, failing to recognize a government official in the ragged and unkempt Sulieman, refused to stop bombing fish after being ordered to do so, had their boat boarded by a cutting-out party and were unceremoniously slung into the sea. This was the subject of official correspondence between my office, Foreign Affairs in Cairo, and the Saudi-Arabian Minister in Egypt, which I believe is still proceeding merrily. I forget the amount of compensation claimed, but whatever it is, it is well beyond Sulieman's means.

Sulieman's second exploit concerned a small party of Travel-mongers—those who travel for profit, not pleasure

—who were endeavouring to get into Saudi-Arabia, late the Hedjaz, with the avowed object of visiting Mecca. I had been warned to look out for them and turn them back, but they slipped past my frontier post near Akaba, and when I heard that Sulieman had met them and was sponsoring the party I feared the worst. If it was adventure to write about that they were looking for, he was the man to supply it, but there was a considerable amount of doubt as to whether he possessed the qualities that would also extract them safely. More by luck than judgment the party was just prevented from setting forth in three very unstable dug-out canoes to cross the gulf and land on the farther shore, Sulieman having told them with his normal mendacity that Mecca, the Holy City, was " just round the corner," when actually it was some 650 miles distant.

When sent for to explain his behaviour he showed his usual *savoir-faire*, not to say natural cunning, by completely taking the wind out of my sails in this fashion :

" *Wallahi!* I never knew they were forbidden to go. They came to me and said they were the friends of His Excellency the Governor. On hearing this I flung myself on the ground and kissed the hem of their garments, saying with truth that if it were the desire of the Governor that I should die I would willingly cast myself into the sea. When they said they desired to visit Mecca, how could I refuse, seeing that they were Your Excellency's friends ? If I have erred it was out of love for Your Excellency and a desire only to obey your commands and help your friends."

Well, after half an hour of this sort of thing laid on by a practised hand even an Attila is apt to go all soft, crumple up and forget his spleen. I am certainly no Attila, for, though a plausible rogue does not take me in, he always excites my admiration, not to say envy.

Sulieman figured in many amusing situations, for unlike

the average Arab he was bursting with energy and initiative and always carried out his instructions with such enthusiasm and zest that he usually caused my undoing as well as his own, together with a complete disintegration of the scheme in hand. One Christmas when we had taken a large party to Taba at the head of the gulf he was indefatigable as usual, and, having discovered that the party wished to bathe but were naturally too terrified of sharks to attempt it, he explained how this could be done in safety.

" On the shore side of yonder island, Faroan, to which I will take you in my boat, there is a stretch of sand some sixty paces wide on which the water is but three *diras* deep (about four and a half feet). The sand is white, the water is clear, and it is possible for a watchman with keen eyes such as I possess to stand on the rocks above and see everything that moves, even the smallest fish. Beyond the sand the water is deep and here the sharks lie, but I shall be responsible for the safety of the party, and if I see so much as a fin move from the deep water I will call out in a very loud voice a warning that a shark is coming."

We therefore went out to the island and found everything as Sulieman had described. The water was gin-clear and unruffled and, though the deep blue depths beyond the sand-belt looked ominous and capable of hiding anything, it was sufficiently far away to enable a swimmer, if warned of danger, to reach the shore in safety. It was a most perfect day for bathing and the most ideal spot; there was not a breath of wind, the sun was blazing in the sky, and the water looked delightfully fresh, cool and clear, whilst the going underfoot was hard white sand and not jagged rocks.

We put on our bathing-suits and waded in whilst Sulieman climbed to a high point of rock overlooking our beach.

" Fear not," he cried, " I, Sulieman, am on the look out

and there is no man in the Gezeirat el Sinai who has eyes like mine. If danger comes I will cry out in a loud voice."

For the first few minutes the party experienced a rather creepy, fearsome feeling, for the thought of a high wedge-shaped fin suddenly appearing abaft one's beam, to be followed by a sudden tearing grip on one's leg, was rather alarming, and, whatever precautions one may take, bathing in shark-infested water is always a nervous business. After a while, however, we forgot our fears and the party, revelling in the cool water after the burning heat of the day, had gradually worked out till they were perilously near to the edge of the white sand and the gloomy depths beyond, when suddenly there came a wild screech from Sulieman, who at the same moment sprang to his feet and waved his *kufiyah* (head-shawl) frantically.

Immediately there ensued one of the most marvellous exhibitions of high-speed swimming that the world has ever seen. As one man the party swung round in a flurry of foam and tore madly for the shore with arms and legs churning the water in overhead strokes, trudge strokes, and in fact every stroke known to the civilized world, including several new ones specially improvised for this dreadful occasion. As the swimmers rose to their feet in shallow water with heaving breasts and gaping mouths Sulieman came down from his perch.

" Why have you come in ? " he asked calmly.

" The shark ? " we gasped, " where is he ? "

" I have not seen one," said Sulieman. " I was only calling out just now to my brother-in-law on the shore and telling him to go and fetch my camel."

*   *   *   *   *

Perhaps the queerest and most intriguing character of all

was Atrash, the deaf man, who also came of the Mezeina tribe and was in fact a distant cousin of Sulieman's, whom he hated with an intense hatred. There was some reason for this, as Sulieman had arranged a marriage between his sister and Atrash, forgetting to mention to the bride that the bridegroom was a deaf mute. One can feel nothing but sympathy for a wife when she discovers that none of her breakfast-table remarks, instructions and admonitions go home, and though deafness does not figure as cause for divorce in the Arab world any more than it does in our own, despite Mr. Herbert's recent Bill, Sulieman's sister decided it was not good enough, so packed up and departed. Atrash was not greatly worried about the flitting of his bride, but he was considerably concerned over the loss of the £12 dowry he had paid, and demanded its return. Unfortunately Sulieman had drawn this, and as he had celebrated the nuptials in Suez had nothing to show for it beyond the resulting "hang-over." All this had happened long ago, but as Atrash had only managed to collect about fivepence of the £12 in eight years he naturally felt rather aggrieved about the affair, and for this reason it was difficult to have a really cheery fishing party if the two were present. No matter how good the sport might be, the topic of conversation sooner or later got round to money and matrimony.

Actually, of course, Atrash could not talk, for he was a genuine deaf mute and came of a family where all the males suffered from this disability, though the females were normal in every way. He could, however, give utterance to various noises such as a high-pitched squeal like that of an angry elephant which showed that he was annoyed, another squeal on a different and more musical note to denote the fact that he was pleased, and a whole series of grunts that referred to such things as the ways of fish, suitability of baits, and the state of the weather.

For really important occasions, however, Atrash used special deaf and dumb language invented by his family which was so easily understood that I passed with honours in it after half an hour's conversation. The sign for a woman I discovered was the hand swept down the face from the eyes to the chin, i.e. the Mohammedan *yashmak*, and for a man a quick pluck at the chin to denote a beard ; and these two gestures were used to show the sex of animals as well. A camel he depicted by turning his head round and roaring at his load—a typical camel gesture— whilst a goat was a sweep of the hand to denote horns and a sudden twitching of the nose. Fish were shown by a waggle of one hand and a rapid measurement to show size by placing the forefinger of the right hand on the left arm ; wind or a gale by puffed-out cheeks, and a calm by a sweep of the hand ; the time of day was merely an indication of the point in the sky where the sun would be. I think, however, the most amusing and the cleverest of all was the sign for an ibex ; this was an extended sweep of the hands to describe scimitar horns, a pluck at the chin for the beard, and the forefinger of the right hand twiddled rapidly in the vicinity of the posterior to denote that animal's nervous little tail.

I found Atrash infinitely more knowledgeable about the ways of fish and their haunts than any of his *confrères* on either side of the gulf and can only conclude that his dis- ability, that shut him off from so much of that which was going on in the world, gave him time to study his trade in all its intricacies. He had not only an extraordinary good brain and quick intelligence, but he was also able to under- stand every conversation that was going on near him. This was not a question of lip-reading, as he got the gist of matters equally well if people were speaking English and not Arabic. In fact, I strongly suspected that Atrash had developed a gift of second sight combined with thought-reading, for whatever part of the southern shores of Sinai I visited Atrash would be there waiting with a volley of grunts and squeals and a palm-leaf basket filled with the exact type of dead bait I required. These places were some of them over a hundred miles apart, i.e. Taba at the head of the Gulf of Akaba, Ras Mohammed at the apex of the Peninsula, and Abu Zeneima some seventy miles south of Suez in the gulf of that name; but Atrash always seemed to know what my movements would be far better than the occupants of my police posts, who were sometimes taken badly by surprise—and an unprepared Arab police post is a totally different matter from a prepared one. Given one hour's warning and the average police post in Sinai could put up a show of smartness, efficiency and surrounding order and cleanliness that would cause a Company Commander of the Grenadier Guards to go green with envy; omit the warning, however, and the scene was usually so entirely different and so painful that one prefers not to describe it. A mere half-hour's warning or less always caused a curious atmospheric phenomenon—namely, a cloud of dust on the horizon even on the calmest day that gradually settled as one drew near. The settlement of the dust always coincided with the exit and disappearance into thin air of various vague Beduin figures carrying palm branches. This had nothing to do with the proverbial Eastern triumphal reception but was merely the disbandment of a hastily raised and quite unpaid corps of sweepers. On seeing this I wondered often what the effect would be if the constables in a village in England were suddenly to rush into the street, cuff every passer-by soundly over the head, shove a broom into his hand, and set him to work tidying up the police station, adopting all the time an outraged attitude that it was entirely the sweeper's fault the

The Author with the Bardawil family of fishermen
Arranging the folds of the cast net preparatory to throwing

[*See page* 203]

Suliman at Faroan Island

[*See page* 220]

building and its surroundings had got into such a shocking state of neglect.

Atrash was easily the most poverty-stricken and *maskeen* of all my disreputable fishing friends. The meaning of the Arabic *maskeen* is difficult to explain, as it indicates poor in every sense of the word—down-and-out, hopeless, and usually unjustly treated into the bargain, and poor old Atrash seemed to be all these, despite the fact that he was extremely intelligent and quick off the mark. Deafness is a terrible disability, as one commands only the most grudging sympathy from those who hear, and the usual attitude is that deafness goes hand-in-hand with imbecility and obstinacy.

Atrash's poverty was such that all he possessed in the world were his cast net and a home-made garment constructed from a gunny sack, and his food was the fish he caught and a small red berry that grew on a certain seashore scrub bush. Bread or flour in any form he seldom ate, except on those occasions when he joined me on patrol and fed with my police and car drivers; yet he seemed to keep in good condition, and if I moved down the coast forty miles he would turn up in the evening wreathed in smiles carrying about a hundredweight of fish and langouste he had caught on his way down the coast.

With the cast net he was a dry-fly purist rather than one of the " chuck-and-chance-it " brigade, for he fished the rise. That is to say, his little deep-set eyes saw considerably farther into the water than the average eye, and when one detected him running up the seashore with sudden pauses and crouches, holding the net at the ready, he was actually stalking some big fish that was quite invisible to the ordinary eye. And when he finally cast, he very seldom failed to net his quarry.

Despite his skill, however, his state of poverty remained unchanged, until one day some three months or so before I left Sinai for good I went down to Abu Zeneima on inspection and found two Italian steam trawlers anchored in the harbour. Ashore there was a scene of great excitement, for two Arab boats were at work with seine nets and a big crowd of Beduin were hauling on the drag ropes, yelling lustily.

I walked down to the seashore to see the catch brought in and, judging by the rate at which the corks were travelling, it was going to be a big one. The noise was deafening, for everyone was shouting at the top of his voice; but far above the tumult and confusion I could hear the high squealing note of Atrash. As I drew nearer I saw him among the mob of heaving men, but he was not hauling himself—far from it; armed with a small switch of palm branch he was running up and down the line of toilers, screaming in their faces and beating them over the shoulders. This is one of the peculiarities of the Beduin world; a blow delivered in anger during a squabble is a deadly insult that can only be wiped out in blood, but a hearty crack over the back with a stick when one is engaged in heavy toil is a friendly encouragement and esteemed as such. It is a recognized thing that Arabs cannot indulge in manual labour unless someone is yelling and beating them at intervals, and once when some of my tribesmen were engaged in a purely voluntary job of cleaning out an old cistern they asked me to supply a *reis* (head man) to keep them at it and beat them if necessary.

Directly Atrash saw me he ran up to make his salutations, and then, explaining hurriedly that he was a busy man, he rushed back to the gang to continue his yelling and beating. The two nets were brought ashore with a veritable miraculous draught of fishes, for they were filled to bursting-point with grey mullet and the haul I estimated was worth something like £15.

I asked my police sergeant who was in charge of the boats and nets.

" Atrash, Effendim," he replied.

" What, Atrash ? " I asked, in amazement. " Not that little deaf man ? "

" Yes, Atrash and no other," he said. " *Wallahi*, he's a big man now ; he's been working with these Italians for some three months and sells his catches to them. He's already bought two boats and two nets worth about £50 and everybody on the Sinai coast works under him and obeys his commands."

That night I went to call on Atrash and found him living in a tent and dispensing coffee to his men. To see Atrash in a tent of his own was rather on a par with finding one of London's unemployed living in a suite at the Ritz, and to make matters more amazing he was playing the part of a coffee Sheikh—a sure sign of the greatest eminence in the Arab world. It was satisfactory to find that this sudden rise in the social scale had in no way affected the manners of my old friend, and his welcome was as cordial as ever. It is such a pity one cannot end the story of Atrash on this note of a man of means and made for life. Unfortunately for my peace of mind an urgent matter took me to Taba some five days before I left Sinai, and there to greet me on the shore, clad in his old sack again and carrying his cast net, was Atrash—right back where he had started. It is useless to try and find a reason or explanation for these sudden rises to eminence and equally sudden returns to poverty that sometimes occur in the Beduin world. In Lancashire, I believe, they say " Clogs to clogs in three generations," but the Arabs are quicker than that. I imagine there awakes within them some latent urge and dormant ability to achieve great things, some hint of that lost energy that caused them to capture the whole of the civilized mid-East in the seventh century, and then just as success is within their grasp they realize the futility of worldly possessions and let everything go by the board far more quickly than they acquired it.

CHAPTER X

RAMADAN AND RELIGION

Religion should extinguish strife,
And make a calm of human life.

COWPER.

T O most of those unacquainted with the East and its
ways Ramadan is understood to be a month's fast
kept by Mahommedans only in much the same way as
we observe Lent, and that as it is a part of the Moslem
creed it is no immediate concern of the Christians resident
in the country. This unfortunately is not quite correct,
for, though the Christians themselves do not keep the
fast, both their servants and neighbours take particular
care to see that they are not allowed to forget for one
moment that it is *Ramadan Kareem* and that all good
believers are setting an example to the infidels.

The Christian employer of domestic staff will be called
in the morning anything from half an hour to two hours
late, will find the water in the bathroom stone-cold, his
coffee at breakfast undrinkable, and his eggs uncooked.
On setting out after this delightful meal a blear-eyed and
corpse-like chauffeur, who has been up all night, will fail
to start the car for the simple reason that there is no petrol
in the tank and on arrival at the office, which during
Ramadan does not open till 10 a.m., the Mahommedan
members of the staff will be found to be in a lethargic
and stupid state and quite incapable of finding any file or
giving a coherent answer on any subject.

At night after a badly cooked dinner served by half-witted servants he will be kept awake by the ceaseless chatter of *boabs* (doorkeepers) at his gateway and by passing parties of revellers moving from one heavy midnight meal to another, and if this does not have the required effect of depriving everyone of slumber artillery salvos are fired at midnight and 3 a.m. to summon the faithful to prayer and meals, whilst drummers and " knockers-up " move up and down the streets till one hour before dawn. Fortunately for the general well-being of the country there is a very high percentage of Copts, or native Christians, in all the important departments, and as they do not keep the fast the machinery of the government continues to " tick over " until Bairam comes to end the month of torture.

It is bad taste to criticize the religion of another race, but the drawback about Ramadan is in the first place that, though possibly admirably suited to the Arabs of A.D. 600 for whom it was intended originally, its rigid observance is absolutely impossible for the hard-working man of to-day if he wishes to maintain his ordinary standard of efficiency and energy. Secondly, one imagines that Mahommed the Prophet ordered the fast, not only as a form of religious penance, but more particularly from the point of view of general health, and it is in this respect that the average observer of Ramadan to-day defeats its purpose entirely by eating far more than is the case normally.

There is not the slightest doubt that all people who can afford to do so eat far too much. The average Englishman with his three hearty meals a day would crack up at forty-five but for the fact that he works off his surplus fat by hunting, golf and every form of active exercise. In the East well-cooked meals are just as attractive as in England and rather richer, but the desire to take exercise is not so marked. Nearly every Englishman in the East, realizing that his health depends upon it, forces himself to ride or to play some strenuous game every day, but the Oriental, though he eats quite as much, is naturally averse to exercise.

When one studies the routine of prayers ordered by Mahommed, one is struck by the fact that they savour more of physical exercises than devotions, and it seems safe to assume that the Prophet, finding the wealthy merchants of Mecca and Medina in a lamentable state of general health due to over-eating in a hot climate, evolved a religion that would not only purify their souls but exercise the muscles of their stomachs at the same time and so improve the state of their digestive organs.

The religion calls for five lengthy prayers during each day, the first at dawn and the last after the evening meal, and at each prayer *rakkhas*, or genuflexions, consisting of a complete prostration of the body from the knees with the head touching the ground, are ordered—the total number during the day being thirty-two, and thirty-two complete bendings and stretchings make a very fair exercise for a middle-aged or elderly man. The prayers, moreover, demand personal cleanliness and, if the devotions are carried out properly, not only the hands but the mouth, ears, neck, arms, head and feet are washed thoroughly. The attention paid by the Prophet to these details suggests that he was not merely an inspired religious teacher but a physical culture expert also. The Ramadan fast, if carried out as ordered, may be a trifle drastic, particularly as regards abstention from water during the day, but few modern doctors would find much fault with a system of practical starvation for a whole month in the case of heavy eaters and drinkers. Again, to prove the wisdom and foresight of the Prophet, the prohibition of pig-flesh was an essentially sound move as pork is a most unsuitable food for a hot climate. If beef or mutton should become tainted in the great heat it is merely unpleasant to eat but not dangerous, whereas pork that has turned bad is a virulent poison. In the East the pig is merely a scavenger and, as his flesh is never in a particularly healthy state, one may surmise that Mahommed from time to time saw whole families wiped out by ptomaine poisoning and wisely prohibited the swine as an unclean beast.

The Arabs with whom Mahommed had to deal were mostly merchants and camel-drovers whose mode of life made the observance of the fast moderately easy; if it is possible to sleep away the hours of daylight the fact that one has to go without food or water is not nearly so burdensome as it is if one is compelled to work at a desk with difficult problems to solve or has to wield a shovel in a sun-scorched field. In the Prophet's days it was the unwritten law that no one did any work in Ramadan; the faithful dozed and slept through the heat of the day, keeping a languid watch on their shops or flocks of sheep and grazing camels; and at night they broke their fast and paid ceremonial visits. In fact all Arabia went out of business for a month and enjoyed itself, for the true Mahommedan obtains a vast amount of pleasure and satisfaction from his religion.

In the middle ages this system worked admirably for then nations had not to worry about the all-important question of balancing exports and imports, labour troubles and maintenance of the gold standard, but the strict observance of Ramadan is an absolute impossibility for a civilized country to-day if it wishes to take its place among the important Powers of the world. The government cannot possibly carry on efficiently if for one month out of the twelve the greater part of its staff is too languid to work properly; when the police are only half awake and hope vainly that evil-doers are in the same helpless state; and when the Army of the nation shuts up shop on the first day of Ramadan and does not function again until after the feast of Bairam. The same state of affairs pertains in the business world, and purely Egyptian commercial concerns, though they do not close down, realize that it is impossible to expect any efficient work whilst the fast is in progress, and this is one of the reasons why most of the important trade of Egypt is in the hands of Greeks, Italians, Frenchmen and other foreigners.

The rulers of the Egyptian nation realize fully the situation, but are powerless to do anything, as any suggestion that the fast of Ramadan should be modified to meet modern conditions would raise a storm of fanatical disapproval in the country and the *Qadis* (religious judges), *Imams* (priests) and *Fikis* (junior schoolmasters) would arise in their might against the profane iconoclasts; and the power of the religious teachers in the country is very considerable when any questions concerning the orthodoxy of the Faith are involved. The far-reaching reforms introduced into Turkey by Mustafa Kamel during the past few years with official disapproval of Ramadan, the prohibition of the yashmak and the compulsory wearing of hats could not possibly be introduced into Egypt where fanaticism only needs a spark to start a blaze. Possibly with the increase of education in the country the great mass of the people may eventually see for themselves that the observance of the fast is not in keeping with modern conditions and should be modified, but that day is far ahead.

If Ramadan were kept more in the spirit as taught by Mahommed the results would not be so regrettable, but if one of the ideas of the Prophet was to give overworked stomachs a rest the observance of the fast to-day has

233

entirely the opposite effect. After a day spent in slumber and lethargy the faster makes a heavy and lengthy meal at sunset, he then strolls round to see his friends and eats sweetmeats and drinks coffee for several hours ; after this he has a short sleep and at midnight is called to eat a second terrific meal, he then dozes for three hours or so and awakes to make a third meal—his breakfast—an hour before dawn. After this he sleeps till about 9.30, when he crawls out to his office or his work and the state of his interior by this time is beyond belief. Halitosis is the order of the day, and it is necessary to ask one's Muslim staff to stand at least three yards from one when conducting one's business during Ramadan.

The drawback to the Mahommedan faith is that the observance of this fast is not the concern of the individual alone, but every devout Muslim conceives it his duty to ascertain if his neighbours are doing the same, and is not above lodging official complaints about backsliders who have been discovered munching a slab of bread and an onion in a dark corner or surreptitiously puffing at a cigarette. I remember a junior official in my office, who suffered from this pharasaical feeling, and who in Ramadan used to bring before me for punishment members of the police force whom he had detected in the heinous crime of having a midday snack or a pull at a water *goola*. I have always held the view that a man's soul is entirely his own property to do with as he will, and if he wishes to go to purgatory in the hereafter it is entirely his own affair and he is the only one who will suffer. Moreover, the official in question had not risen from his bed until 9.30 a.m. and proposed to return there sharp at 1.30 p.m., and the policeman had probably been on patrol in the desert since the small hours of the morning. Hypocrisy and phariseeism are the most despicable and irritating of the ordinary failings of the human race, and one of the most glorious moments of my life was when I walked into this particular official's office towards the end of Ramadan and discovered how he kept the fast. The door was locked, but as all locks in Egypt are inefficient and either open at once without the aid of a key or refuse to open however often the right key or any other key is turned in them, I walked right in and found my devout friend making a hearty meal off three hard-boiled eggs and a square yard of native bread. Had he been an ordinary individual who minded his own business I should have discreetly ignored the food and beat a hasty retreat, but as it was I felt something was due to him and said, " Hallo, Mahommed effendi, you've turned Christian, I see. Have you started to eat pork yet ? " But both his mouth and his heart were too full to reply.

In Christian countries if an individual fails to live up to teachings of his religion it is regarded as his own affair and he does not lose caste or social position because of his attitude, but for an Egyptian to fail to observe the Ramadan fast is on a par with an Englishman letting his Club down with a R.D. cheque or being caught cheating at cards. There are a number of younger Egyptians who have been educated in England or on the Continent and who agree with Mustafa Kamel that the strict observance of the Mahommedan religion is a definite bar to progress and civilization. These men are sufficiently broad-minded to see that the Ramadan fast is a survival of the seventh century and the care-free life of the Arabian desert, but owing to the attitude adopted by their friends and colleagues in the service they are morally forced to come into line, or in any case to keep up an outward pretence of being good Mahommedans.

The old mediæval idea that Ramadan is a month to be

235

devoted solely to religion still pertains and people who
are quite lukewarm about the faith normally get touched
by fanaticism during these thirty days of fasting. If any
disaster occurs owing to forgetfulness caused by the
distraction of the fast, such as twenty tons of cement
left out to be spoilt by rain, a new car seized up through
being run without oil, or a pen of pedigree chickens dead
from starvation, the attitude adopted is that the disaster
has occurred in God's service and almost suggests that
the Deity has derived some personal satisfaction from the
loss. Certainly the culprit does not feel in any way to
blame, but rather assumes the attitude of a man who has
deserved well of his God in that he has given tangible
proof of his devotion to the Faith. All this is terribly
riling for the well-meaning British official who tries to
carry on the work of the country and who sees sometimes
the labour of years wasted owing to the lethargy and
stupidity that the Ramadan fast brings in its train.

> " The Christian riles and the Aryan smiles
> And he weareth the Christian down."

When Ramadan came in the dog days of summer it
did not affect the efficiency of the country to such an
extent as at other seasons, for owing to the departure of the
Ministers and their offices to Alexandria for the hot season,
the absence of most British officials on leave, and the
entire lack of funds for works due to the normal delay
in passing the Budget, the period from May to the end
of August has always been regarded in Egypt as a slack
time during which little is expected of one's staff except
to carry on routine. Now, however, Ramadan comes in
mid-winter; it lasts thirty days, it is followed by the
Bairam holiday of five days, and two months later there
is the second Bairam festival of another five days together

with a multitude of minor feasts such as the Ceremony of the Holy Carpet, Coptic New Year and Shem el Nessim, so that it is absolutely impossible to get in more than a month's solid work during the cold weather before the period of fasts and *eids* (festivals) is upon one, and once that has started it is little use trying to carry on with the training of the Army, the construction of roads and other public services.

At the time of writing the zenith has been passed and with its difference of from four to five days annually the Mahommedan year by about 1950 will have put Ramadan back where it really belongs—the dog days of summer—and all will be well again from the point of view of the government and the employers of labour. The change, however, will not be so welcome to the fasters who must abstain from water during the interminably long days of a hot summer, nor to the Mecca pilgrims who will have to perform their bareheaded devotions in a temperature bordering on 115°.

I have heard Christian missionaries say that Islam is gradually dying out in Egypt, but in my opinion the wish is father to the thought. I can safely say I saw no sign of it and during my service in the country I was struck by the devotion to the Faith shown by all races and almost all classes. There are, I admit, a few, very few, of the intelligentsia and senior officials in the big cities who are not very devout believers, but among the *fellaheen*, the shopkeeper class and the Arabs the Mahommedan religion has as strong a hold to-day as it had a thousand years ago.

Actually there would seem to be little or no reason for missionary effort in a Mahommedan country, and this opinion is based upon the fact that so far as Egypt is concerned it is unlikely that more than a dozen real converts have been made during the last half-century. By real converts I mean men of some standing and those in full possession of all their faculties, and I do not include kitchen boys and the domestic staff of missionary stations whose religious views are biased by their employment and whose adherence to Christianity is to say the least temporal.

I do not wish to argue as to the respective merits of the Christian and Muslim faiths—personally I prefer Christ's teaching to that of Mahommed—but the fact remains that the two sects worship the same God though our conception of the Deity is Occidental whereas that of the Mahommedan is definitely Oriental, and if a Mahommedan lives up to his religion there is nothing much wrong with him. The trouble with the Muslim is that the percentage of hypocrites is rather high, and there is a tendency to believe that so long as the necessary prayers and genuflexions are performed one's behaviour for the rest of the day and night does not matter. This state of affairs existed in Europe in the Middle Ages, and in fact hypocrisy has not died out yet in England, but in any case hypocrisy can only be due to one cause—lack of understanding, intolerance and inefficient education; it is not the religion itself that is at fault. A Mahommedan who lives up to the teaching of his faith is every bit as good a man as a devout Christian.

The only weak spot in the Muslim faith is that regarding the plurality of wives, and here again one must remember the religion was devised in the first place for a primitive race where not only do women age quickly, but where they also outnumber the men. Polygamy is still admirably suited to the nomad Beduin, for with them a wife of forty is usually prematurely aged and past both work and child-bearing, and the old wife has no great objection to the introduction of another and younger woman to relieve her of some of her heavier duties. With the Beduin, plurality of wives solves the question of surplus women and their maintenance, for the nomad has the sterling quality of accepting responsibility for all his relatives. Among the Arabs there is no such thing as a poor rate and outdoor relief, for every man regards it as his duty to support not only his own wives, but also the widows and children of his brothers and cousins.

With the educated classes in Egypt, Palestine and Syria polygamy is dying out rapidly and is, moreover, regarded as bad form. Among the lower orders of the settled population however the position of women still leaves much to be desired, but there are at work in all these countries organizations for the emancipation of women run by Egyptian, Syrian and Palestinian ladies, and the time is close at hand when, so far as women are concerned, the Mahommedan faith will set its house in order.

I always resisted missionary effort in Sinai, for in the first place I regard it as savouring of impertinence to suggest that the religion of the Arabs is all wrong, and that our own should be adopted in its stead; secondly, the Arabs on the whole are an extremely moral and decent-living race, and except for their idleness compare very favourably indeed with any Christian community; and thirdly, I am absolutely certain that if missionaries worked consistently in Sinai or any other Arab country for twenty years they would not succeed in making one convert. I have not travelled very widely, but in the few countries in which I have sojourned I have been struck by the abortiveness of our missionary work abroad, though I admire the spirit which prompts missionaries themselves and the personal courage and endurance they display under every hardship and disadvantage. In Egypt it is a definite failure so far as Mahommedans are concerned, and, moreover, causes offence to the inhabitants; among the Arabs it is completely useless and might lead to dangerous situations, whilst in South Africa it is an understood thing that no one employs a Christian convert as a servant or workman if the unspoilt product is available. These are facts that are patent to everyone in any way conversant with these countries.

Missionary Societies, of course, hotly refute these statements and render reports of the work they are carrying out which to say the least are misleading. The fact remains that a considerable proportion of the money expended in foreign missions is to all intents and purposes wasted and, considering the conditions existing in some parts of the United Kingdom, it is nothing short of a scandal that huge sums should be spent annually abroad when there is a very crying need for it at home. It is to my mind an intolerable and unchristian situation that children in the distressed areas in the north of England and Wales are actually short of food and clothing, and shiver at night for want of proper bedding, when the money that might improve their lot is being thrown away on missionary work with the Mahommedans who resent it.

I take it that the missionary fraternity base their case on Christ's exhortation to go forth and spread the Gospel abroad, but it must be remembered that the world in those days was a very much smaller place than it is to-day. "Abroad," used in the sense in which it is employed in the New Testament, merely means throughout the countryside and does not refer to other nations outside Palestine. In any case Christ could have been referring only to Egypt, Syria and possibly Rome itself, which at that time was certainly in need of some form of religious revival, and it is inconceivable that He would say the same to-day. His teaching was based entirely upon peace and goodwill, love and charity, tolerance above all things, and what we call to-day common horse-sense. He hated pomp and show of any kind and He had time to spare for every sinner and backslider. The only types for which He had no use whatsoever were the intolerant, the Pharisee and the hypocrite. This was His teaching, and what have we Christians made of it during nineteen hundred odd years? More people have suffered death and the tortures of the damned in the name of the Christian faith than from any other cause—the brutalities of the Crusades, the burning of Joan of Arc, the Inquisition, the wholesale massacre of the inhabitants of Mexico and Peru, St. Bartholomew's Eve, the executions ordered by Queen Mary and Queen Elizabeth, the religious intolerance of Ireland, Pogroms of Jews in Russia and Poland, the Kikuyu Controversy, and last but not least the unseemly fights in the Churches of the Holy Sepulchre and the Nativity in Jerusalem and Bethlehem where Christian priests, squalling like cats, rend each other's vestments, tear down sacred emblems, and are whipped into order by Mahommedan police ! Does it not savour somewhat of hypocrisy that we should endeavour to teach Mahommedans a religion the correct interpretation of which we have been unable to decide for ourselves in nearly two thousand years?

CHAPTER XI

THE WADI GEDEIRAT

Build to-day, then, strong and sure,
With a firm and ample base ;
And ascending and secure
Shall to-morrow find a place.

LONGFELLOW.

SOME sixty-four miles south of El Arish in the rugged
limestone hills on the Sinai–Palestine frontier there
is a small stream of water that rises at the narrowest part
of a deep valley and flows along a gravelly bed before it
gradually soaks away into the ground as is the habit of
desert springs. At least this was the condition of the
valley when I first visited it in 1922, but since then things
have altered somewhat.

The desert in which the stream rises is particularly
harsh and forbidding for it is a country of precipitous
and broken mountains, rising from gravelly uplands, and,
except for twisted and stunted scrub growth in the valleys,
entirely devoid of vegetation. The limestone ranges that
rise from the plain are in process of disintegration, owing
to the high winds that are a constant feature of this part
of Sinai ; and the sand-storms that blow with great violence
in the early spring have scoured away the loose soil from
the hillsides, causing sudden cliffs and jutting crags that
stand out white and polished against the pale dun of the
surrounding country. It is not a land in which one
would expect water, but, owing to a catchment area some
thirty miles away to the north-east and a tilt in the strata
with a fissure in the rocks by Gedeirat, a spring fed by the

winter rains breaks to the surface in the rocky valley and
runs westward in the form of a small brook.

It is a matter of luck that this flow of perennial water
is in Sinai and not in Palestine, as, when the dispute with
Turkey over the Sinai frontier arose in 1906 and the
boundary was fixed by a commission of Turkish and
British officers, the Turks showed a marked desire so to
delineate the line that every well and spring within reasonable distance of the frontier came within their territory.
By the time they had worked up from Taba on the Gulf
of Akaba, however, their activity in examining the country
personally had become less and less, so that when Colonel
Owen, who knew of the existence of this spring, drew
the line of the boundary east of the Wadi Gedeirat the
Turks, imagining that nothing of interest existed in this
rough and precipitous waste, accepted it without inspection.
It is said that when they discovered later that they had
handed over one of the few reliable water supplies of this
desert, they adopted the attitude that the British commission had deliberately deceived them and thrown dust in
their eyes, which is something of a compliment, for it is
not easy to throw dust in the eyes of a Turk.

When I first saw the Wadi Gedeirat there were about
six acres of cultivated land which the local Arabs irrigated
by means of a small mud dam that they constructed every
year after the winter floods. The place, however, had a
bad name for fever, which was understandable, for every
little pool by the side of the stream was a squirming mass
of anopheles mosquito larvæ. Partly for this reason and
partly because the Arab has an ingrained loathing of
hard work, no attempt was made to extend the area of
cultivated land and practically all the water was, therefore,
allowed to run to waste in the sand of the desert. The
perennial water and the presence of corn attracted a number

of the desert partridges; the Chikor, which is found all over the Middle East, and the Heys, a smaller bird which is common in the Himalayas, and it was those desert partridges in large numbers that first attracted me.

One day whilst resting high on the hillside overlooking the valley after a hard morning's shoot, I noticed a big square mass of old masonry on the southern slope of the hill that was obviously an old Roman reservoir. It was filled to the top with silt and the sides had fallen away in places, so that previously I had imagined it was the ruins of a large building, but from my position above I now saw it for what it was, a stone water-tank. The question then arose as to how the Romans managed to fill it as it was nearly fifty feet above the level of the valley. Gradually as my eyes got used to the uniform greyish-yellow of the limestone rocks I traced the line of the ancient water-course that had brought water to the reservoir a thousand years ago and, following it up on foot, I came at the head of the valley to the remains of the dam that had at one time raised the level of the stream.

I then climbed the high hillside again, and knowing what I had to look for, I managed to pick out in the tumbled mass of boulders the whole system of the Roman irrigation with its side channels, the outline of fallen orchard walls and the rows of scattered stones on the steep slopes that at one time had been terracing for fruit trees. A trained archæologist would, of course, have seen all this in a glance, but to the ordinary man it is not easy to decide if a row of boulders is merely a freak of nature or the ruins of some building.

It then occurred to me that it would be most interesting and fascinating, not to say useful, to reconstruct in some way the old Roman system of irrigation that thirteen hundred years ago had provided a livelihood for a village of a thousand inhabitants or so. The need for something of the sort was apparent, for the Arabs of this area depend for their existence on rain crop barley which is only a definite success once in five years, and to say that they live always in a state of semi-starvation is no exaggeration. If they were provided with an irrigation system that would enable them to make certain of their winter barley, and to grow also a summer crop of maize or millet, it would constitute a very definite bettering of their lot, though whether this peculiar people would appreciate efforts on their behalf was another matter.

It was easy to understand how this fertile and intensively cultivated valley had gradually returned to its original state, with the stream in the centre cutting out a deep channel below the level of the land and ultimately running to waste in the sand. During the later Roman period, between the third and sixth centuries A.D. there had been a wave of prosperity in the Middle East and settlers from the cultivated lands of Palestine and Syria, and possibly also time-expired soldiers of the Roman Empire, had taken up land in the barren areas south of Beersheba and Gaza, exploiting the existing water supplies to their fullest extent and building small townships on the cultivated sites. Then had come the Arab invasion of the seventh century with the occupation of these areas by nomad Beduin from Arabia, and this prosperous civilization was swept away. In all probability these desert townships, of which Gedeirat was one, hung on for many years after the invasion, but there was no strong central government to protect them from raiding nomads; their markets for produce ceased to exist; and enterprise and initiative died out as it always does under Arab rule. Gradually the irrigation systems began to disintegrate, the grazing animals of the nomad broke through the orchard walls and destroyed the trees, until finally the surviving inhabitants evacuated the ruins or died out, and the sites returned gradually to their state of hopeless desert.

I have no dislike of the deserts. I have lived in them for eighteen years and can appreciate their vastness, the purity of the keen air, their beauty at dawn and sunset and their wonderful star-lit nights. At the same time, I see no reason why a desert should be allowed to remain a desert if it can be turned into anything else ; and a desert that was once a cultivated land is in my opinion a reproach if not " unto Israel " at least unto the man responsible for it. This being the case I felt that something must be done about Gedeirat, and on our return to El Arish that evening by car I discussed it with my wife, pointing out at the same time the impossibility of accomplishing anything owing to the lack of funds and the unlikelihood of obtaining them. Wives always encourage husbands to go ahead with their pet hobbies as it keeps them quiet and contented, and the female brain is much quicker and more fertile than the male variety, and, incidentally, a little less scrupulous. She reminded me that there was £700 in the budget of Sinai for anti-malaria work, and what better place for its expenditure than the Wadi Gedeirat, where mosquitoes swarmed in clouds and malaria was rampant.

One of the peculiarities of the Egyptian Government is that, although it allows mosquito-breeding swamps to exist in every depression in the fields outside the chief cities, and particularly by the side of the railway embankments, it willingly grants hundreds of pounds for the removal of some small swamp in the desert that might infect with malaria a section of a Beduin tribe if it were foolish enough to camp in the vicinity. As a matter of fact, it is always foolish enough to do so, for proximity to drinking water is of more importance than health and, moreover, the Beduin so far has been unable to bring himself to believe in Sir Ronald Ross's theory of the malaria-carrying mosquito. It is absurd to credit a fairy story of this description, for it is a recognized fact in instructed Arab circles that malaria is caused by eating unripe dates.

As the Wadi Gedeirat clearly came within the category of a mosquito-breeding haunt, and, as the construction of a dam at the head of the valley would hold the water back and prevent the formation of isolated pools below, I decided to put the work in hand and kill two birds with one stone. The dam after all was the only possible method of dealing with the water and checking its flow, and one could easily cope with the mosquito larvæ in the big pond that would form by the introduction of that jolly little Egyptian fish, the Bolti. The Bolti, as far as I can see, belongs to the perch tribe, for he has lateral dark stripes down his sides and a prickly dorsal fin, and he will thrive and reproduce his species to an extraordinary extent in almost any type of water. It matters not a jot to him if it is definitely saline, slightly brackish or perfectly fresh, for he is most accommodating and, immediately after his introduction to a stream or pool, he makes himself at home and proceeds to breed to such an extent that in a few short months the water is a moving mass of small fry. The fry, which are in a constant state of ravenous hunger, work their way up into the grassy fringes of the pools and round the stems of the reeds and rushes, so that it takes a most redoubtable mosquito larva to escape their attentions. I had enlisted the services of the Bolti fish in other and more difficult areas, and I knew that I could rely on him to play his part.

The dam was constructed by Haj Ali, the government

mason at El Arish, and when the history of the Turkish Empire is written and their misdeeds during the Great War recounted, it should be placed on record, and to their credit, that after their invasion of Sinai in 1915 they left Haj Ali behind them. He had been conscripted in his home town of Tripoli and in due course had found himself on the Sinai front, where he worked as a mason on the various water supplies that the invading Turks constructed in the desert. During their hurried retreat from Murray's advance in 1916 Haj Ali was overlooked and left behind and, being an Arab by birth, was taken on at the conclusion of the war by the Egyptian Government as chief mason and builder. Good masons are not uncommon in the East, but Haj Ali's great attribute lay in the fact that he was willing to work " with worn-out tools," and if, for instance, only one sack of cement was available on some isolated job in the desert, instead of the three for which he had indented, he attempted to make it do by manufacturing home-made lime on the spot, or employing some workable make-shift. Such men occur but rarely in the East or elsewhere in the world, and so Haj Ali's name should be writ large upon the scroll of those who served and served well. As a matter of actual fact he holds the same view himself, for on every bridge, culvert and dam he has constructed in Sinai one finds scratched in the cement an Arabic date and under it

حج علي (Haj Ali).

On the whole he is quite a modest, unassuming man, but he does not like anyone else to take credit for his work.

The dam was built from ready-cut blocks of limestone which the Turkish masons had left behind them at Kosseima, where they contemplated building a railway station. Having the stone ready at hand effected a great economy and the actual construction only cost about £150 of the £700 at my disposal. To celebrate its completion and its filling with water the workmen under Haj Ali were treated to a sheep—a form of *backsheesh* that is expected in the East, and which can be put to good account, because, although the actual animal only costs from thirty shillings to two pounds, one can get twice that value in work out of the gang by promising it on condition that the job is finished in some specific period. I have often wished when undertaking a construction in England that one could obtain the same results with this quite inexpensive animal. According to time-honoured custom, the dam was smeared with the blood of the slaughtered sheep—a proceeding which invariably brings good luck and the blessing of Allah in its train.

When the dam filled up as it did in a day and a half a huge pond a hundred yards long and thirty wide was created, which was entirely satisfactory, but what was not quite so satisfactory was the discovery that the barrier was not absolutely water-tight. I consoled myself by the reminder that even the Assuan dam has a certain amount of seepage, but as something like one-sixth of my supply of water was finding its way through the coarse gravel beneath the concrete foundations, I imagine that my loss was considerably greater in ratio than that experienced on the Nile at Assuan. Haj Ali, who viewed the seepage as a blot on his escutcheon, rose to the occasion by constructing a second and much lower dam some fifty yards below the first, and from this led the escaping water into the big channels that ran from the dam to the reservoirs, so that by this means we harnessed the whole flow of the stream.

The reactions of the local Beduin towards the work

were puzzling. When appealed to they expressed the most fervent gratitude for the efforts of the government, but underlying this flow of praise one could detect a certain uneasiness at this activity in the heart of their beloved desert. This stream of water that the government had secured and harnessed must mean a change, and all change is abhorrent to the nomad. Also there were misgivings that it might mean additional manual labour, and that is a serious matter. This was the general outlook, but one or two of them with more initiative saw possibilities of increased prosperity and one day a funny little man, all eyes and beard, asked me if iron pipes would be of any value in the work. On hearing that they would be the greatest possible boon he said:

"When the Turkish Army was here they led this water in big iron pipes to Dheiga, fifteen miles away. After the war a Jewish contractor bought these pipes from the Egyptian Government and he covenanted with the Arabs to dig them up and bring them in by camel to the railway at El Arish. I myself was one of the Arabs who worked for him. The work was hard and the payment poor, for the Jew was ever a hard man, so when we became weary we reported that the work was completed and all the pipes delivered. This was a false statement, for we left behind three miles of these pipes that are still in the ground."

Although the little Arab had lied to the Jewish contractor he was not lying to me, for on investigation I found things as he stated, and some two feet below the surface at the spot indicated were nearly three miles of excellent eight-inch cast-iron piping, and this wonderful find, worth anything from £800 to £1,000, put the Wadi Gedeirat reconstruction scheme with its insufficient financial backing firmly on its feet. It was possible by employing the pipes not only to run the water from the dam to the reservoir without loss by soakage, but also to carry subsidiary channels across gorges to good land beyond and to extend the irrigation system half a mile below the reservoir.

The reservoir was then cleaned of the silt of ages, which filled it to the brim, and the old Roman plaster lining, which had fallen away in patches, was stripped off and a layer of twentieth-century concrete substituted. The concrete was later faced with a lining of cement and " Pudlo," a patent water-proofing mixture, and the reservoir was ready for the flow from the stream and probably far more water-tight than when the Byzantines constructed it somewhere about the third century A.D. I felt something of a Philistine when I lined a sixteen-hundred-year-old construction of vast cut stones with the prosaic and unpleasant-coloured concrete of to-day, but I consoled myself with the thought of the acres of dun-coloured desert that would become green as the result.

The reservoir, which was twenty-five yards square and ten feet deep, took a day to fill, and when I saw the enormous store of water I was nervous that the old masonry, after centuries of neglect, would not stand the strain. Water-engineering when one is not a water-engineer by profession is full of surprises, and only recently I had constructed a stone reservoir in El Arish for the town supply which, after an imposing and successful opening ceremony, had carried on the good work by opening up itself. The first warning we had of the disaster was a stream of water flowing through the village by night, entering the houses and washing the people out of their beds. Water, however, is so popular and so esteemed in desert areas that, like kings, it can do no wrong, and a *contretemps* of this description, which would cause intense irritation in England and letters of complaint to the Rural District Council, was regarded in El Arish as a welcome and pleasing visitation.

The reservoir at Gedeirat, however, had been built by the Romans, a race who apparently never suffered from parsimonious Headquarters, and it stood firm under the enormous pressure and not one crack in the masonry opened up. From the outflow pipes cement channels were led in various directions across the valley floor and, immediately the water began to flow to the fields, a gang of prisoners was sent down from El Arish prison to rebuild the orchard walls that had fallen into disrepair centuries before. Last but not least, with the few remaining pounds left over from the original £700 grant for anti-malaria purposes, the old stream bed was filled in to remove larvæ breeding pools and both the reservoir and the dam were stocked with the inimitable Bolti fish.

* * * * *

Years of tuition and careful training has caused my conscience to become both accommodating and open to reason, and, although the original aim and object of the scheme had been the re-creation of a Roman agricultural colony, I persuaded myself that if one had undertaken the freeing of this fever-stricken valley of its pests and nothing else the method adopted would have been very similar to that which I had used. A stream a mile long could never have been kept clear of larvæ as, though they will not thrive in fast-running water, every camel passing by the brook leaves a deep footprint that immediately fills with water, and a camel's footprint appears to comprise all the necessary qualifications for a thoroughly successful mosquito hatchery. The only possible thing to do would be to dam up the water and control its outlet, and the best method of controlling its outlet would be to use it up for agriculture.

The obvious and simplest solution of a difficulty of this description would appear to be the employment of a man who inspects the water-logged area every day and fills with sand all the pools that have formed, but this system definitely does not work in Egypt. There are two reasons for this, one being that if a man is given a permanent job that necessitates eight hours' hard work a day he will perform it satisfactorily, if it only requires four hours the work will be patchy and oft neglected, and should it only demand half an hour of his time *per diem*, then it is obvious that it is so unimportant nothing need be done about it and the labourer sleeps away the hours of daylight in unbroken slumber. The other reason is that no one will believe that the little wriggling brown worm that lives in water is really a mosquito—it is an insult to an Oriental intelligence to suggest such a thing—and so the jolly little larvæ are left to grow to maturity and spread disease.

I remember once when undertaking the draining of a swamp in Sinai I was given the services of what is called in Egypt a Health *Sol*. The actual meaning of the word *Sol* is Sergeant-Major or Warrant-officer, and a Health *Sol* is therefore a Sanitary Inspector with a military flavour. The military flavour is necessary in Egypt, where a Sanitary Inspector, interfering with age-old customs that date back to the Pharaohs, such as throwing dead dogs and manure into the village water supply or using the back of the mosque as a latrine, is apt to raise resentment from the justly incensed population, and he is therefore given a uniform and senior military rank to enable him to carry out his unpleasant task without risk of physical violence.

This particular *Sol*, who was also an anti-malaria expert,

was given some twenty labourers to carry out the drainage scheme and in due course reported the task finished. I went down to inspect and at first sight the work looked excellent, for a deep ditch carried off the marsh water to a large sand-dune that completely absorbed it and several subsidiary channels led into the main drain from both sides.

"All work completed, Saaht el Bey," said the Health *Sol*, saluting smartly. "The drains are very excellent and no more mosquito."

I walked along with the *Sol* to examine the work more closely and I noticed that the main drain had a small notice-board on it that read "King Fuad Drain." I was not certain if his Egyptian Majesty would appreciate the honour of having a swamp drain called after him, but it is after all intention that really matters in this world.

A second drain was called after the Director-General and a third—a very shallow insignificant one—after me. One is naturally interested in one's godchildren, so I inspected my own drain closely and found to my horror that, owing to the fact that there was practically no flow of water, the small trickle at the bottom was a moving mass of mosquito larvæ. I then looked at the drains of the Director-General and His Majesty and discovered that they were in an even worse condition than mine. In other words, the Health *Sol*, by digging his little drains that refused to run, had created far more breeding haunts for mosquitoes than had been the case when the marsh was lying in its virgin state.

The *Sol*, when this was pointed out to him, at first refused to see the mosquitoes, but when I ladled fifty or so into the palm of his hand he had to admit he noticed something. He was disconcerted for a moment, but it is difficult, if not impossible, to disturb Egyptian official complacency for any length of time.

" Oh," he said delightedly, " but they are not anopheles but only culex, and I was draining the marsh to free it from anopheles only."

Of course it is the anopheles variety that causes malaria, the culex being only capable of infecting one with elephantiasis, but my friend had quite ignored the fact that a breeding haunt for one species will do equally well for the other. However, I offer no explanation of the occurrence for so frequently in Egypt one meets the inexplicable, chiefly in the minds and outlook of the minor official, and as my friend seemed entirely satisfied with his work, I sent him back to his beloved Cairo the next day, and with the small amount of money left unexpended filled in his drains again.

One other episode of this nature, proving that the Egyptian eye will not see the mosquito larva, concerns the small frontier police post of Kosseima. Here until a small swamp was drained malignant malaria was common, but with the removal of the marsh the post was free from the disease for several years until it broke out again with six cases of fever in a month. The sergeant in charge was a recognized expert on anti-malaria work, and he had with him at the post a trained Tamurgi (a dispenser with military rank), also a man with experience of mosquito fighting. I therefore sent an Egyptian doctor to inspect, but he also failed to find any reason for the recurrence of the disease. I then went down myself and was taken round by the sergeant, who explained to me volubly that he had examined every inch of ground in the vicinity without finding a trace of water, and this was correct, for the marsh itself was completely dry. Just behind the police barracks, however, there was a small cement reservoir used for watering a plot of garden should the police feel sufficiently energetic to raise a few vegetables. Unfortunately the particular post on duty at the time were not horticulturally minded, and no garden existed, with the result that the tank had been left half full of water for some six months or more, and no one had taken the trouble to look over the wall. The two feet of stagnant green water at the bottom was so packed with anopheles larvæ that it was almost too thick to run through the outlet pipe, and it is no exaggeration to say that sufficient mosquitoes had been hatching out every night to infect every living soul in the Nile Valley with malaria.

Here again it was difficult to find an explanation, but twenty years in the East has enabled me to follow the workings of the Oriental mind a certain distance, though I am not presumptuous enough to pretend I can go all the way. The theory in the episode, I think, was based on the fact that the mosquito being a product of the wild breeds only in pools provided by nature, and that the insect should be so lost to all sense of decency and right feeling as to hatch out in a reservoir made by the hand of man for irrigation purposes was, of course, unthinkable. My reason for believing that this may be the explanation is based on another mysterious mosquito plague that occurred at Tor, the Pilgrim Quarantine station in south Sinai. Here in rows of modern buildings the returning pilgrims from Mecca are detained for several days before being allowed to proceed northwards to Egypt, Palestine and Syria—a very necessary precaution, as before the institution of the quarantine all the plagues of the East were spread over the Mohammedan world annually by this intermingling of races from every part of the world in the home town of the Prophet Mohammed.

Years previously I had been given a grant to clear up a series of mosquito hatching pools to the north of the town, and this was carried out so successfully than the

Radwan and two barracouta of forty and thirty-five pounds
Mullet jumping into net barrier placed across inlet to Bardawil Lake

[*See page* 216]

The Wadi Gedeirat, ten years ago, when the work had started. The first
irrigation channel shows in the front of the picture
A garden in the Wadi Gedeirat five years after the trees were planted

[See page 272]

ponds completely disappeared. Then suddenly an accusation was made that my staff were neglectful as the mosquito had returned in large numbers. The Department of Public Health accused me, so I accused my man, the Mamour (local Police Officer) at Tor, and he accused the head of the gang in charge of the clearing operations. Who this gentleman accused and abused I do not know, but, after some bitter recriminations and any amount of hurt feelings, the Quarantine people made a complete recantation by admitting very reluctantly that they had forgotten to empty the cisterns in their various buildings after the last pilgrimage season, and that they were hatching out their own mosquitoes in these receptacles and turning them out in thousands on the spot. The mosquito does not figure very prominently here at home in England, but in the East he is a very potent and ever-present power of evil, and, among other things, has disturbed long-standing and happy *liaisons* between departments and shattered many a warm official friendship.

Here in England I must admit that the mosquito puzzles me as in my part of the world—the New Forest—he is almost as plentiful as in Egypt. Every little stagnant pool and every rain-water butt is full of larvæ in the late summer months, and there are always a large number of the winged insects flying about the house. I have frequently gone to bed and counted a dozen or more settled on the ceiling, yet I have never known a case of these mosquitoes biting.

They are, so far as I can see, of the culex variety, though I have once or twice seen anopheles, and the culex in Egypt, the south of France and elsewhere are most rapacious and inveterate bloodsuckers, so much so that if there is one in the room at night there is not the slightest possibility of sleep. Here in England one can turn in cheerfully

K

with a swarm dancing round the window-panes and all will be well.

I have heard people complain of being bitten by mosquitoes, but I feel very doubtful about it as they have never bitten me. I am not impervious to bites from insects, as the river midge frequently drives me mad when fishing the evening rise, the biting fly of the New Forest sends his bradawl through my socks as I sit on the lawn, and the bot, or horsefly, if he gets a chance, will give me a jab like a thrust from a stiletto, but my old enemy, the mosquito, seems to be a most benign and peaceful individual in this country.

I have been told that on the Sussex coast the mosquitoes are really a pest and that some people actually sleep under nets. One theory to explain this is that this particular mosquito was imported from the Baltic by timber ships that unloaded at Shoreham. He is probably the same species, the culex, but his upbringing has been on different lines.

* * * * *

Now that I had achieved my object by damming the stream, filling the reservoir of the Wadi Gedeirat and providing the irrigation channels, I imagined the heaviest and most difficult part of my work was over, which proved to be a vain thought, for I had quite overlooked the mentality of the Beduin Arab and his natural cussedness. With the enthusiasm of the agriculturist I had counted on the local landowners hailing the completion of the irrigation works with pæans of joy, and in my mind's eye had seen them rush to their ploughs and mattocks to take advantage of the flowing water on the land, but nothing of the sort occurred. Instead there was a series of idiotic and childish squabbles based on every conceivable form of petty obstruction. Some plots, it appeared, were shared by three or more brothers and cousins, and, though one half wished to plough and sow seed, the other half refused to agree; others were owned by some man who had not been seen for several years and his agent or nearest relative was afraid to do anything; others, again, were mortgaged and neither the mortgagor nor the mortgagee could be found; and in several cases individuals not only refused to do any cultivation themselves, but also prevented the water flowing through their land for the benefit of others below. In other words, my work on behalf of the local Arabs, so far from meeting with approval, had caused the utmost antagonism and obstruction.

I went down to Gedeirat as often as I could find time to try and smooth over the various difficulties that cropped up like mushrooms whenever I had turned my back, and then discovered that the whole of the obstruction was being created by one man, an evil, saturnine-looking creature called Obeid. He himself had a very considerable share in several of the plots watered by the reservoir and had got into his muddled Arab head that the scheme had been originated by the government with the idea of eventually depriving the Beduin of their lands. He had, therefore, worked upon the feelings of the tribesmen so successfully that every move I made was cleverly countered by Arab obstruction, and Arab obstruction is very ingenious and very difficult to overcome, because one is allowed to arrive at a solution amid murmurs of what passes as universal approval only to find that fresh barriers and difficulties have arisen overnight.

I finally went down in what might be called a nasty frame of mind with the idea of either settling the trouble for good, or estreating the land from the Arabs at a valuation and selling it to the inhabitants of El Arish, who were only too willing to take it over. We had a heated meeting that unfortunately for Obeid took place on the edge of the reservoir, which was brimful of unused water. I may also add that it was a bitterly cold day with a biting wind from the south-east. The arguments had been going on for some time, consisting of silly recriminations between various landowners, and then Obeid came forward to harangue the people and he went a little too far, making a remark that just overstepped the limit allowed to public speakers. I noticed that he was right on the brink of the reservoir at that moment, so took a sudden pace forward in his direction and, as I expected and hoped, he jumped back, going head over heels into the icy water, where with his big black goatskin *abayah* spread out on the surface he flopped and squalled like an old wet hen. This not only finished Obeid and his machinations, but also settled the Wadi Gedeirat troubles for all time. Ridicule is the most deadly weapon one can use in the East, and Obeid having made himself a figure of fun at a moment when he thought he was at his best, swaying the multitude with his oratory, the meeting broke up with roars of laughter. Obeid was dragged out of the water by the police and, getting on his camel, rode off in a huff to other lands of his in south Palestine and was not seen in Gedeirat again for many years, by which time the whole valley had come under cultivation.

The first thing I undertook was the construction of a government garden, in which it would be possible to grow everything in the way it should be grown with the idea of providing an object lesson. This, I learned by experience, was of little value because, the Arab argues, cheerfully and complacently, that of course the government can succeed because it has knowledge, labour and resources behind it, whereas he, lacking everything, can therefore accomplish nothing—a typical Beduin attitude which is most difficult to overcome.

In the government garden, assisted by the very able henchmen of Mr. Brown of the Horticultural Department, we planted olives of every variety from every country, oranges, grape-fruit, plums, peaches, apricots, figs, lemons, and last but not least, vines. I had expected many unforeseen drawbacks, for the desert is a harsh and unforgiving task-mistress and keeps many trump cards up her sleeve, such as unexpected diseases and plagues, and frequently an underlying layer of salt that after irrigation rises to the surface like hoar-frost and destroys all growth. Wadi Gedeirat, however, was not real virgin soil, for it had been most fruitful in the past and merely required the minimum of cultivation to produce unexpected results. The olives made the most prolific growth, attaining the height of over twelve feet in their third year and yielding two bushels of fruit in their fourth, whilst the vines were exceptional in every way, for not only did they produce the most remarkable quantity of grapes, but their flavour was finer than anything grown in Egypt. In fact, everything succeeded beyond my most sanguine expectations with the exception of the orange and the grape-fruit, their yield and growth being below the average, because apparently the citrus family require a certain humidity in the air which the high desert lacks.

Among other things I experimented with was asparagus, which had already proved a success both in El Arish and my previous station, the Oasis of Kharga, but in the Wadi Gedeirat the growth of this vegetable was phenomenal in every way. Not only did the plants arrive at maturity in twelve months, but the shoots were equal in size to those giant growths that one finds in tins emanating from California, and combined with their size all the succulence of the British-grown variety, which is lacking in the huge Californian product. This, however, was an entirely private enterprise, for I realized that much water must flow beneath Kasr-el-Nil bridge before the desert Beduin would produce in large quantities for the Cairo and Jerusalem markets an expensive vegetable, of which they had never heard and which they regarded as not only useless but as a subject for ribald laughter.

I found as I expected that orchard planting with a race that have no conception of any growth beyond barley and the desert fig was going to be no easy task and, after a few experiences of Beduin husbandry, I accepted the situation and laid out their gardens for them with skilled labour from El Arish. I shall never forget the first Beduin " garden " I saw in Gedeirat. It was about an acre of land just below the dam, so had a constant supply of water, and the soil was rich with the accumulated silt of ages. It was, however, full of rushes and a spiny scrub growth rather resembling a straggling thistle. The little Arab who owned the plot had taken an interest in the reclamation work from the start, and was in fact the informant who had put me on to the buried pipe line. When the fruit trees arrived from the Horticultural Department he was the first to apply for some, but his efforts to plant them were pathetically inefficient. He had not troubled to remove any of the dense mass of undergrowth in his plot; the trees were planted so that though the centre of the roots was inserted in a hole the important parts, the ends, were sticking up in a fringe all round; and most of his water channels ran uphill. The Nile Valley *fellah* and the cultivator from El Arish have a most wonderful natural eye for levels, and will run a water channel a distance of two hundred yards or so that is correct to an inch, but the poor haphazard old Beduin, with his age-old contempt for agriculture, created irrigation systems that suggested the efforts of children on a sandy shore at home.

Even when the whole valley had come under cultivation and the Beduin were reaping the results of their labours one struck some queer cases of racial cussedness. One man who had a particularly nice little plot of an acre refused to do anything to it until he was warned that, if it was not under cultivation within a week, it would be sold to someone else. He thereupon turned the water's full force on to the land one evening and left it running across it all night, with the result that the next morning the plot was gone. The swift-flowing water had eaten away great chasms some six feet deep into the soft loamy soil and the raw boulders of the old watercourse were sticking up out of the scored-out desolation in all directions. This is rather typical of the Beduin, who is a vindictive man, and his attitude is that " if I do not wish to use my land no one else shall." This primitive desire to hang on to one's quite useless possessions at all costs regardless of whether they can be put to any use, and the enhanced value they obtain immediately anyone else wants them, is apparent in all small children, and the mentality of the Beduin is very similar to that of a child.

On the other side of the picture was the enthusiasm of the government blacksmith who was working in the valley laying the pipe line. He suggested a subsidiary pipe line with a syphon running across a deep gorge to a small plot on a high point some distance away. It seemed to me that the small area that could be irrigated was hardly worth the expense of the pipe line, but he was most emphatic in pointing out that it was. According to him, it had the richest soil in the valley and was well worth the expense.

"It was a Roman garden once," he explained, "the walls of it merely need rebuilding and when I get the pipe to yonder point the water will run in the channel that the Romans made. The Beduin who owns that land will do well."

It was so refreshing to find a congenial spirit showing interest and enthusiasm that I agreed to the extension, but omitted to ask the name of the lucky Beduin land-owner. It transpired when the work was completed that half of it belonged to the blacksmith himself, and he had acquired it by the simple method of arranging beforehand that the landowner should give him half if he should be able to persuade me to agree to the pipe extension. This may sound very irregular, but in the East little " rake-offs " of this description add spice to existence and are considered as quite correct and above-board. The only weak spot in these little ramps is that the perpetrator always imagines fondly that he has thrown dust in one's eyes whereas once one has grasped the lines on which the Arab mind works most of their little devices are plainly apparent and, in the few cases where they are not, there are a whole army of people ready to give the intrigues away, for there is no such thing as secrecy in the Arab world.

Actually one had to close one's eyes to more or less shady methods of acquiring land in the valley owing to the peculiarity of the Arab character. He is a backward man and most conservative and he cannot be driven, neither can he be led, but he can be coaxed in the right direction by the employment of wiles and devices, or what might be called ju-jitsu methods. My idea was to get the whole valley cultivated with olives and vines at any cost, as once it had come into full bearing I hoped that the scheme would carry on of its own accord, but the difficulty was to get the Arabs sufficiently interested to perform the necessary hard labour of planting, watering and weeding during the preliminary period before there was any return.

The Arab has a natural aversion to anything that is open and above-board and plain sailing. If a man had a plot of land right on the main supply of the irrigation channel it was too easy and his efforts lacked both enthusiasm and initiative, but, if by any chance he could acquire the land of someone else by Arab guile and trickery, this added the spice of chicanery to the work and he would show the greatest industry and keenness on a plot of this description.

This side of the Arab character I had grasped years ago over the question of tomato culture in the El Arish district. The northern part of the Peninsula supplies a large number of tomatoes to Egypt and Palestine, but in the past the price fetched was very low owing to the fact that the local tomatoes were of such inferior strain and so very wrinkled and misshapen. I bought quantities of first-class tomato seed and issued it free with exhortations, but my efforts were treated with lethargy and silent contempt and then my old Turkish gardener said: " If you want to get the people to grow those fine tomatoes of ours you should not ask them to do so. You want to make an order saying that these tomatoes are reserved for *bashawat* (pashas) and *nas kobar* (upper class) only and any Arishy found growing them will be severely punished. If you do this no man will be happy till he has acquired the seed."

I did not actually make such an edict as all my Province Orders had to go to Cairo for approval and a command of this description might have been misunderstood, but I let it be known generally that no seed was to be issued to the people in future in any circumstances. This had an instantaneous and most invigorating effect and my old gardener spent nearly all his time smuggling small packets over the garden wall with his fingers on his lips. " *Wallahi*, here is a parcel of the seed," in a hoarse whisper. " But on your life say nothing to anyone, for if the Bey hears I have given this away he will discharge me from the service. And when I say ' given away ' I speak with reservations for the risk I run is great. Let us say three piastres." By these underhand ruses we disposed of many ounces of " Toogood's Superb " and now the whole of the crop produced in north Sinai is of this variety and none other. The cream of the joke was my old gardener's keen delight in being able to deceive and throw dust in the eyes of his own people, making three piastres over every shady deal, though this part of the performance he imagined was unknown to me.

" Sixteen packets I disposed of to-day," he would say with glee, " and I tell every man that he will receive a year's imprisonment if he is detected."

An amusing episode of a similar nature occurred over a plot of very rich land that lay above the dam. In Roman days the water level had been slightly higher, but this particular little lot of three acres now lay too high to be irrigated by gravitation. As it was exceptionally rich soil I put in a ram, one of those queer contrivances that employs the force of water on a drop to send up a matter of one-eighth of the supply to almost any height. I have never been able to understand quite what the principle is and so it is small wonder that the Arabs failed to grasp it.

One of these rams was installed in the stream bed above the dam and all the Arabs were collected to see it installed and watch it at work. When the mechanism began to operate with a steady tick-tock of its internal works and the water spurting out of the pipe, there were deep-throated " Allah's " presumably of satisfaction, and

I hoped that with the new supply of water these three acres of fallow land would immediately come into cultivation. Nothing of the sort occurred, however, and it then transpired after many lies and evasions that the machine was an evil and godless contrivance, for as it consumed neither oil nor petrol it must be worked by a devil.

As everybody avoided the ram and its water supply it eventually clogged up with dirt through neglect and a mechanic was sent down from El Arish to clean it. He initiated into its mysteries the little Arab who had found the pipe line and who by this time was becoming a most intelligent cultivator and rapidly rising in the social scale. He realized when he looked inside the ram that it was in reality a most simple contrivance, quite devoid of all devils and evil machinations of any kind, and suggested that for a very small sum each month he would look after it and keep it in order. The offer was accepted and unto this day the little Arab, who is now known as Willie, keeps the ram free from dirt with the aid of a large and rusty spanner which he keeps in his tool-box—a big scrub bush—and it is not only his monthly pay that causes him to maintain the machine in such excellent working order for the fact of the matter is he is now owner of all the land watered by it. As he explains with a satisfied grin, he bought it up cheap during the period when the actual landlord was afraid to go anywhere near the place because of the evil spirit who lived inside the ram. "*Wallahi*, these Beduin, being ignorant, will believe anything, but," proudly, "I am a mechanic and of course I knew that no devil existed—but merely a clever idea of the *Frangis*."

I started the Gedeirat irrigation scheme in 1926, so that when I left Sinai in 1936 it had been in existence for ten years, and some three hundred acres had come into cultivation with hundreds of olive trees in full bearing and several thousands more in varying stages of growth. The saying that Rome was not built in a day applied very much to a scheme of this description, for, as I expected, there was no real enthusiasm for the work until the first Beduin had marketed his crop of olives and turned the cash proceeds over wonderingly in his palm. Then, when it transpired that there was really money to be made over these queer bitter fruits, every man proceeded to extend his plot, and to level off fresh desert land until finally one found irrigated orchards a mile away from the dam at the head of the stream. This when I left Sinai was the extreme limit that the small stream could supply, though in course of time, if the Beduin devote all the water to trees and cut out irrigated cornland—and they are very partial to the maize they grow in the summer months—the flow will be sufficient for double the area that is at present planted with olives and vines.

When one considers the vast irrigation works of the Middle East, such as the Assuan dam and the reclamation of the Lake Hule district in Palestine, the little Wadi Gedeirat with its gardens is of no importance whatsoever and pales to comparative insignificance. Its only claim to notice lies in the fact that it is one instance of settling the Beduin nomad on the land and thereby providing him with a sufficiency of food; and it is the first attempt to reconstruct the many disused irrigation systems of the late Romans in this part of the desert.

My efforts were not entirely altruistic, for one gets an enormous kick out of defeating the desert, and there is far more satisfaction to be obtained from half a dozen olive trees one has forced to grow where nothing grew before than from a wonderful rock garden one has created in England from plants supplied by the nurseryman. The Wadi Gedeirat was a constant source of interest and delight, for it is a most inspiring sight to see groves of trees where previously there was only rocky barren desert, and the effort was highly spiced by the fact that nothing was easy as the desert does not surrender its wastes willingly, neither does the Beduin become a cultivator without a stern struggle against enslavement.

At the back of my mind is the uneasy feeling that the experiment—though successful—has something of the nature of the child's watch in it. It goes splendidly so long as there is someone present to keep turning the key that sends the hands round. But what will happen if the motive force is withdrawn? My successor is a keen horticulturist and he has seen the scheme from its start as he was a regular communicant at my winter partridge shoots in the Wadi from its earliest days. All will be well so long as he is there in Sinai to turn the hands round. But when he is replaced by an Egyptian Governor, as is intended, I wonder if the propelling force will still be in existence. The dam may crack with a heavy flood, the fencing will wear, blight and insect pests will attack the trees, and waiting patiently outside the garden walls are those Philistines and iconoclasts of the cultivated world —the goats and camels of the Arabs. They are barred from the feast at present, but let there be one hint of slackening up—one short week of inattention—and the flocks and herds will be in, and the three hundred fertile acres will return to their original state of desolation, for there are only three strands of barbed wire to hold the fort.

* * * * * *

The success of the Gedeirat reclamation work justifies the hope that something may come of the Jewish proposal to start a settlement in what is called the Negev area of Southern Palestine. Negev is Hebrew for " south," and

I believe that when the scheme was suggested originally the idea was that the whole of the southern portion of Palestine from a line drawn north of Gaza to Beersheba should be included. The originators of this proposal appear to have been under the impression that the area was to all intents and purposes depopulated, and had over-looked the fact that in the northern portion of the Negev there is a large and virile population of settled cultivators in the villages and Beduin, both nomad and semi-nomad, living in the open country. It is not easy to arrive at the exact figure, but it may be taken as somewhere between 50,000 and 80,000, and also one must take into account the fact that the people of the town of Gaza are quite as fanatical and intolerant as those in Nablus and Hebron. The adding of this portion of the country to a Jewish state, therefore, would only increase the existing bitter-ness. It would also affect the real Beduin of the desert, and so far one might say that his interest in the Jew-Arab trouble in Palestine has been merely academic, for he has not come in actual contact with the Jewish settler. He hears a lot about the hard lot of his fellow-countryman, though he is by no means certain that the Palestine villager is a countryman of his, and a certain number of Beduin from Trans-Jordan and southern Palestine have gone into the troubled areas for a little amusement. Things are dull among the tribes now that raiding is frowned upon.

In the country beyond, however, that lying south of a line drawn through Auja and Beersheba, and bounded on the east by Trans-Jordan and on the west by Sinai—an area of some four thousand square miles—you have a stretch of wilderness that is almost entirely depopulated. I estimate that there are not more than a thousand Beduin living there to-day, and this is a generous estimate. These people, who scratch a patch of winter barley, burn a little charcoal, and graze a few goats and camels, are the poorer off-shoots of the big tribes. They live in a state of such penury and want, it is no exaggeration to say that they are perpetually on the brink of starvation.

The queer part about this barren country, which now cannot support a thousand Beduin, is that in the past, and not so very far back in the world's history, there was a thriving Roman settlement here with at least six big, stone-built towns each with a population of from five to ten thousand, and prosperous enough to support two or three churches and a monastery as well. In addition there are in these rough limestone mountains and deep valleys the ruins of many small hamlets and farmhouses, terracing along the hillsides for vines and olives, and a number of *harabas,* or underground cisterns, of great size, carved out of the natural rock. One way and another this district at a most conservative estimate must have supported a population of not less than fifty thousand people.

The suggestion of settling this area causes a considerable amount of antagonism from those people who say : " Nobody has managed to make anything of this country in the last thousand years, so what is the use of trying ? " or alternatively : " There are so many other areas in the world better worth developing that it is a waste of time and effort to spend money on so bare a country." For the people who make the first remark one might call attention to Raleigh's first attempt to settle people in Virginia. It was a most lamentable failure, but no one can say that the colonization of America has not been a success in the long run, for there are roughly two hundred and twenty million colonists there to-day who just manage to make both ends meet. To the second category of objectors one might say, the fact that there are better lands available elsewhere is not quite the point. The Jews, strangely enough, have a marked choice for Palestine as it happens to be the land of their origin.

It is admitted that Jewish settlers might find things easier in every way in Australia, Canada or one of the South American states, but the fact remains that they wish to create a state for themselves in Palestine and nowhere else, and moreover they have given already definite proof that they are willing to suffer hardship, penury and dangers provided they can live in the land from which their forebears came. One has only to look at the barren sandhills and malarious marshes that the Jews have won back to cultivation during the last few years to realize that the race have pioneers of the right type to eke out a living in the most unpropitious circumstances.

If therefore the Jews are anxious to tackle the particularly stiff proposition of re-creating the Negev, why throw cold water on the scheme at the start and try to prevent it? The Jews will find the capital so that no one will lose by it but themselves if it is a failure, and as the land to-day is practically depopulated and the Arabs themselves have done nothing towards reclaiming it in fifteen hundred years, it is a dog-in-the-manger policy to refuse to allow the Jews to make the attempt if they wish to do so.

There are various arguments against the prospect of success, and one is that the climate has changed and the rainfall is less. Against this is the considered opinion of all the geologists and surveyors who have worked in this area and who hold the opinion that the climate has not altered in any way in the last two thousand years. My personal opinion is that it has deteriorated slightly—say to the extent of one rainfall a year, and one rainfall at the right time may make much difference. However, my experience is based on eighteen years only and this is all too short a period in which to come to a definite conclusion. The Arabs say that the weather runs in cycles of thirty years, thirty wet followed by thirty dry, and we are just coming to the end of a dry period. This is corroborated by an old monk at the Monastery of St. Catherine in Sinai, who is said to be over a hundred years of age. He has seen two complete thirties and is drawing to the close of his third. From what I saw of him, he is likely to see several more, for there is nothing much to worry one up at this mountain monastery; no Air Raid Precautions and no income-tax returns to fill in.

Another theory is that the high winds have caused erosion of the soil and that the rich top spit of tilth ploughed by the Romans has been blown away by the wind, leaving the unfertile gravel beneath. This is a state of affairs that is causing trouble in the Middle West of the United States, in Canada and in some parts of Australia. So far as one can see, there never was much natural good soil for the wind to erode, and that the Romans obtained their tilth artificially by damming wadis and terracing hillsides to collect the deposit brought down by floods. That which has been lost can easily be regained, and in some parts of Sinai new terracing and dams have accumulated nearly a foot of rich silt in two years.

Then there is the view that this extensive settlement was caused by the convergence there of several big trade routes, and that the roads from Akaba, then Eloth and Suez, met at this spot on their way to the markets of the north. There is much in this view, but at the same time these extensive settlements lived on the crops and fruits they raised whatever may have been the original reason of their creation. The Jews of to-day ask very little. They do not expect to re-create old trade routes; the majority of them merely desire to exist and to live a life of peace without racial hate and interference.

The inhabitants of these now deserted towns: Auja, Rahieba, Khalasa, Abda, Esbeita and Kurnub, did not rely on wells for their water supply but on the rain water that they collected in these underground *harabas* and in surface reservoirs built of stone. Apparently these were sufficient for their requirements, and the cleaning out and repair of all these water catchment systems would not be a very great nor expensive undertaking. The infrequent wells and springs in the area are not very satisfactory; in some the water is fresh but in others it is definitely brackish. It should be borne in mind, however, that no attempt has been made to bore for artesian water south of Beersheba. The fact that there are natural springs rising to the surface in various parts such as Gedeirat, Kadies, Weiba and others proves that subterranean water exists, and if several good supplies are struck by means of deep bores the success of a settlement here is assured.

There is of course no question of a land flowing with milk and honey. It is a harsh country, but it can be tamed and softened; it is subjected to high winds and sandstorms, but belts of eucalyptus, casuarina and wattle will act as windbreaks; it is a hot country but it is dry and healthy. It will never be a great corn-producing area, neither will it be famous for its luscious fruits, but it is a country where land-starved Jews, deprived the right to exist elsewhere, will be able to live in peace and derive the satisfaction, the most complete satisfaction in the world, of turning a barren desert into a producing land.

Twelve years ago the Wadi Gedeirat in Sinai was in precisely the same state of hopeless desolation as these other towns in southern Palestine, and experiments there have proved that the soil is rich and that certain fruits and cereals will thrive and crop heavily. The result has been achieved with a race lacking all knowledge of cultivation and, one might say also, all desire to cultivate. If this could be done with Beduin, one may ask what might have been achieved with settlers possessing capital, experience and a definite incentive of winning a living for themselves and a home for their families.

The weak spot in all emigration schemes is home-sickness, and having suffered from it myself I know what it means. It is this longing for home that causes so many emigrants to lose heart and to feel a growing distaste for the new and barren country they are trying to open up. One wonders how many emigrants to Australia and Canada have thrown up the sponge from this cause and nothing else. With the Jewish emigrant this failing is entirely absent. There is no question of home-sickness when home means Germany where the Jew is denied all rights as a human being, Poland where pogroms may occur at any time, and Roumania where the return of the Fascists to power means terror to the Jewish race.

One last point in favour of this scheme for handing over the empty quarter of southern Palestine to the Jewish settlers is that, strategically and from the purely selfish point of view of the British Empire, a small wedge of Jewish territory between Arab Trans-Jordan and Egyptian Sinai with the port of Akaba included might be no bad thing. In time of war the inhabitants would be probably between the devil and the deep sea, but the Jew has lived for two thousand years with the devil on one side and the sea on the other that this will not act as a deterrent and he will survive.

The point is that a Jewish state would be in all probability a pro-British state—at any rate for some considerable time to come. Gratitude among nations is admittedly a very doubtful and unreliable quality, and one can put about as much reliance in gratitude as one can in any solemn pact or treaty made between two nations—in other words, none. Nations, however, do not forget wrongs quite as readily as they forget assistance and friendship, and there are certain big Powers in Europe for whom the Jews are unlikely to have any warm feelings in the future.

There has been and always will be a considerable amount of flirtation with the various Arab peoples on the part of potentates and dictators looking for expansion and world-power. Most of us will remember the ex-Kaiser's ardent and successful courtship of the Mid-Eastern Arabs in the days prior to the war, and now we learn that the real devout lover and true friend of the Arab race and the defender of the Muslim faith is none other than Mussolini of Italy. Judging by the photographs we see of his visits to Libya, the Libyan Arab appears to believe it, but of course one must make some allowance for the fact that the Arab is always polite and is a first-class actor on all occasions. The fact remains, however, that the Arab is definitely susceptible to advances if the advances are sufficiently ardent and convincing, and in time of war, or just prior to the outbreak of hostilities, they are all that and more.

CHAPTER XII

THE ROAD TO JERUSALEM

Had you seen this road before it was made,
You would lift both your hands and bless General Wade.
AN IRISH ENSIGN.

GOVERNMENTS on the whole are not vastly interested in deserts, nor are they particularly concerned about the state of the inhabitants providing they
behave themselves, so that there were seldom funds of
appreciable size for any public works in Sinai or the other
areas in which I served. The most important thing in
Sinai was, of course, the road across the Peninsula that
links Egypt with Palestine and incidentally Africa with
Asia and Europe; but the apathy shown towards the
project when I first mooted the suggestion was only
equalled by the lack of enthusiasm towards its improvement and maintenance some ten years later when it had
come into being.

Actually neither Palestine nor Egypt was interested in
the slightest degree in the scheme, in fact one might go
further and say that they were markedly hostile. In the
early days of the Mandate Palestine was definitely railway-
minded; a large overhead price had been paid for the
track constructed by the British Army in 1916 that runs
from Kantara on the Suez Canal to Lydda, with branches to
Jerusalem and Haifa, and the government was chiefly
exercised in its mind as to ways and means to make this
railway pay. This being the case, a road across Sinai
making a car-run from Cairo to Jerusalem a possibility

would be a definite blow to passenger traffic, and so
Palestine was apathetic and did little or nothing towards
the upkeep of their sector from the frontier at Kosseima
to Beersheba. They had every excuse for this as Egypt,
despite my harping upon the subject, took no interest
whatsoever in her sector that traversed Sinai.

Egypt's attitude towards the road was that it might offer
a line of escape to her tourists. In the halcyon pre-War
days a most useful, wealthy and easily satisfied class of
tourist used to visit the Nile Valley; they came every year
in their thousands, they had ample means, they wore
helmets with green veils, donned blue glasses on sunny or
sunless days, and they sat all day on the verandahs of the
various hotels with odd visits to the Pyramids and to the
Mouski, spending money freely all the time on gharries,
sham " antikas," dragomans and refreshments. They
were quite willing to stay " put " in Cairo or Luxor for
three of the winter months and they showed not the
slightest desire for a change. Egypt believes firmly that
these desirable tourists still exist and desires to bring them
back again to the fold, but the trouble is these tourists,
like so many other relics of Victorian and Edwardian days,
died during the war and we shall not look upon their like
again. They have been replaced by much more energetic
people who desire to see all there is to be seen under their
own steam if possible, and Egypt must reconcile herself to
the fact that the tourists who now make the journey to
Cairo will desire to see Jerusalem and Damascus also. A
road that will enable tourists to visit these places by car is
therefore an attraction, and, moreover, a track that provides
a means for departure can also be used for the purposes of
arrival. Until quite recently Egypt put the motorist who
used his car for a long run in much the same category as a
man who travelled on the railway without a ticket; he was

almost regarded as a malefactor and every difficulty was put in his way to prevent him travelling about the country in his own vehicle.

The opening up of the road across Sinai from the frontier near Auja in Palestine to Kubri, the ferry on the canal north of Suez, was not a task of very great magnitude. The Turks during their occupation of the Peninsula in the early stages of the war constructed a metalled highway from the Palestine border to Hassana in the centre of the Province. From Hassana a level plain of gravel intersected by small wadis, or dry water-courses, required very little work to provide a possible track on which one could average twenty-five miles an hour. This gravel plain extends for fifty miles and then the road enters the Mitla mountains, where it meets and follows the route of the Mecca pilgrims—the Wadi el Haj—along which in the past all the pilgrims from Egypt and farther west travelled on their journey to and from the Holy Cities of Arabia.

This age-old highway had been cleared of boulders and made up for camel traffic by various Sultans of Egypt who have interested themselves in the welfare of the pilgrims, and in the early part of the nineteenth century a considerable amount of work was carried out to enable Ibrahim Pasha to march through with his army and artillery for the conquest of the Hedjaz.

The Orient is often alluded to as the unchanging East, and extreme conservatism is a marked characteristic of most of the races who have embraced Mohammedanism, but the pilgrimage to Mecca stands out as a most remarkable exception, for in twenty-five short years the old pilgrim route to which so much care and attention was devoted in the past is now entirely dead. With the exception of a few miserably poor and extremely religious devotees of the Faith who wander through on foot, taking years over the journey, every pilgrim to the Holy City now travels by rail, motor or ship.

Twenty-five or thirty years ago the setting forth of the pilgrimage, which took place in the last month of the Arab calendar, was one of the great events of the year and a huge concourse of men and camels foregathered at Cairo in preparation for the journey across the desert to Mecca. Statistics are not available, and moreover the number of pilgrims who travelled by road in those days varied considerably from year to year for a variety of reasons, but those who started from Cairo were probably not less than ten to fifteen thousand.

The route from Cairo led straight across the desert to Suez, crossed the canal by ferry north of the town and then struck out into the sand-dunes of the Sinai wilderness. As the track here became lost in drifting sand, conical pillars were constructed to mark the road till it reached the gravel uplands by the Mitla pass. Here the road wound down into the rocky gorge known as the Wadi el Haj (Valley of the Pilgrims), and for the next fifteen miles the outcrops of rock, which are frequent, are worn into smooth grooves by the passage of thousands of camels' feet.

At the end of the wadi or gorge at Sudr el Heitan, where the existing motor highway strikes the pilgrim route, the road went straight across the desert towards Nekhl, and here the winding tracks of the Darb (camel paths) with the rocks polished and shining by the tread of countless camels' feet are plainly visible and will remain so for many centuries to come.

Nekhl was one of the watering-places on the road, and here there are two enormous cisterns constructed in the ground which were filled in preparation for the Pilgrimage by means of two bulls, who were sent annually from Suez for the purpose, and who worked on a water-wheel for three months every year to raise the water required for the vast crowd of men and animals.

The total distance from Cairo to Mecca by road was approximately one thousand miles, and as the vast caravan, consisting largely of aged men and a certain number of women, could not travel faster than two and a half miles an hour, the distance covered in a day was seldom more than twenty-five miles, so that under the most favourable conditions the pilgrimage took the greater part of four months. As many, in fact the majority, of the men who undertook the pilgrimage were not only aged but probably had not ridden on a camel for many years, the terrific strain of this fatiguing journey across the desert, undertaken at times in the terrific heat of the summer months, accounted for a very large number of deaths by the road.

Some idea of the numbers who died can be obtained from the small heaps of stones denoting hurriedly made graves that lie thick all along the pilgrim route. The very large piles of stones that one sees, however, are not graves but are spots where every true believer was supposed to contribute a boulder as he passed. The reasons for this were various, such as hurling a stone to curse the devil, to pay devotion to a *menhel el muluk* (alighting place of angels), or merely to construct a cairn to show the road.

In the midst of the Wadi el Haj there is one spot where a few acacia trees grow that is marked by some thirty or forty huge piles of stones thrown by the pilgrims. This place, according to the Arabs, is devil-haunted and the dwelling-place of *afrits* (evil spirits), and the legend relates that a pilgrim was murdered here by marauding Beduin, who always lurked on the fringe of the pilgrimage to loot stragglers.

In those days the Egyptian and Turkish Governments paid out a large sum annually to the Sheikhs of all the

Beduin tribes on the route to ensure the safe passage of the pilgrimage. This form of blackmail was called the *surra*, and as the Sheikhs did not always distribute this fairly there were usually disaffected members of the tribes who were prepared to carry out a raid; and individuals from outlying tribes who would commit a robbery in another Sheikh's area for the dual purpose of obtaining loot and serving an enemy a bad turn.

Now along this well-worn track, where countless thousands have toiled and suffered in the past, jolting along on padding camels in an inexorable sun, one may travel at forty miles an hour in a modern car with perfect safety, and of that vast throng that once used the track, see only one poor little ragged pilgrim trudging along on his thousand-mile walk with his satchel on his back.

The opening up of this ancient road for motor traffic presented a certain amount of difficulty, particularly on the first twenty miles from the Suez Canal to the Mitla Pass in the ragged range of hills that runs southwards towards the granite mountains of the south. The trouble here was that it was a sand-dune area, and sand is quite as difficult an enemy to fight as water and equally surprising, for there is no limit to the action that drift-sand will take if its free course is interfered with. Such a thing, for instance, as a stray tar barrel left out inadvertently in the centre of an open stretch of gravel may in a few short months produce a dune forty feet high and a hundred yards in depth that will effectually bar the progress of any car. When constructing a road through a dune area one must be most careful to leave no jutting obstructions that will invite sand to collect, and avoid at all costs anything in the nature of cuttings as this is merely asking for trouble. A really strong south-easter, such as all Egypt experiences on several occasions in the spring months, will fill a six-foot cutting with fine blown sand in half an hour—a neat little job of work that will take twenty men a couple of days to clear.

Dunes invariably owe their origin to some small obstruction like a scrub bush or stray rock which causes the fine particles to collect on the leeward side. If the desert's surface is perfectly smooth the travelling sand, which scurries along with the wind in a film of pale sickly yellow, will continue its movement until some depression or barrier causes it to deposit in much the same way as silt in flood-water behaves. There is very little one can do to cope with an embryo sand-dune once it has started; sometimes the removal of its origin will cause it to disappear, but usually once the trouble has begun the dune itself continues to grow like some evil thing or cancerous growth. One remedy that is sometimes efficacious is the erection of sheets of corrugated iron with a clear space of about four inches between the bottom of the sheets and the ground. This causes a draught that puts the deposited sand on the move again, but the remedy has usually only a local effect and the dune forms again some twenty yards to leeward. When writing of sand I do so with considerable feeling for I have inadvertently caused many flourishing and vigorous dunes to form in Sinai, a particularly fine one being created by a palm-branch hedge I erected around an olive garden.

When I first opened up this stretch of country for motor traffic I had so little money available that there was no question of road construction and the track was mapped out from the Canal for the first part of the way up the bed of a wadi which the flood-water kept clear of sand, and after that it wandered in snake fashion on firm gravel going between the straggling dunes until it reached the Mitla range of hills where the heaped sand constructed a definite barrier. Across this wire netting was laid on a cleared track on which coarse desert grass and small scrub bushes had been placed to form a foundation. This provided a possible but perilous track because sand is definitely cussed in its action and, if defeated by having a road made over the top of one of its dunes, it frequently decides to do nothing further about that dune and in fact proceeds to remove it to some other spot so that one's wire or clay road eventually becomes a narrow ridge with a sheer drop on either side.

The road, however, was just possible and our patrol cars with their high clearance could negotiate it, but when would-be pioneers from Cairo began to essay the risky journey to Jerusalem there was much trouble. Frequently a driver would lose his head in the most difficult part of the road and drive off the edge into bottomless drift-sand, or some British make of car with a particularly low clearance would catch in a mesh of the wire netting leaving it in a tangled and broken heap.

As the years went by I obtained driblets of money for this road and, occasionally by urging its claims to King Fuad himself or some more far-seeing Prime Minister than usual, I would be granted a really substantial sum like £5,000. The British Press in Egypt and the local branch of the Automobile Club too were most helpful and continued to din into the ears of the railway-minded Cabinet the necessity for this trans-Continental route, and every year saw some particularly awkward bit of country crossed by a permanent road of stone with a surface of disintegrated limestone, black shale or clay. This surfacing material depended upon what could be found in the desert within reasonable distance of the track, and I had two police non-commissioned officers, who worked in charge of road gangs permanently, and who were remarkably clever and ingenious in discovering pockets of suitable dressing.

The disintegrated limestone, which was usually found a foot or so below the gravel surface of the desert, consisted of loose, flaky bits of limestone that became powdered by the passage of cars, hardening up after the first rain to set like cement. This was the best possible material, but it was not always available and the next best thing was a black shale that also hardened up after becoming wet. If both these materials were non-existent the surfacing was done with clay, of which there were many varieties from stiff blue to dark red and pale yellow. This latter was the poorest of all as it rutted badly in wet weather and was only used by my N.C.O.'s when they could find no other.

The two policemen did not work together, but during the busy season in winter were put in charge of different sectors with fifty or sixty Arab workmen under them. One was named Zraik and the other Azrak, and there was intense and almost bitter rivalry between them. In Egypt the police believe firmly that their future promotion is entirely a personal matter, and that if the person at the head of things is pleased there is no limit to the heights to which a man may rise; they knew that the road was my particular hobby and they strove to the uttermost not only to get the greatest possible amount of work out of their gangs, but also to devise improvements of their own initiative. The discovery of the binding properties of these desert clays and shales was due entirely to their experiments.

This feeling of rivalry, being a very useful incentive, was carefully fostered and when I went out on inspection of the work the car-drivers entered into the spirit of the thing. We would first of all examine the three kilometres made by Zraik since the last inspection and then travel on another thirty miles to look at Azrak and his construction. I would then overhear the following conversation between Azrak and Abdel Bassit, my driver:

"Do you think the Bey is pleased with my work?" Azrak would ask anxiously.

"*Shwai-shwai*" ("Just a little"), Abdel Bassit would reply, grudgingly; "but, my God! you ought to see the work Zraik has done farther back. Kilometres and kilometres of road just like Cairo. The Bey is very pleased with him."

On our return we would stop again to see Zraik and the same anxious inquiry was made and here Abdel Bassit would say:

"Your work is not bad, but, *ya Salaam!* you would never believe what Azrak has done farther on. We went so fast on it the telegraph poles looked like the teeth of a comb. The Bey says he will promote him at once."

One of the results of this sowing of the seed of rivalry was that I had to interfere occasionally to stop the unfortunate gangs being overworked, and this sort of thing is unusual in Egypt. On the occasion of the next visit after some specially chosen words of that arch-leg-puller, Abdel Bassit, the gang would parade with woebegone faces and complain that they had been worked ten hours a day with no Friday off on which to wash their clothes.

One year as we were nearing the end of our works programme we found ourselves in possession of several tons of cement surplus to requirements and this was used up in the construction of a series of small bridges across the deep water cuts in the Wadi el Haj. Rain, which is such a blessing to the desert generally, is a most destructive factor to amateur road construction because the last thing the water tries to do is to soak into the parched soil. As the heavy drops fall they form tiny trickles, the trickles join others and become runs, till finally at the lowest point a surging yellow flood some four feet deep goes tossing and tumbling towards the sea. These small spates, that may last only an hour, cut out with sharp precipitous edges all that portion of the road that has been constructed across the water-courses. These unexpected cuts were a trap for the unwary as it was quite usual when travelling at 45 m.p.h. to suddenly find ten yards ahead of one that the road suddenly ended in a yawning chasm five feet deep.

It was an old Sinaitic custom if a careless driver took one of these in his stride and turned his car over to perpetuate the feat by calling that particular spruit after him. One of the deepest and most sudden of these in the vicinity of the Mitla Pass is called to this day *Wadi el Sitt* (The Watercourse of the Lady), and here my wife turned a Ford car completely over with no damage to anyone or anything except the hood. My drivers, some of whom had two or three wadis to their credit, named Wadi Mohammed the First, Wadi Mohammed the Second, and so on, took a particular delight in naming this one after my wife immediately they were satisfied she was not hurt in any way. The question of hurting feelings did not arise.

Experience had taught us the disintegrating effect of a sudden, violent flood of water on masonry after ten months of sun and intense dryness. This has the result of weakening the cement joints so that bridges of shaped stone almost invariably break in some vital spot, and therefore the small culverts and bridges we made were constructed of one solid block of concrete. The method employed was to place a wooden arch or frame in the bed of the stream and over this the mason, Haj Ali, would erect a lattice-work of iron rods, lashing them together with lengths of old barbed wire from the Turkish and British trench systems which are dotted all over Sinai.

On top of this the concrete was shovelled until the bridge was finished and then the wooden frame was pulled out to be used again in the next wadi. Small culverts of this description could be made very rapidly and very economically, and no flood that Sinai could produce would shift a vast block of concrete some ten yards long and six yards wide.

As the road continued to improve the tourist traffic increased from five cars in the year 1926 to fifty cars in one day in 1935, and grudgingly the two governments concerned awoke to the fact that the road actually existed and was being used to such an extent that it was useless to fight against the march of progress any longer. One of the reasons why the road became so popular was the very ordinary and most appealing one of expense. The return railway fare from Cairo to Jerusalem is £8, and if a lowly paid Government official or business man wished to see something of Palestine or, conversely, Egypt, it meant if his family was of any size a very considerable outlay for tickets, particularly as the journey necessitated the taking of sleepers also. If one travelled by road in one's own car four people could make the return journey at a cost of approximately £3, for the actual distance from Cairo to Jerusalem is 334 miles only.

Gradually as the road became better known it was the recognized thing in Egypt to spend either the Christmas or Easter holidays touring not only in Palestine but also in Syria, and there are no countries in the world where the sightseer can find so many " sights " to enthral him. No matter what one's special period may be, from Hittite to late Saracen, there is something of more than considerable interest every twenty miles of the road, and if the trip is made in the spring there is the added advantage of seeing the highlands of Palestine and Syria rioting with mountain and desert wild-flowers.

Newly-made road over the Mitla Pass
The Pass to the Gulf of Akaba—a stretch of " one in three " before the road
was made

[See page 281]

Rolling the sand and bitumen mixture with a light camel roller
The labour gang at work on the trans-Sinai road

[See page 294]

When the pass at Akaba was made negotiable for cars, and this was no easy matter for the great plateau of Sinai here drops 2,900 feet in a mile and a half, it was possible to do what is known as the Grand Tour. This meant a run through Sinai to Jerusalem, thence via Haifa to Beyrout and Latakia, then across the north of Syria to Aleppo, and from Aleppo to Damascus with the Krak des Chevaliers and Baalbek on the way. The return is made via Amman and Kerak to Petra—"The Rose-red City half as old as time"—and thence via the head of the Gulf of Akaba, up the precipitous pass, and across Sinai by the southern route to link up with the main road at what is now known as Sudr el Heitan junction, a very imposing name for a blank bit of desert where two roads meet. After this tour, which can be done in about ten days, the sightseer will return with twenty spools of over- and under-exposed films and a brain so muddled up with Greek, Hebrew, Roman, Nabataean and Crusader periods that only a most exhaustive study of ancient history can sort out for him.

In 1935 the Egyptian Government suddenly became road-minded. The Cairo–Suez stretch of desert road was macadamized and turned into a speedway and I was granted £9,000 for the proper construction of a road in my most difficult sector—the sand area between the Canal and Mitla Pass. The money allowed was quite insufficient for anything in the nature of macadam and we therefore decided to use the "mix-in-place" system invented by the Shell Company of Egypt. At the risk of boring those readers who are not vastly interested in road construction this novel and economical method of making a motor-car speedway is so unlike any other form of road work that it is worth describing.

Mix-in-place, as its name suggests, consists of mixing the sand of the desert with a light bitumen, a waste product of ordinary fuel oil, so that the sand becomes black and glutinous. The mixing is carried out in a large machine similar to a concrete mixer and the result is then laid on the desert which has previously been levelled off to take it. The following day, when the tarred sand has set slightly, it is tamped down by hand rammers, then rolled by a light roller drawn by a camel and finally about ten days later a three-ton petrol roller is run over it. The result is a marvellous smooth and moderately hard road that will stand up to all light traffic and on which one can travel at any speed which one's car can attain. The lasting properties of these makeshift and inexpensive roads is more or less unknown, but there are certain stretches in Egypt that have stood up to ten years' constant wear and it seems that, with a light re-dressing of bitumen every three years or so, they may last almost indefinitely. They, however, will not carry heavy lorry traffic and cart or other solid wheels will destroy them utterly in a very short time.

Over the question of lorry traffic in Sinai I congratulate myself on having been in the " Wise Virgin " class, for I foresaw in the earliest days that no roughly constructed desert road was going to stand up to lorries, and as I failed to see why I should have my spine permanently jarred because a few grasping merchants wished to save on camel transport, I prohibited the passage of any vehicle carrying more than one ton. Having made this order before any lorries had started to run, or thought of it, there was no question of hardship to owners of heavy vehicles and omnibus companies who had already started services, and, knowing the extent to which the thin end of the wedge operates in the Orient, I was absolutely adamant over the question of special permits for anything heavy, or for distinguished parties desiring to make a journey in an omnibus or char-à-banc. I aroused much antagonism over this and was called a conservative obstructionist and other things less complimentary.

Here in England the heavy industries, the brewers, and the petrol and oil companies, by employment of this same time-honoured thin end of the wedge, have put such vast and ponderous vehicles on the road that the greatest brains in road construction and foundation have been quite unable to keep pace with them, and their length and height are such that the ordinary motorist finds considerable difficulty in passing them. If our road authorities had been in the " Wise Virgin " class some twenty years ago these Leviathan vehicles would never have found their way on to our highways and motoring would have been in consequence much pleasanter and less dangerous, our road upkeep bill might have been halved, and our railways would have benefited by the transport of heavy materials that should never have been allowed on ordinary highways.

My unyielding attitude over the question of lorries, moreover, was not dictated solely by a selfish desire to travel over my Province in reasonable comfort and ease, but also because a very large proportion of my population existed solely on the camel and its earnings as a transport animal. It is quite the usual thing in the Arab world for a widow or a divorced wife to be given a camel as a means of support and on the 1s. 6d. or 2s. a day this animal will earn on the caravan routes the woman and her children will exist in moderate comfort. The lorry is now upsetting the old Beduin method of life entirely, and to enable one merchant to make treble profits by using mechanical transport not only is every desert track turned into a series of dust-filled pot-holes of incredible depth, but the very keystone of Arab life is being destroyed. To force the Beduin off the camel standard is a far more serious matter in Arabia and Sinai than the devaluation of either the franc or the dollar is in France or America as to all intents and purposes it means the end of the nomad people.

The £9,000 grant was not available until the 1st October, 1935, and as the financial year in Egypt ends on 31st March it meant that the whole of the twenty miles had to be constructed in six months. This would not have been difficult in the ordinary way, but unfortunately Mussolini became tiresome in the autumn of 1935 and worried many people, from Haile Selassie and Sir Samuel Hoare to quite inconspicuous people like myself. Sanctions were then extremely fashionable, though they were not thought so much of a few months later, and Mussolini applied sanctions to me by refusing to allow the Shell Company to transfer their Mix-in-Place machines to Egypt from Italian Libya where they had been working for some months. This meant that I was not only late in starting work but that for a considerable time I had to carry on with one mixer instead of two.

Labour was supplied by engaging gangs of Saidis, the brawny, hard-working inhabitants of Upper Egypt, and over these cheery, inimitable workers I have no complaints whatsoever, for they were superb. There was a vast amount of solid digging to be done, for as the road went through sand country there was no question of maintaining one's levels by the simple method of cuttings. The track had of necessity to be carried from one high point to the next by means of embankments and these embankments were made by the age-old Pharaonic method of labourers filling, carrying and dumping small baskets of earth.

It was a most inspiring sight to see the gang which numbered some four hundred men working like furies in a cloud of sand and dust that rose up to the sky, the diggers hacking away with rapid strokes of their mattocks and the basket-carriers running in long lines from the pit to the

embankment with every man roaring at the top of his voice
the chorus of some Saidi chanty :

> Kam leylah—kam yom,
> Sittah leylah—sabah ayam,
> Khokh wa tina—baladina,
> Biddiarowa—baladi.

The words when translated are not particularly inspiring
and are of the " Want to get back to Dixie " school of
song :

> How many nights—how many days,
> Six nights—seven days,
> Peaches and figs in our home-land ;
> I want to go back to my own country.

When I had discovered how many square metres of embankment and how many metres length of Mix-in-Place
the gang could do in one day of real hard labour, I made
an arrangement by which the " knock-off " whistles would
sound immediately this piece of work was completed. This
had a most electrifying effect, for the gang then worked
like fiends possessed and the basket-carriers sprinted, doing
the hundred in even time, so that usually a very exhausted
but happy crowd was able to knock off work to rest and
coffee-making by three o'clock in the afternoon.

The men engaged on what was known as the " Tolba el
Iswid " (the Black Gang), namely those mixing and carrying
the bitumenized sand, were paid 6d. a day more than others
as a " dirty allowance." This additional pay was fully
earned as they were stained both as regards skin and
clothing that particular dirty shade which is known in
women's dressmaking circles as " nigger-brown," and as
this bitumen is water-resisting I can only conclude that
the colouring lasted till the skin wore away.

As the work progressed and the long black streak of
road crept farther and farther into the desert one enjoyed a

feeling of complete satisfaction of something accomplished when one sailed along at an easy 60 m.p.h. through forbidding sand-dunes and loose gravelly slopes where previously one had toiled and strained with stuck cars and boiling radiators, taking often from two to three hours negotiating a stretch of country that one now ran across with ease in twenty-five minutes.

Two days before the dreaded end of the Financial Year and the closing of accounts the gang, by working overtime, reached their goal, the stretch of bitumenized road in the Pass itself that had been completed two years previously. The very wonderful hard-working gang of Saidis with fat wallets, but not nearly so fat as they deserved, then broke up to return to their home country about which they had been singing so lustily for six weary, toilsome months in the desert which must have been anathema to them.

Nearly all my pleasantest memories of Egypt seem to be connected with the people, the very lovable, loyal and hard-working *fellah* who has the wonderful quality of showing a vast enthusiasm, keenness and never-failing cheerfulness over some work that cannot possibly be of the slightest interest to him. These husky Saidis are born and bred in the rich corn, cotton and sugar lands of the upper Nile Valley, and to them the stretch of harsh sandy desert in which they toiled must have meant annihilation's waste ; but because they were being paid an additional $2\frac{1}{2}d.$ a day " hard lying " money they thought they were being generously treated indeed and therefore gave of their best. It is such a pity that governments, being tied hand and foot by regulations, cannot countenance that very irregular form of emolument, the bonus.

When I left Sinai this trans-Continental road, though very far from perfect, was an accomplished fact and, unless a particularly violent rain-storm had caused unexpected cuts and disintegrations, there was nothing to prevent the ordinary touring car from making the journey from Cairo to Jerusalem in ten hours. For those who do not care for such strenuous travelling a small Rest House, glorified by the name of the Central Sinai Hotel, was constructed in 1935 at Hassana, which is roughly half-way between the two cities. Here the traveller can put up for the night and, after warming himself over a big open fire-place in which desert scrub burns furiously, can go to sleep in the wonderfully invigorating air of the desert. Hassana is not one of the most attractive spots I have seen, for it consists of nothing but a well and a few police buildings in a particularly harsh stretch of desert, but the air in this lonely outpost is so dry and so pure that one wakes up in the morning with that seventeen-year-old " All's right-with-the-world " feeling; and when one is over fifty years of age it is not every day that one can recapture the enthusiasms, raptures and morning appetite of one's long-past and much-regretted 'teens.

CHAPTER XIII

THE ARAB AND HIS PIPE

What a blessing this smoking is !—perhaps the greatest that we owe to the discovery of America.

HELPS.

A MOST attractive and human side of the Beduin is his love of his pipe and tobacco. Possibly Messrs. Dunhill would disapprove strongly of his smoker's outfit, which is primitive to say the least, but it is in keeping with the man and the conditions under which he uses it. His pipe, which in the old days he called the *gallioun*, but which is now designated the *beeba*, the Arabic form of the English pipe (Arabic having no use for the letter " p "), consists of a bowl carved from a soft stone that is found near Teima in Central Arabia and in some cases is of grey-coloured clay. The stem is of considerable length and this the Beduin manufactures himself from any wood available. Almond wood is used in the best circles, but this is rare unless he lives in close proximity to Palestine where the tree is grown extensively. Shoots of the wild fig bored out by means of a hot skewer serve the purpose, but the wood is soft and easily bitten through, and the same applies to the oleander, which is indigenous in all the deep valleys of Trans-Jordan.

There is a very good story about oleander pipe-stems and a little Arab with Dunhill ideas. When I first opened up the Wadi Gedeirat for cultivation, which I have described in another chapter, a row of oleanders was discovered growing in this Arab's garden. As this tree is not

296

indigenous to Sinai I asked about it and the Arab, Sobeih by name, afterwards christened Willie, admitted he had planted them. As I did not know at that time that oleanders could be used for pipe-stems, I was very much surprised that anyone should take the trouble to fetch plants, some hundred and fifty miles, from Trans-Jordan. Willie mistook my surprise for annoyance and thought there must be some order against oleander-growing—*Hakoomas* (governments) are always making ridiculous interfering edicts of this nature—so when I asked why he had grown them he said with ready mendacity that he had done so because they were beautiful and sweet-scented.

As the desert Arab has not the slightest trace of an eye for beauty and as decoration of anything by means of gardens is utterly beyond his ken, I was amazed and delighted that I had found at last a member of the race who could enjoy flowers and pleasant scents. To show my appreciation of his efforts I put a gang of men on his garden, laid it out for him in the best horticultural style, and gave him some hundreds of selected fruit trees. For several years he traded on his reputation of having an eye for beauty, wearing a puzzled smile on his little wizened face, and then the unhappy disclosure was made that he was growing the oleanders for the entirely sordid and mercenary reason of selling the shoots at half a *piastre* each as pipe-stems.

Arab tobacco, like that of the Boers of South Africa, is very dry and crumbly and the Beduin's pouch must therefore be capacious. Most of the best people use the complete skin of a kid that has died at birth and this is fashioned with the hair outside. It makes an extremely large *kees* (bag), but, as the Beduin is always setting forth on journeys to look for straying camels or to attend the hearing of protracted law-suits and may be away anything from three days to six months, it is necessary to be prepared for all eventualities.

Matches are a luxury and, being expensive, are not purchased, though if a box can be obtained from a passing traveller it is duly appreciated. Hung round his neck on a thong of home-made leather are his *lares atque penates*, consisting of his seal, with which he will willingly sign any deed, mortgage, complaint, or " round Robin," a small pick for cleaning out his pipe, and lastly, most important of all, his flint and steel.

The steel is a narrow strip of metal bent in the shape of a triangle and the base, which is about an inch wide, provides the striking surface. There is no difficulty about flints as the greater part of the desert in which he lives is strewn thickly with them, and the largest and sharpest can always be found under one's valise at night or beneath the seat of one's trousers if one squats round a camp fire. There is something of the Neolithic man about the Beduin, for, besides using the flint in conjunction with the steel, he will, if he has no knife handy, quickly knap a suitable flint and use it for cutting rope or skinning animals.

His tinder is a portion of an old cotton garment and he prepares it by hammering it into shreds between two stones. To light his pipe he grasps the steel in the first finger and thumb of his left hand and between the first finger and second he holds a prepared piece of tinder. Then, with the right hand, he strikes a sharp glancing blow with a flint, and immediately there is a spark followed by a tiny wisp of smoke from the tinder.

The really intriguing and awkward part of the Beduin smoker's outfit is his tobacco, and here the government and the Arab unfortunately do not see eye to eye. Tobacco and its seed, which, according to Doughty, was first brought to the East by English traders in the days of

James I, can be grown easily over the greater part of Arabia, and for the last three hundred years the Beduin has been accustomed to cultivate his own tobacco in any suitable corner of the desert where a depression of good soil receives rather more than its share of rain water. Unfortunately the governments concerned with the Arab's welfare either prohibit tobacco-growing altogether or only permit it under licence, and anything that requires a licence is of course purely ridiculous in the Beduin's eyes.

The Egyptian Government adopt a most uncompromising attitude because a considerable part of their revenue is obtained from the tobacco monopoly, and its cultivation is regarded as one of the seven deadly sins. The tobacco that the Beduin grows is precisely what one would expect from a haphazard cultivator working in a sterile waste, and in other words is abominable. It is used in its rough state with the leaves dried on their stalks and is an unhealthy greenish colour. When smoked it gives off such a rank and penetrating smell that no other race but the Beduin could possibly smoke it, and if it were used to adulterate or mix with other tobacco for cigarette manufacture the firm who adopted the venture would go out of business at once.

There is, therefore, no valid objection to the poor old Beduin growing his own tobacco. He is far too needy to buy any that has paid duty and would not appreciate its quality if he did. If he is prevented from cultivating it he has to go without and only the confirmed smoker realizes what this means. I have always found it most difficult to reconcile my loyalty to the government that employed me and my fellow-feeling for a brother addict of the weed, especially when that brother is a desperately poor man with few other consolations in his hard life.

Luckily, I managed to establish the fact that tobacco

seed, which is like the finest dust, has the quality of remaining dormant for years, and in the course of generations of its cultivation has blown all over the " desert's dusty face."

As a proof of this I could always point to a normal occurrence in my own vegetable garden where half a dozen or more healthy plants sprang up every year. Nasr, my old gardener, and I used to have a joke about this phenomenon annually, as I would adopt the attitude that he should go to prison for three years for cultivating tobacco, and he would retaliate by saying that as I was the owner of the garden the severest sentence should be given to me and that he, as a mere hired hand, would get off with something very much lighter. The great charm about the jest was that it was a hardy perennial, and Nasr really only appreciated a joke when it was well flavoured and seasoned by age. It took him some time to taste the full savour of a new joke and get its meaning, and the situation was always aggravated by the presence of his junior, Mohammed, who invariably saw the point long before he had grasped it, and that sort of thing is so bad for discipline and derogatory to dignity.

If tobacco would grow in this fashion in a garden that was dug over every year, it stood to reason, therefore, that a trifle more than the normal rainfall in some secluded wadi would cause wind-blown seeds to sprout of their own accord. So that if a thriving patch of tobacco plants was found tucked away in some hidden corner of a mountain gorge it was an understood thing among the Sinai Police that no attempt should be made to find the owner of the plot, even if there should happen to be recent marks of a mattock. Undoubtedly the cultivation was an act of God and to tamper with it in any way would savour of sacrilege.

These were the general lines on which we worked in

Sinai, but it was all very difficult as from time to time we had serving in the Police or Camel Corps some enthusiastic young Egyptian officer from the Nile Valley who, imbued with the tradition of the criminality of tobacco-growing, would show his keenness by discovering a cultivated plot and arresting its owner, who was usually one of my star-turn Sheikhs and a very old friend to boot. Sometimes the case had gone too far for me to quash it and scotch it at birth, and if once the papers concerning the " crime " had reached Cairo it meant that the most drastic steps had to be taken to save from long imprisonment and utter financial ruin some dear old gentleman who had quite unwittingly broken the laws of the land in his efforts to keep his *beeba* filled with home-grown tobacco.

On one occasion a case went so far that I had to go personally to the Minister of Finance to try and persuade him to see things from my point of view. He was not easy for he held the view that if the Arabs were prevented from growing their own tobacco they would buy cigarettes that had paid duty. When I pointed out that they were far too poor to buy the cheapest cigarettes he, from the comfortable angle of £2,000 a year, considered this nonsense. However, as he said the tobacco could be bought by dishonest manufacturers and used to adulterate other brands, and this gave me an opening. I produced a bag of the much-discussed tobacco and rolled him a rough cigarette, asking him to try it and see what he thought of it. He took a deep draught of the foul-smelling weed, gave a cough and a strangled scream of anguish and then said, "Have it your own way, but don't say anything about it."

One was always at a great disadvantage when one went to plead with the " Great Ones " of Egypt for the rescue of some miserable old Arab from the clutches of the law,

because it was quite impossible for an Egyptian to understand one's motive; and they felt certain there must be
some reason for the trouble one took. It was so manifestly
absurd and ridiculous in every way that a senior official
should concern himself as to whether a poverty-stricken
Arab went to prison or not. I used to wish I had the
gift of thought-reading so that I could have had revealed
to me the various theories that were suggesting themselves
in the Egyptian mind: "Is this official concerned in
tobacco-growing himself and is this one of his employees?"
Or, "Is he keeping the old Sheikh's daughter and trying
to save the old man for her sake?" Or, possibly, "Is
the Sheikh in a position to blackmail him over something
and he must save the Sheikh to save himself?" The
under-dog in Egypt from the days since the Pyramids
were built by forced labour has been so low down in the
social scale and so entirely miserable in his outlook,
that the general attitude is one or two more blows from
fate cannot matter much to him, so why worry?

As to the carrying of dried tobacco one had to be
more careful as there were plenty of "cads" willing to
"let the side down," mostly from the townspeople of El
Arish. The "Gentleman's Agreement" was that an
Arab could carry a pouchful, and as these pouches were on
the generous side this meant they could travel with two
or three pounds of the weed. One day, however, an El
Arish townsman was brought in with a large sheepskin
packed tightly with quite superior tobacco grown in
Palestine, and when asked to explain matters stated with
much emphasis that he was merely carrying a "pouchful"
sufficient to last him a week—or possibly a fortnight!

One of my favourite Sheikhs in Sinai smoked neither a
pipe nor a cigarette because, according to his statement,
the doctor had knocked him off both on account of his

health, but had agreed to his smoking cigars. A doctor with expensive views like these might be a positive godsend in Mayfair, but he and his attitude towards luxuries seemed a trifle out of place and incongruous in Sinai. The result was that the old man never had a smoke except when I provided him with a box of Indian cheroots from the N.A.A.F.I. canteen.

One year the Mohammedan festival of Bairam coincided with our Christmas Day, and as I always gave the old Sheikh a box for his Bairam present I wired to a friend of mine who was coming up to stay for the holiday to bring with him a box of cheroots. My friend, thinking the cheroots were to form part of the Christmas fare and festivities, was of opinion that something a trifle better than mere Indian weed should be provided, especially as he would be asked to smoke them himself. He therefore brought up a box of fifty Coronas, and nobody was pleased. My friend was disappointed that he did not get one and was horrified at seeing Coronas presented to an old Arab ; I was displeased at having to pay a very high price for my annual gift ; and the old Sheikh after three draws and a spit said : " *Quies khalis, walakin el jinss et tani ma el shereet assmar ahsan min da.*" (" Very nice, but the other kind with the brown bands are better than these.") !

CHAPTER XIV

POETS AND EXILES

It's the white road westwards is the road I must tread,
 To the green grass, the cool grass, and rest for heart and head.
To the violets and the brown brooks and the thrushes' song
 In the fine land, the west land, the land where I belong.

J. MASEFIELD.

I SUPPOSE it never occurred to the nineteenth-century
poets how unhappy and dissatisfied they were going
to make the present-day exiles when they wrote so charm-
ingly and convincingly of the English country-side some
eighty years ago. One can recall the lines : "The year's
at the spring, and day's at the morn" with complete
equanimity and agreement when one looks out from one's
bedroom window on to the green of an English birch
grove, but when one sees instead twisted, camel-gnawed
fig-trees one can only draw unhappy comparisons and
think of those glorious days before one went East. The
point is that one might be more or less satisfied with
stunted fig-trees and drift sand if the poets had not gone
out of their way to din into one's ears all that one was
missing at home.

In some ways I feel I owe a debt to Robert Browning
for the many hours of happiness I have obtained from a
ragged copy of his poems that travelled with me everywhere, but I have a definite grudge against him for " Pippa
Passes," and the effect it had on me when I remembered
on some particularly foul day during an Egyptian April
the lines that run .

304

The hill-side's dew-pearled :
The lark's on the wing ;
The snail's on the thorn.

Spring in Egypt and its deserts is without doubt the most unpleasant of the four seasons of the year as it lacks everything with which we connect the magic word in England. In the first place it heralds the approach of summer, and there is nothing about an Egyptian summer to look forward to except escape from the country on leave home. Summer in Egypt means twelve hours of unbroken blazing sunshine every day for five interminable months, and as it is the sort of sunshine that makes the metal portions of one's car so hot that they cannot be touched with the hand it is not of much use to even the most hardened sun-bather. In the second place spring in England, even a second-rate one such as we experienced this year, means a general quickening of life throughout the countryside. The primroses show in the dead and rotten leaves at the foot of the hedgerow, the bracken and ferns thrust up their fronds, and the birds open the day, however grey and gloomy it may be, with a crash of song. In Egypt, however, as Keats said, " no birds sing " and spring instead of heralding life is the harbinger of death to all growth unless artificially watered. Throughout the last few months of winter even in the harshest deserts a faint film of green has been apparent on the gravelly wastes, whilst on the uplands and grazing areas there has been a sprinkling of scarlet anemones, almost a blue-bell sheen where the small desert iris has established itself, and over all the gay pink and white blossoms of the asphodel. For an all too short time the desert has blossomed, perhaps not quite as the rose, but has nevertheless put up a brave show considering its natural sterility and the shortage of rainfall.

Then comes the first hint of spring in early April, and it arrives at a time when a glance at the calendar reminds one in England now—

> That the lowest branch and the brushwood sheaf
> Round the elm-tree bole are in tiny leaf,

but in Egypt what has one?

The first spring morning in Egypt makes its presence felt by a dryness of the nose and mouth and a prickly sensation of the skin when one awakes. One looks out from the window, or through the tent-flap if one is unlucky enough to be out on patrol, and sees that there is a greyish-yellow haze over the horizon and that the rising sun instead of being a blazing orb of gold looks rather like a cake of yellow soap at the bottom of a basin of dirty water. There is no breeze, not even the customary faint cold air that comes in from the high desert at dawn, but every now and again one will notice faint scurries of lifted sand and tiny dust devils writhing and dancing among the scrub. Then come little puffs of hot wind that scorch and these grow stronger and more regular until at eight o'clock the wind is in full blast—a roaring, burning, sand-laden gale from the south, and one knows that the Egyptian spring has arrived!

The thermometer goes steadily upwards until by midday it may be anything from 102° to 112°, and all the while the gale roars along carrying with it not only the dust and sand of the desert, but the powdered clay from the wadi-beds, and the dried filth from the villages and camel-lines. The doors and windows are closed and shuttered and every precaution taken to keep within the house the cool, clean air of the night before, but the south wind of Egypt will penetrate into and drive out anything. Gradually the temperature within the house rises, the air becomes thicker and staler, and a film of yellow dust collects on the furniture, until by evening everything within the room is a uniform dun colour.

After sunset the wind will drop and a ghastly breathless night will follow during which one's pillow-case will feel as if it had come straight from the iron of the *muckwagi*,[1] and the sheets will be harsh and gritty. One awakes to another day which will be precisely the same as its predecessor except that the thermometer will be two degrees higher and the wind stronger and more dust-laden, whilst the third day will be even worse. Just before sunset on this the last day the wind will show a tendency to follow the sun and will work slowly round to south-west. Then suddenly with a bang it flies into its accustomed quarter, the north-west, and after this it all depends how far one is from the Mediterranean before one experiences that delightful sense of coolness and humidity that comes with a wind from the sea. Life during these horrible three days of scorching heat is a burden, but it would be more or less bearable if one did not think of lines such as " From a lone sheiling on a misty island " and others that breathe of the softness and moisture of spring at home.

This is the normal herald of spring in Egypt—a burning *Khamsin* wind from the south bringing with it all the stored heat of Central Arabia and the southern Sahara. The word " *khamsin* " means " fifty," and the theory is that from this first hot wind there will be a period of fifty days during which one may expect constant burning *simoons* that always last three days and sometimes very regrettably extend to six. The Mohammedans have a festival to commemorate spring which is called " Shem el Nessim," the Scent of the Breeze, and it is the custom

[1] Laundry-man.

on this day for complete families to crowd into any conveyance—some thirty or forty on a flat springless cart, called an *arabeah*, or a slightly smaller number into an equally springless Ford—for a long happy day in the country to smell the zephyrs of spring. As *Shem el Nessim* almost invariably coincides with one of these hot winds, it might be called more appropriately Shem el Khamsin, for the holiday-makers, instead of breathing in the scent of flowers, get their lungs well filled with all the dust and garbage that has accumulated on the surface of the soil during the preceding months.

The effect these hot *khamsin* winds of spring have on the garden, the crops of the Arab, and the desert flowers is devastating, and in a few short hours all the green growth and colour are gone, with the country looking as if it had been swept by fire. Yellow patches appear on the lawn, the sweet peas droop and shrivel, the trees take on a dead greenish-yellow tinge, and one realizes that one is on the threshold of the summer of one's discontent. It is in this atmosphere and among the wreckage of one's garden that one remembers what spring can mean in England, and one is filled with a wild longing to be home to see for oneself the things that Browning and others wrote about so convincingly.

After every *khamsin* wind with the ruin it brought in its train and its burning discomfort I experienced always a sudden detestation of the Mid-East and everything connected with it, and for this frame of mind I blame the poets quite as much as the weather. They caused me many unhappy hours when I thought of all that I was missing at home, and seeing how short life is I used to wonder if it were worth while to lose so much that could never be regained. Browning was one of the worst offenders at causing these attacks of nostalgia and home-sickness, but there were others. Francis Thompson with his lines—

> Where the thistle lifts a purple crown
> Six foot out of the turf,
> And the harebell shakes on a windy hill—
> O the breath of the distant surf,

used to bring back memories of Sussex downs, the plaintive wail of the kittiwake, and the murmur of sheep, and I longed intensely for the scent of thyme and hated Sinai with an intense loathing. Then there was Masefield, another culprit, with his

Twilight it is, and the far woods are dim, and the rooks cry and call.
Down in the valley the lamps, and the mist, and a star over all.

This brought back to me so poignantly the real country-side of England and that soft evening mist with its hint of blue that is so different in every way from the very pronounced *shaboora*, or fog, that sometimes follows the Egyptian sunset. Yes, I hold Masefield responsible for much unhappiness.

These poets that made " the heart-strings crack " were not confined to those who are household names, for in *Punch* from time to time appeared lines by modern contributors who wrote the more convincingly because being exiles themselves they really experienced the feelings about which they wrote. Since the day when I saw " Flanders Fields " in a copy of *Punch* during the war I have realized that it is in our leading humorous weekly that one must look for little gems of verse that find a response in the heart of the ordinary man and probably shock to the core the new poets who write the modern stuff that sounds like a car missing on two cylinders.

A *Punch* poet who caused me my most violent bout of home-sickness was G. C. Tew, who was responsible for the following during a heat-wave in June, and a particularly ghastly heat-wave it was.

Vultures in a brassy sky,
Starving cur and carrion fly—
Theirs this aching land, where I
Nothing own save memory.

The chalk-stream slides through the old grey bridge
   And swirls round the stones where a chestnut bough,
Low hung, spreads shade for the dancing midge
   And the dimpling trout—in England now ;
      But I'm here, when it's summer at Home.

From the ford below come children's cries
   As they laugh in the shallows ; and knee-deep kine
Swing restless tails at the teasing flies,
   In England now. God ! Why is it mine
      To be here, when it's summer at Home ?

The voices cease as the clear light dies,
   And a mist creeps up. Shall I walk to the inn
Where warm lamps glow, or wait for the rise
   Which may come with the dark ? Ah ! I'm here for my sin—
      I'm here, and it's summer at Home.

Here was the heart-felt cry of the chalk-stream fisherman who could find nothing in the East to console him for the days he was missing on his favourite river at home. For Gilbert Tew I harbour no resentment, instead I experience only that fellow-feeling that makes us wondrous kind. One hopes only that when he returned home in these days of wealthy syndicates, sewage effluents and tarred roads, he found his trout-stream all he had imagined it to be during those days of burning heat or the sticky nights of the monsoon.

Perhaps the exile has a tendency to dream of an England that he knew some twenty years ago and to forget how much things have changed since he first saw the lighthouse of Port Said come up suddenly from the unbroken horizon of the sea. Often too when one has been dreaming of the glory of a spring at home, with the thrushes and blackbirds in full blast and the blossom on the bough, there has arrived a letter from a friend in England : " I envy you your lot in a warm and sunny desert. Here we are having the most damnable spring and the thermometer on the lawn last night registered fourteen degrees of frost. My early potatoes——" But usually one reads no further, for no one really worries about another man's early potatoes, and besides, one refuses to destroy one's sweet imaginings and cherished ideals on account of one peevish letter, for sooner or later one feels that England will justify herself.

Possibly Egypt offers some consolations for the spring one always missed, but personally I require an enormous number of Pyramids standing out against a westering sun to compensate me for one *khamsin* day experienced and one English spring morning lost.

INDEX

313